DATE DUE

HIGHSMITH   #45102

Retarded Kids Need To Play

A publication of
Leisure Press.
597 Fifth Avenue; New York, N.Y. 10017

Copyright © 1983 Leisure Press
All rights reserved. Printed in the U.S.A.

No part of this publication may be reproduced
or transmitted in any form or by any means
electronic or mechanical, including photocopying, recording,
or any information storage and retrieval system now known
or to be invented, without permission in writing from the publisher,
except by a reviewer who wishes to quote brief passages
in connection with a written review for
inclusion in a magazine, newspaper, or broadcast.

Library of Congress Catalog Card Number: 82-83929

ISBN: 088011-097-X

Book design: Diana J. Goodin
Cover design: Tanya Edgar
Text photographs: Frank and Cyntha Hirst
Typesetting: The Graphics Connection; Oakland, California

Retarded Kids Need To Play

A Manual for Parents and Other Teachers

Includes ideas and programs for involving retarded children in physical activities.

Cyntha C. Hirst, Ph.d.
Elaine Michaelis, M.S.

Department of Physical Education
Brigham Young University
Provo, Utah

LEISURE PRESS

NEW YORK

CONTENTS

	PREFACE	5
1	PHYSICAL ACTIVITY IN SPECIAL EDUCATION	7
2	EVALUATION OF MOTOR PERFORMANCE	16
3	MOVEMENT EDUCATION	28
4	ACTIVITIES FOR BABIES	31
5	MOVEMENT EXPLORATION ACTIVITIES	49
6	PERCEPTUAL MOTOR ACTIVITIES	70
7	RHYTHM AND DANCE	75
8	MOVEMENT EXPLORATION USING EQUIPMENT	81
9	EXERCISE THEORY AND PRACTICE	98
10	LOW-ORGANIZATIONAL GAMES	124
11	SPORT SKILLS	128
12	STUNTS AND TUMBLING	192
13	APPARATUS ACTIVITIES	217
14	AQUATIC ACTIVITIES	236
15	TRACK AND FIELD	257
16	ACTIVITIES OF OUTDOOR PLAYGROUND EQUIPMENT	270
17	COMPETITION	283

PREFACE

In the United States today, there are more than six million mentally retarded persons. About half of these are school-age children and teenagers. Many of the parents of these retarded school children are eager to take an active role in the educational experiences of their retarded son or daughter, but they may not know how to do this. The United States Government guarantees educational opportunities to all children in the United States through the local school systems, so parents of mentally retarded children no longer have to pay private school tuition or special day care center fees for the education of their retarded children. These children are part of the public school enrollment, and activities for them must be included in the school program.

The schools, however, cannot be expected to do the whole job of educating these special children. If the school-age mentally retarded population is to reach the highest possible levels of achievement in life-time skills, parents must help, counsel, and support the efforts of the public school teachers. In some instances, the parents will need to lead the schools in educating these children.

This book was written for the parents of retarded children, and for any other person who will be involved with teaching sport skills and physical education to the retarded. The progressions and sequences are organized to range from the most simple skills (with basic analysis of the skills), to advanced or complete stunts or skills. The organization will provide parents and other teachers who do not have professional knowledge in the field with information about a variety of activities so they can function as a team to provide beneficial physical education experiences.

Parents of the retarded child should play with their child and provide all forms of childhood play before the child is of school age.

The child should have dancing lessons, swimming experiences, music lessons and experiences with other children. The child should also know many of the basic activities of running, throwing, catching, going to parties, going to the zoo and staying overnight with grandma. Parents of the retarded child should then work closely with the school teachers so the physical education curriculum will be rich in variety. This will help to insure that the sequence of activities will allow the children to develop and be able to perform to the best of their abilities.

The purpose of this book is to present a program of physical education activities which will help the retarded child develop those physical education skills necessary for enjoyable living. An attempt has also been made to integrate the development of family play activities and school physical education activities with academic experiences so that all will enhance the total learning for the child. The activities all have directions to follow. The child will be able to learn the advantages of following directions and of being obedient to the parent's and/or teacher's instructions.

It is not expected that any one pair of parents can be skilled enough to conduct all the activities in this book. The progressions for each type of activity are organized so the parents can find a starting place for their child, and can assist the professional teacher in designing a program of physical education activities that will be rich and fun for all children of any skill level. By including a complete and total curriculum with a great variety of activities, parents can help to guide and lead, if necessary, the physical education development of their child.

The authors express their appreciation to all the children who served as models, and for their willingness to appear in this book. We also appreciate the parents of the models who gave permission for the photographs to be used in the book. The help of professional consultants like Barbara Merrill, of the Oakridge School, and Sara Lee Gibb, of the Brigham Young University Dance Department, is also greatly appreciated.

1
PHYSICAL ACTIVITY IN SPECIAL EDUCATION

Children differ greatly in their ability to adjust to the school situation. Some children enter school, enjoy every day and progress as expected. Others do not progress as expected, and the school experience is very unpleasant. Their intellectual ability, habits, attitudes, and expectations vary considerably. Children come to school from a variety of environments and have many different experiences as a base for future learning. This makes the job of the teacher and the job of the parent in the learning process very difficult. Many learning problems may be attributed to a lack of readiness skills, slow developmental processes, a physical handicap, or an emotional disturbance; the child may be culturally deprived, or underenriched; or the child may be mentally retarded. This book will deal with the problem of teaching physical education skills and play activities to the mentally retarded child. The teacher may be professionally prepared in the pre-school or elementary school, or that person may be the parent of a mentally retarded child who is willing to get involved in the child's educational development.

As the learning experiences are presented in the formal school setting, it becomes apparent that some pupils do not seem quite able to learn in the same way others learn. These difficulties begin early in the school experience and can be noted in the "readiness" activities that precede formal instruction of subject matter. As the school year progresses, these children fall further and further behind in some areas of learning until they are not able to participate on the same level as the rest of the group. The longer they remain in this situation, the more confused they become, and the more often they are faced with their failure to achieve. The complex environment in which we live demands learning. Learning is difficult enough when most outside influences are positive and few are negative. For a child whose physiological and/or neurological processes do not operate normally, very special help becomes necessary. Our civilization, while increasing its demands for knowledge, is decreasing the opportunities for a child to gain the necessary experiences for basic skills. For example, one common problem among children entering school is the lack of basic perceptual motor skill experience. This is because children must ride to school rather than walk to the neighborhood school. They watch television instead of doing demanding home chores or participating in physical activities. Children stay inside the house because open fields have disappeared into housing complexes, and children rarely participate in physically demanding play or recreational activities that build the perceptual motor skills required by the more complex activities of reading, writing, and mathematics. These opportunities must be provided by the parent apart from classroom hours.

Traditionally, education has been presented to children via spoken language. In the developmental pattern of children, the small muscle skills and the abstract thinking aspects of personality functioning do not appear for quite some time after birth and require considerable practice before they become apparent. Physical play is the central interest of the child and is a means of learning. Therefore, activity and movement can and should be a prime method through which learning experiences are provided by the teacher and the parent.

Not only is physical activity a valuable teaching aid, but it is also a necessity for good health, because without physical activity one loses the desire to be active in play and movement experiences. Physical activity keeps the body systems functioning efficiently and provides energy for the play activities from which a child can learn.

OBJECTIVES OF PHYSICAL EDUCATION

Physical education is defined in PL94-142 (The Education for All Handicapped Children Act) as being the development of: (1) Physical and motor fitness, (2) Fundamental motor skills and patterns and (3) Skills in aquatics, dance and individual and group games and activities. This definition provides a curriculum guide that should be followed.

Each child in school is to have an individualized educational plan (IEP) that is designed for his or her special educational needs. Evaluation of motor performance objectives are a necessary part of this plan.

It is important in any program of physical education for the teacher and the parent to have the general educational objective clearly defined. The first objective of a physical education program should be *the development of physical fitness*. Strength and endurance of the muscular, circulatory, and respiratory systems are essential for efficient performance of the motor skills that are a part of all sport and dance activities. The second objective is *the development of neuro-*

muscular skill. The motor skills of each activity must be learned before the student can enjoy the activity. The skill must be presented in a clear and concise manner so the child can learn the skills. The third objective is *a knowledge of activities for use in leisure time*. Students should be taught activities that can be used after school and when they no longer attend school. The fourth objective is *the knowledge of rules of behavior and of the rules required by the game*. How to behave during the game, good sportsmanship, and how to play the game are essential parts of learning physical education activities.

These objectives can be applied to most activities in physical education programs. Some physical education activities stress one objective more than others. Some activities are especially designed to develop physical fitness and have very little to do with rules of the game. Other activities may be very good for the development of a specific skill and not for developing physical fitness. It does not matter whether the program is for pre-school, the elementary school, junior high level, senior high level, or university or adult level, or if the activity program is being conducted at home by the parents, these objectives should be used to develop the activity program. The objectives should be planned and worked into the activities so the student has the opportunity to understand why he is participating and how he will benefit from his participation.

VALUE OF ACTIVITY

Physical Development. Physical activity enhances muscular strength, muscular endurance, balance, coordination, agility, good posture habits, and flexibility. Interest in one's physical condition, skill ability, and general well being is stimulated, and the ability to relax in an appropriate setting may also be learned. Injuries during physical activity will be less severe or absent entirely if children have proper development.

Emotional Stability. Play activities provide opportunities for emotional expression and the release of tensions and aggression. The development of courage, initiative, alertness, trust, confidence, willingness to risk, and attending to an assigned task can result from successful experiences in group and individual games and activities.

Creativity. Play provides experiences for creative expression and helps to develop an appreciation of beauty and the aesthetic qualities of life. Play experiences provide the opportunity for a child to experiment with and to provide his own play, and to change a presented skill or game into a creative experience.

Skill Development. Opportunity is provided through activity to develop skills basic to future participation in directed learning experiences of organized sports and leisure time activities. Awareness of talents and abilities fundamental for future development may be acquired. Satisfaction with one's self and feelings of self worth can result as motor skills increase.

Social Relationships. Children learn to perform as members of a group and learn cooperative social skills when they are part of a family, a member of a class in school, or have a position on a team or squad. Through play experiences, the child can learn about the world around him and the laws governing his relationship to the world. In our society, the ability to perform basic motor skills is important to the child and often dictates acceptance by his peers and opportunities to participate in school and neighborhood peer group activities. The child needs as many experiences as possible to improve his background, and these experiences should be mostly successful ones.

Intellectual Development. Motor experiences, motor experimentation, and learning are the foundations upon which the child learns about himself and the world, and they are the premise upon which knowledge is based. It is logical that behavior builds upon lower forms of behavior. There is evidence that the scholastic achievement of all children, not just mentally handicapped children, can be improved by supplementing a proper program of physical education.

Self Image. Children form images of themselves based to a great extent upon understandings gained from what their bodies can do. This image is basic to the developing personality. Remedial physical development work is capable of activating dormant potential for personality development. If a child knows that he can do a number of skills, he then reflects this knowledge when performing these skills. A positive self image can be acquired as the child increases the number of motor skills that he can perform successfully.

DEVELOPMENTAL PERCEPTUAL SKILLS

It is apparent that readiness to learn regular academic subject matter involves certain basic skills, physical development, and emotional maturity. These skills are the background for the ability and desire to learn concepts of the standard curriculum, and for desirable physical performance. Many of these skills are expected of normal children before they reach school age. Since new learning is based upon earlier learning, a slow learner or a retarded person may experience increasing difficulty. An opportunity to attain these skills must be provided for children with learning problems in order to facilitate fruitful learning experiences.

Motor Skills. Basic motor skill activities using large muscles of the body are involved in tasks such as drawing or writing. This task requires the ability to control the body, to move the fingers, hand, and arm in a coordinated manner, and the ability to differentiate a specific movement pattern out of a general total movement.

Laterality. The human body is neurologically and anatomically designed as a bilateral (two-sided) organism. The sides of the body are innervated separately, which makes it possible for unified or separate movement of the respective side (right or left) of the body. The development of the concept of laterality in movement as it relates to direction in space is fundamental to understanding one's environment. Laterality is learned through experimentation with body movement and the realization of possible interaction between the two sides of the body and space. Laterality can be developed by movement exploration, balance beam activities, rhythms, marching, aquatics, ball skills, and conditioning exercises.

Laterality is not "handedness." It is the awareness of the two sides of the body and their differences. A child will need to develop dominance by developing one side as the leading side. Before learning to write, a child must be able to control both sides of the body separately and simultaneously. The development of laterality is important to distinguishing the difference between similar letters such as "b," "d," "p," and "q."

Directionality. Horizontal, vertical and depth dimensions follow the understanding of laterality. Kinesthetic awareness is the means by which these concepts are developed. Visual responses are matched with the kinesthetic sense of feeling body parts move to coordinate and evaluate movement. By experimenting with movement patterns, a child learns what movements he must make to touch an object at his right side, behind him or over his head. The coordination of the stimuli from the eyes and the information gained through kinesthetic activity is very important. In order to learn this, a child must make a series of matches between positions of the eyes and positions of the hand in relation to an object. Directionality is dependent upon the development of laterality. Motor activity is the means by which these concepts are learned. It is important that motor learning opportunities be provided and directed toward the development of these skills. Directionality can be developed from movement exploration activities, balance beam activities, ball skills and rhythms.

Posture. Posture is the maintenance of body position with reference to its center of gravity by the innervation of antigravity muscle groups. All other movement patterns develop out of basic posture, which is the means by which we relate to our environment. The ability to adjust body positions efficiently and purposefully is important to this relationship.

Body Image. Our body is the point of reference from which we organize and construct the relative impressions we receive into a coherent personality. A false conception of one's body image will result in faulty actions and faulty perceptions of others. The body image is a learned concept that results from experimentation with body parts and the realization of their relationship to each other and to the external environment. The development of laterality and directionality is an important aspect in the development of body image.

Discrimination. The ability to select desired items from among the mass in the environment is a skill children must have if they are going to learn academic skills. Discrimination is divided into five categories: perceptual, visual, auditory, spatial and quality. The child will learn to make choices and to be selective and inventive in his selections through a well organized program of physical education activities.

- *Perceptual Discrimination.* The ability to distinguish the visual characteristics of objects and to discriminate the meaning of verbal sounds is important. The feel of the motor skill transmits to the performer information about the activity and the performer's ability to perform.
- *Visual Discrimination.* As a child develops the ability to discriminate the details of the mass before him, he progresses toward a higher form of perception. As he learns to discriminate the details he also must learn to differentiate details and organize them into form. The ability to differentiate is very important to a child who is trying to analyze forms and learn to read.
- *Auditory Discrimination.* To understand language, a person must be receptive to auditory stimulation and be able to discriminate one sound from another. When he is able to do this, he can attach meaning to the sounds and understand the combinations of sounds appropriate for language. School experiences and home experiences should provide opportunities to associate language with activities.
- *Spatial Discrimination.* Information about space is gathered through clues that must be interpreted to obtain a concept of space. Kinesthesis is the most direct source of information about space. We compare, select, group, and organize characteristics that become concepts about space.
- *Quality Discrimination.* Concepts concerning motion, quality, time, comparison, and location are necessary for learning. A background involving the concepts of fast, slow, when, what, before, after, thicker, thinner, up, down, and so forth is necessary for learning.

Language Development. Language usage is developed primarily in the home. Children from culturally deprived environments may lack good language development experiences and children from bilingual homes or culturally rich environments may develop extremely good language skills. It is important that an opportunity to express observations and experiences be provided so children learn to use these skills. Many games and activities children play are conducive to natural involvement of verbal skills. Singing games, counting scores, using appropriate terminology, and verbalizing accomplishments or decisions will help stimulate the use of language.

Language Concept Development. Language concept development is necessary because without some type of language the teacher cannot give instructions. Children need to know what words mean, what signals mean and what is expected when words are used.

Memory. One of the important variables involved in the perceptual process is that of consistent input for similar experimental situations. Since a great number of a child's experiences are movement oriented, it is important that any single experience be consistent with the desired learning experiences of the total learning situation. Activity also provides a good opportunity to reinforce learned concepts related to the current activity period.

Group Association. Social development and adjustment to the group and to group activities are important for the slow learner if he is to participate effectively in society. Learning to share with his family members and friends and to work and play with other individuals is especially necessary. The ability to follow directions, to obey rules and regulations, and to accept group decisions and discipline are desirable characteristics that may be developed through group activities. There is always the hope that the retarded child will be invited to the party and that he will already know the rules to the game, the accepted responses and how to behave.

Motivation. Motivation is dependent upon the ability of the teacher to help the child overcome the feeling of inadequacy and to promote success. Coordination of activities to promote understanding and the practical application of concepts already learned will help keep the child's interest and reinforce learning. The activities must be meaningful and should encourage the child to discover the relationship between the learning situation and the playground. Variety in teaching activities that require continued practice is necessary for continued interest. Activities should be centered around the abilities and interests of the children.

PRINCIPLES OF TEACHING

The use of sound teaching techniques is important when teaching any child. However, because of the nature of the retarded child, good teaching techniques are mandatory. These principles of teaching should be observed whether the teacher is a professional or a parent without any professional preparation. The following suggestions may prove helpful in teaching skills to the retarded child:

- The children should be ready to learn the specific concept or skill being taught. When a new concept or skill is to be presented, the initial step is to develop a need for it. Next, provide sufficient positive practice or repetitions to make its use accurate and efficient. Numerous situations should then be introduced where the skill is required, thus providing review and application.

- Instruction should be at the child's level. Verbal directions should be few and very simple, and given without "talking down" to the child. The child will need a model to copy or follow.
- Instruction should always start with what is familiar to the class and proceed to the new skill.
- The activity should be meaningful and have value to the child. Skills and concepts should be taught through the use of socially meaningful situations and materials. Activities should be presented in terms of the individual's needs and objectives.
- Plan to have guaranteed successes. Nothing contributes to interest in an activity more than does legitimate success.
- Instruction should be organized and taught systematically to provide for transfer of learning.
- Repetitions and practice should be used to ensure learning and retention. Practice periods should be short, and new activities should be presented early in the instruction period.
- Demonstrations and leader participation are good teaching devices. Kinesthetic guidance through correct actions is effective in establishing more efficient patterns of movement.
- Geniune praise and encouragement are valuable motivators.
- Class periods should be well organized and supervised.
- Skills should be presented in a progressive plan by building skill upon skill.
- Opportunity should be provided for children to use learned academic skills as they relate to and integrate with the physical activity being presented.
- Class organization should provide for active participation by all, be varied in appeal, provide for different attention spans, provide purposeful practice, and create interest in the activity.
- Safety should be considered in planning the activities.
- Progress slowly but go as fast as the child is able. When one skill is learned, move quickly to the next. Do not get discouraged. Progress is slow with some, so be happy about the smallest progress.
- Develop a close relationship with the child. Show how pleased you are when he is able to do even the most elementary skill correctly. Let him show you many times the skill he has learned. Let him show other adults and other children. Let him know you sincerely want him to perform, and reward him with praise.
- Be secure in your knowledge of the skills. To participate in this program you do not need to be an expert performer yourself, but you should be able to analyze the skills you are asking the child to do.
- Keep the lesson fun. The child will learn faster if he enjoys what is being done. Entertainment is not a primary objective of a physical education program, but enjoyment is a tool that increases learning.
- Keep the instruction period short. The child can only practice up to

his own limits of concentration; these limits may be broadened, but only the child can determine this. Allow his attention to wander only after he has really tried to perform. When his attention does wander, change the skill, help him with another activity, but return to the desired performance before the instructional period is over.
- Be patient, but be forceful. Help the child succeed by encouraging him to perform the skill on which you are working.
- Develop group instruction as soon as possible. The sooner a child can function in a group, the sooner he will be able to live in a group.
- Demand good discipline. A child will learn more if he is required to be well behaved. He will also learn better how to function with a group when good behavior is required. Use firmness and fairness, but remember you are dealing with a child.
- As far as possible, use the same instructor each day. A child responds better when he feels secure with the instructor. He should not have to adjust every class period to another teacher.
- If you need to touch a child during the lesson, tell him about it before you do so. If he is expecting you to take hold of his hands, he will willingly permit you to. If he is surprised, he may pull back, and you will have to repeat the procedure.
- Be enthusiastic and have fun yourself.

The activities presented in the following chapters have been planned to provide desirable learning materials to meet the needs of the special child with learning disabilities and to provide for total development. When the child is able to participate successfully in these activities, he should be guided into programs with normal children.

MAINSTREAMING

A mentally retarded child should be placed for his education into regular educational classes whenever the child will benefit more by being in the classroom rather than special education classes. There will be times when an educable retarded student will be able to function with the regular classes, and there will be times when he should be in a special classroom. The teachers and parents should decide together how and when to mainstream a child in order to make the school experience a true learning experience.

It is the objective of education to prepare all children for life experiences; a retarded child should also have this opportunity. The child should be placed in the least restrictive environment to maximize the educational experience. The evaluation team of teachers, parents and administrators are responsible for this decision.

At all times, the retarded child should be mainstreamed in family activities. He can take part in and be a contributing member in most family activities in the home and in the neighborhood.

2
EVALUATION OF MOTOR PERFORMANCE

Evaluation of motor performance in physical education activities for mentally retarded students is very important because evaluation is one part of the triad of diagnostic teaching—skill presentation, skill evaluation and skill correction. Evaluation of motor performance provides the parent and the teacher with opportunities for giving praise to the child, for correcting the skill, for recognizing achievement, and for advancing the child to a more difficult skill or group. Each of these opportunities aids in improving the child's self image and increasing performing ability. Parents should be aware of the importance of evaluating motor performance, and should encourage the school personnel to include motor performance evaluations in testing plans.

Evaluation of motor skills is an important part of the Individual Education Program (IEP) for children in special education. Physical education skills are measurable with results that can be observed. These evaluations should be included in all IEP discussion and goal planning sessions. The tests provide a measurement tool against which performance can be compared. The results of the tests should be noted on the IEP, goals for improvement should be set, and activities for remediation should be planned into the child's physical education program. The person or team of persons responsible for implementing remedial activities should be noted and be responsible for including the activities in the child's program.

Parents should be included in the evaluation planning sessions so that specific activities can be included in the home as a supplement to the school program.

A child's motor performance should be evaluated in the following areas:
- physical fitness,
- motor perception and basic movement skills, and
- sport skills.

Test results should be noted in each of these areas, and goals and activities should be planned to correct skills where performance is faulty, and to strengthen muscles if the tests indicate a child is muscularly weak.

Physical Fitness Evaluation

There are two approaches to measurement of physical fitness—the use of standardized tests and the use of teacher-made tests.

Standardized Tests. Standardized tests provide norms and performance standards against which individual performances can be measured. Many of these tests provide recognition and award programs that give motivation and recognition to the child.

The American Alliance of Health, Physical Education, Recreation and Dance, The Joseph P. Kennedy Foundation, and the President's Council on Physical Fitness and Sports are three groups that provide programs and tests specifically for the evaluation of physical fitness levels of mentally retarded people. The test items included by all three agencies are:
- the flexed arm hang,
- sit ups,
- standing long jump,
- softball throw,
- 50 yard dash, and
- the 300 yard run-walk.

The *AAHPERD Special Silver Award* is for children who achieve at the 50th percentile on 5 of the 6 items of the test. The *AAHPERD Special Gold Award* is for children who achieve at the 75th percentile on 5 of 6 test items. The *Kennedy Foundation Champ Award* is for children who achieve at the 85th percentile on all 6 test items. The *AAHPERD Progress Award* is a certificate for children who participate and improve their performance. The tests and award requirements are included in a publication authored by Johnson and Londeree.[1]

The *Kraus-Weber Test of Minimum Fitness*[2] is a pass-fail test that includes six items evaluating abdominal strength, back strength, and leg flexibility. The test items are:
- **Sit up**—with legs straight and a partner holding the legs down,
- **Curl up**—with legs flexed and a partner holding the feet down,
- **Leg lift**—while lying on the stomach with partner holding hips and shoulders down, raise the legs from the floor and hold 10 seconds,

---

[1] Johnson, Leon and Ben Londeree, *Motor Fitness Testing Manual for the Moderately Mentally Retarded*, Washington D.C.: American Alliance for Health, Physical Education, Recreation and Dance, 1976.

[2] Kraus, Hans and Ruth P. Hirschland, "Minimum Fitness Tests on School Children," *Research Quarterly* 25 (1954): 177-188.

- **Chest lift**—while lying on the stomach with partner holding the hips and ankles down, lift the chest up and hold for 10 seconds,
- **Toe Touches**—standing, bend forward and touch the floor just in front of the toes, keep the knees straight and hold 10 seconds. The results of the test provide the teacher with data for improving these components of physical fitness.

The *Physically Underdeveloped Child* is a test that has been developed by the President's Council on Physical Fitness and Sport[3] and is used to identify boys and girls of ages 9 to 17 who are underdeveloped in some basic area(s) of strength and endurance. The test is not specifically designed for mentally retarded children, but many mentally retarded children are physically underdeveloped, and this test can be used to identify this condition.

ARM AND SHOULDER STRENGTH
Test 1 (Boys)
Pull ups—At a horizontal bar that is high enough for the boy's feet to clear the floor when his arms are fully extended, pull body up with arms until the chin is above the bar, and lower the body until the arms are fully extended.
To pass:
ages 9-12—one pull-up
ages 13-14—two pull-ups
ages 15-17—four pull-ups

Test 1 (Girls)
Flexed Arm Hang—Using a palm facing away from the body grip, the girl hangs with the elbows flexed and the chin above the bar. The legs are straight and the feet are clear of the floor.
To pass:
all ages—hold 5 seconds

ABDOMINAL STRENGTH
Test 2
Sit ups—Child lies on the back with the knees bent and the feet on the floor. Feet should be about 12 inches apart and the heels about 12 inches from the buttocks. Hands are clasped behind the neck and the elbows point outward. The child sits up until the elbows reach the knees. Return to the starting position.
To pass:
all ages—20 sit ups

---

[3] *The Physically Underdeveloped Child*, Washington, D.C.: The President's Council on Physical Fitness and Sports.

RECOVERY INDEX TEST
Test 3
Bench Steps—Child places one foot on a 14 inch platform. He steps onto the platform with the other foot and stands erect. He steps down with the first foot and down with the second foot. The rhythmic, steady cadence of up, two, three, four is repeated for four minutes.
To pass:
ages 9-12—Complete the 4 minute exercise.
ages 13-17—Complete the 4 minute exercise, and score 61 or higher on the Recovery Index Text. The pulse is counted for 30 sec. after a 1 minute exercise. At 2 minutes and at 3 minutes the pulse is counted again for 30 sec. The three pulse counts are added together, and the student must score fair or better.

Pulse	Response	Recovery Index
199 or better	Poor	60 or less
171-198	Fair	61 and 70
150-170	Good	71 and 80
133-149	Very good	81 and 90
132-less	Excellent	91 or more

Teacher Made Tests. The teacher can select items that measure physical fitness (strength, flexibility, coordination, agility, balance, and muscular and cardiovascular endurance) and test each component. The teacher should select the items to be evaluated, and then indicate the endurance of or the number of times that the exercise should be done. For example:
- Strength—curl ups (abdominal strength) 5 times. Knee push ups (arm and shoulder strength) 5 times.
- Flexibility—sit and reach (leg and lower back) 1 time and hold 10 seconds.
- Coordination—jumping jacks 10 times.
- Agility—squat thrusts 5 times.
- Balance—hopping on each foot 10 times.
- Endurance—300 yard run-walk 1 time.

The teacher establishes the standards for the class, recognizing improvement and achievement with awards of his/her own design. The results would be entered onto the IEP, goals would be set, and activities would be prescribed for improvement. Parents should be included in this planning so that activities and exercises will be practiced at home as well as at school.

Motor Perceptual and Basic Movement Evaluation

Motor Perceptual Activities are those activities that require or develop an awareness of the body in many noncompetitive movement tasks. *Basic Movement* activities are walking, running, hopping, jumping and skipping.

Motor Perceptual Evaluations

The most widely used test in the area of perceptual testing is the *Purdue Perceptual-Motor Survey*.[4] This text includes:
- the walking board—walking forward, backward, and sidewise,
- jumping—hopping, skipping and patterns,
- identification of body parts,
- imitation of movements,
- obstacle course,
- Kraus-Weber sit up and leg lift tests,
- angels in the snow,
- chalkboard activities of drawing circles and lines,
- rhythmic writing of selected patterns,
- ocular pursuits with both eyes and with each eye alone watching selected light tracks, and
- visual achievement forms of circles, squares, crosses, triangles and diamonds.

Test materials needed for each test item and methods of scoring are given in the test booklet. The test can be used to diagnose deficiencies in motor performance and activities can be designed for correction of the indicated weaknesses.

The *Cratty Test of Motor Perceptions*[5] is a two level test that includes six items at each level. The test items are:
- body perception—copy selected actions,
- gross agility—getting to a standing position as fast as possible,
- balance—standing on one foot,
- locomotor agility—crawling, walking, jumping, and hopping,
- ball throwing—throwing to a catcher, and
- ball tracking—catching a thrown ball.

Level I is more simple than Level II, and the tester is provided with test instructions and scoring values. The test results can serve as guides in the selection of special activities for the child who performed at low levels as evaluated by the test.

Perceptual Motor Test[6] by Paul Smith includes an evaluation of:
- posture,
- balance—bilateral and lateral,
- shoulder flexibility,
- awareness of up and down,
- laterality—bilateral, unilateral, and cross lateral,

---

[4]Roach, Eugene G. and Newell C. Kephart, *The Purdue Perceptual Motor Survey*, Columbus, Ohio: Charles E. Merrill Publishing Co., 1966.

[5]Cratty, Bryant J., *Motor Activity and the Education of Retardates*, Philadelphia: Lea and Febiger, 1974.

[6]Smith, Paul, *Perceptual Motor Test*, Freeport, New York: Education Activities, Inc., 1973.

- preferences—hand, eye, and foot, and
- eye control.

Each test item includes the description of the test, how to score it, and activities that can strengthen the skill if a low score is achieved.

Bruininks-Oseretsky Test of Motor Proficiency[7] is for individual assessment of children ages 4½ to 14½. The test includes pretests of arm and leg preference and tests of:
- running speed and agility in a 30 yard shuttle run,
- balance with eight subtasks while standing and moving,
- bilateral coordination with eight subtasks of the use of upper and lower limb opposition,
- strength with three subtasks of arm and shoulder strength, abdominal strength and leg strength,
- upper-limb coordination with nine subtasks of arm and hand coordination.

The test also includes three tests of fine motor development of response speed, visual-motor control and upper-limb speed and dexterity. The long form of the test will take 45 to 60 minutes to administer. The short form of the test will take 15 to 20 minutes and includes:
- running speed and agility,
- standing on preferred leg on the balance beam,
- walking heel to toe on balance beam,
- tapping feet alternately while making circles with fingers,
- jumping up and clapping hands,
- standing long jump,
- catching a tossed ball with both hands,
- throwing a ball at a target with preferred hand,
- response speed,
- drawing a line through a straight path with preferred hand,
- copying a circle with preferred hand,
- copying overlapping pencils with preferred hand,
- sorting shapes with preferred hand,
- making dots in circles with preferred hand.

Scoring booklets, evaluation norms, and specific pieces of testing equipment are included in the testing kit.

Hirst and Rasmus Basic Movement Evaluation is a test of walking, running, jumping, hopping, and skipping designed for use with young children or with older children who appear to lack skill in these basic movements. Each skill is to be performed by the child and observed by the teacher. The teacher evaluates each performance on a score range of 5 to 1, with 5 being the most efficient score. The child will need the teacher to say, "Can you do this?" and then demonstrate

---

[7] Bruininks, Robert H., *Bruininks-Oseretsky Test of Motor Proficiency*, Circle Pines, Minnesota: American Guidance Service.

the skill for the child. A score of 4 or 5 on a skill indicates an efficient performance with no remedial activities necessary. Scores of 3 or lower indicate some weaknesses in the performance, and activities that strengthen the performance are needed. Provided with the evaluation tool are examples of activities that can provide practice for strengthening skill where deficiencies are observed.

The *Hughes Basic Gross Motor Assessment*[8] (BGMA) is not designed exclusively for the mentally retarded population. It is designed to yield information about gross motor performance for children ages 6 to 12 and can be used to evaluate motor skills of mentally retarded children. The test consists of eight subtests:

1. Static balance—standing on each leg.
2. Stride jumping—feet apart and together several times.
3. Tandem walking—heel to toe walking.
4. Hopping—between two parallel lines.
5. Skipping—in good form and rhythm.
6. Target throwing—at target on the floor.
7. Yoyo catching—catch a ball that is on a string with a container.
8. Ball handling skills of throwing, catching, and dribbling.

Instructions for administering and scoring each of the subtests are included, and worksheets for recording the results are provided.

The *Geddes Psychomotor Inventory*[9] provides both short and long forms for levels of infant, early childhood, primary, intermediate, and young adult. This short form can serve as a screening test, and the long form can serve as a diagnostic assessment when difficulties with the test items are observed. The test items for each level are appropriate for people within each group, and include: (1) balance and posture maintenance, (2) locomotion and basic movement, (3) manipulators, (4) ball handling, (5) body awareness, (6) eye-body coordination, (7) apparatus experiences, (8) selected skill evaluation, (9) perceptual abilities, and (10) aquatic.

Motor Problems Inventory[10] by Glyndon Riley includes: tests of small muscle coordination of finger tapping and voice practice; laterality; gross motor coordination of hopping on each foot, balance, walk, run, and skip; and general observation of behaviors like restlessness, perserverance, distractability, and poor reading and writing skills.

---

[8]Hughes, Jeanne E., *Hughes Basic Gross Motor Assessment*, (Denver, Colo.: Office of Special Education Denver Public Schools).

[9]Geddes, Dolores, *Psychomotor Individualized Educational Programs for Intellectual Learning and Behaviorial Disabilities* (Boston: Allyn and Bacon, 1981).

[10]Riley, Glyndon D., *Motor Problems Inventory*, (Los Angeles, Calif.: Western Psychological Services).

HIRST-RASMUS BASIC MOVEMENT EVALUATION

Part I   **Motor Evaluation**   Circle the number that best indicated the child's performance.

A. Walk—20 feet
1. Rhythm	Smooth	5	4	3	2	1	Rough
2. Arm swing	Opposition	5	4	3	2	1	Unilateral
3. Toes	Straight ahead	5	4	3	2	1	In or out

B. Running—40 feet
1. Rhythm	Smooth	5	4	3	2	1	Rough
2. Arm Swing	Opposition	5	4	3	2	1	Unilateral
3. Feet	Toes forward	5	4	3	2	1	In or out
	Land lightly	5	4	3	2	1	Land heavy
	Balls of feet	5	4	3	2	1	Flat footed

C. Jumping—5 times
A spring into the air from both feet and landing on both feet. The arms move together in the direction of the jump.

1. Take off	From toes	5	4	3	2	1	Flat footed
2. Arm Swing	Up and forward	5	4	3	2	1	No swing
3. Landing	Knees bent	5	4	3	2	1	Knees stiff
4. Direction	Upward	5	4	3	2	1	No lift

D. Hopping—5 times
Begin on one foot and spring from the floor and land on the same foot. The arms move together in the upward direction of the hop.

1. Push off	Right foot upward	5	4	3	2	1	No push
	Left foot upward	5	4	3	2	1	No push
2. Feet	Right from toes	5	4	3	2	1	Flat footed
	Left from toes	5	4	3	2	1	Flat footed
3. Arms	Right balanced	5	4	3	2	1	Unbalanced
	Left balanced	5	4	3	2	1	Unbalanced

E. Skipping—40 feet
A combination of a short hop and a long step, alternating the lead foot after each hop.

1. Rhythm	Smooth	5	4	3	2	1	Rough
2. Height	Vertical	5	4	3	2	1	No lift

Hirst, Cyntha C. and Carolyn J. Rasmus, Brigham Young University, Provo, Utah.

Part II Practice Activities

A. Walking
1. Rhythm—
   A. Step to drum rhythm.
   B. Step to musical beat—marches, waltz, etc.
2. Arm Swing—
   A. Tie one foot and opposite hand together with a loose string and walk.
   B. Step with a high, exaggerated high step.
3. Toe Position—
   A. Walk on cardboard footprints.
   B. Walk with toes curled under.

B. Running
1. Rhythm—
   A. Run as fast as you can.
   B. Run and stop on a signal and repeat.
2. Arm Swing—
   A. Run with arms overhead.
   B. Run with hands on hips.
3. Feet
   Toes forward—
   A. Run on cardboard footprints.
   B. Run in place.
   Landing—
   A. Land on toes when running.
   B. Land heavily and then land lightly.
   Balls of feet—
   A. Run with knees high.
   B. Run in place fast.

C. Jumping
1. Take-off—
   A. Hold onto the back of a chair and jump.
   B. Lean against a wall and jump.
2. Arm Swing—
   A. Jump over one shoe box.
   B. Jump over several shoe boxes in a line.
3. Landing—
   A. Jump from bench to floor.
   B. Jump sideways across a line or rope.
4. Direction—
   A. Jump onto bench from floor with help.
   B. Jump over bench with help.

D. Hopping
1. Push-off—
   A. Hop holding onto back of a chair. Practice with each foot.
   B. Hop from one square into another square for several hops.
2. Feet—
   A. Hop high and low with each foot.
   B. Hop a long way and a short way with each foot.
3. Arms—
   A. Swing arms upward with the hop.
   B. Exaggerate arm swing with hop patterns.

E. Skipping (hop-step-hop-step)
1. Rhythm—
   A. Skip to drum beat.
   B. Exaggerate a high hop and a low step. (Practice hops on each foot if the skip does not come easily.)
2. Height—
   A. Skip fast.
   B. Skip around in circles.

The Teaching Research Motor Development Scale[11] is to measure motor proficiency of moderately and severely retarded people. Activities such as standing on tip toe, standing on one foot, jumping, walking, imitation of movements, stepping over obstacles, ducking under obstacles, passing between obstacles, gymnastic skill, exercises, and various running skills are included. Equipment needs, number of trials, and directions for administering the test are also included. A scoring sheet is part of the scale.

Sport Skill Testing

There are many opportunities on the playground and in the gymnasium for evaluation of sport skills. Anytime a student throws a ball, the throw can be evaluated as to how far the ball was thrown, how accurately it came to the catcher or target, how fast the ball went, or if the starting position, the action, or the follow through of the skill being performed was correct for good performance.

Sport skills can be evaluated in two ways: (1) the *result* of the performance, and (2) the *form* of the performance.

The Result of the Performance. The result of sport skills can be readily measured. How far the ball went, how fast the person ran, how often the ball was hit, how many times the basket was made, how few hits were needed to get to the hole are all easily counted, timed, or scored. Teachers can have tournaments, contests, games, races, and meets. They should keep records and make evaluations of students' performances, improvements, and achievements. Teachers can stress individual performance and competition with the student's own scores so the student is competing with himself before he competes against other students. Awards and recognition can be based on participation and improvement as well as on winning.

Following is a check-list for evaluating sport skills. The list includes skills from many sports and the teacher can use the entire list, or can select specific skills for evaluation as the list applies to the school program.

Specific sports areas can be evaluated; i.e. basketball skills of throwing, catching, shooting, jumping, and running can be evaluated during the winter basketball season; and track skills of running, long jumping, high jumping, low hurdles can be measured as part of the spring track season. The results of the tests should be included in the discussion sessions that are part of the evaluation for the IEP; activities should be included that will strengthen any areas of weakness.

---

[11] Fredericks, H.D. Bud, Victor L. Baldwin, Philip Doughty, and James Walter, *The Teaching Research Motor Development Scale*, (Springfield, Illinois: Charles C. Thomas, 1972).

GAME SKILLS PROFICIENCY RECORD

NAME_____ AGE_____ DATE_____

	Trial Score	Tech. Score	Total Score
1. Roll a ball between partner's legs 30 feet away.			
2. Roll a ball against the wall ten feet away and catch it.			
3. Bounce and catch a ball with partner ten feet away.			
4. Bounce a ball five times with either hand.			
5. Bounce a ball while running 20 feet.			
6. Bounce a ball around three cones, five feet apart.			
7. Catch a utility ball from a throw ten feet away.			
8. Catch a nine-inch ball from a throw 20 feet away.			
9. Catch a softball from a throw 30 feet away.			
10. Throw a ball with underhand toss so partner ten feet away can catch it.			
11. Throw a ball with a chest pass so partner ten feet away can catch it.			
12. Throw a ball or beanbag into wastebasket ten feet away.			
13. Throw a ball 20 feet.			
14. Kick a stationary ball between goal posts 12 feet apart, ten feet away.			
15. Run and kick a stationary ball between goal posts 12 feet apart, ten feet away.			
16. Run and kick a rolling ball between two goal posts 12 feet apart, ten feet away.			
17. Kick a ball 20 feet before it bounces.			
18. Dribble a ball using both feet around a cone 20 feet away, and back.			
19. Hit a ball off a batting tee 60 feet on the fly.			
20. Hit a thrown ball 60 feet on the fly.			
21. Hit a volleyball with a forearm bounce pass to a partner ten feet away.			
22. Hit a volleyball with an overhand hit to a partner 30 feet away.			
23. Serve a volleyball over a six foot net from 30 feet away.			
24. Make a two-hand underhand basketball shot.			
25. Make a chest shot or a one-hand basketball shot five feet away from basket.			
26. Make a basket from ten feet away.			
27. Make a basket from 15 feet away.			
28. Throw a softball 60 feet on the fly.			
29. Catch a bouncing softball before it rolls.			
30. Hit a target with an underhand pitch from 30 feet away.			

The Form of the Performance. The form of the skill performance should be observed by the teacher. Good form that follows the principles of motor performance will result in better scores when the results are being measured. If the teacher will: teach the skill with a good demonstration; allow time for practice; divide the skill into its *starting position*, it *action*, and its *follow-through* for students who need this skill breakdown; allow more practice time; evaluate the performance; and repeat any of the above steps; the student will learn to perform the skill efficiently, and the teacher will be able to identify any part of the skill in which the performance error is being made. Corrections can be made that will result in a more efficient performance.

3
MOVEMENT EDUCATION

Mentally handicapped children may be limited in their ability to perform many motor skills. This inability may be the result of physical handicaps, limited opportunities to participate, or little motivation to develop ability in performing physical skills. The limited opportunity may be the result of a social environment that is restricting for many mentally retarded children. They are often very closely supervised and are kept away from some learning experiences such as lessons in gymnastics or swimming. The lack of motivation may be due to the child's repeated failure during earlier learning experiences when attempting to learn specific skills. Some children with able physical bodies may be afraid to perform activities like walking down the stairs, crossing a bridge or even running down the gym floor, because of fear for their safety, even when performing with a structured approach in movement exploration. These timid children can be led into activities through which they can gain confidence in their abilities, and become more able to perform physical education motor skills.

Principles of Movement

When the basic principles of movement are applied to motor skill performance, the efficiency of performance can be improved. Children do perform more efficiently when proper practice is provided and when the teacher or parent understands the basic principles of movement. The three principles, *opposition*, *total body assembly* and *follow-through*, apply to all movement skills. The teacher must be aware of these principles of movement and apply them in teaching lessons for children in order for the skill to be performed in an efficient manner.

Principle of Opposition. When a balanced maximum effort is desired in the movement, the sides of the body work in opposition.

For example, when throwing a ball for distance, if the ball is to be thrown with the right arm, there is a step forward onto the left foot. This will allow total body involvement, contribute to the throwing action, and maintenance of balance. Walking is another example of opposition of movement. The opposite arm swings forward as each forward step is taken.

Principle of Total Body Assembly. This principle implies that all parts of the body should contribute toward the desired skill performance. For example, in running, the body should lean slightly forward to contribute to the forward progress desired. In throwing, the total body should be used to increase the force of the throw by reaching with the non-throwing arm and by stepping forward in the direction of the throw. All unnecessary movements should be eliminated. In running, the arms should not move across the body, but should reach forward and pull backward. The hands should be relaxed and not cause wasted effort by being held tense.

Principle of Follow-Through. The skill being performed must be finished or completed. The last part of the skill is the follow through. When this is done correctly, the skill will be efficient, but if the follow-through is ignored or in the wrong direction, the skill will not be done well. For instance, the power of the throw will be changed. "Reach for the target" and "Give with the ball" are cues to aid the performer in remembering to complete the skill of throwing.

Elements of Movement

Space Elements
The area around us is space. We move through it with fundamental movements called nonlocomotor movements like swaying and stretching and locomotor movements like running and skipping so that we can experiment with our relationship to this space. This experimenting involves the following:
- **Direction** is the external relationship of the body movements to space—left, right, forward, backward, diagonal, up, down, straight, curved, or spiral.
- **Range** is the size of the movements. It includes the adjustment of the movement to the space size and to the desired objective of the action. Far, near, close, and away are words used to describe range of movement.
- **Dimension** refers to the size of the moving body or body part being used. The size of the body movement should meet the purpose of the movement in an efficient manner. Big, small, wide, narrow, thin, fat, huge and tiny describe body size during movement experience.
- **Focus** should be on the object or on the objective involved. If an

object is used, a ball, for example, the eyes should be on the ball. If an action, for instance striking, is to be carried out, the whole body must concentrate to complete the action.
- **Design** is the pattern of the movement in space. Geometric shapes like circles, lines, squares, curves, or triangles are a part of many dance and sport activities.
- **Level** is the height of the movement. The level of the body should be at an appropriate height for the successful execution of the movement. For example, the angle of an efficient start in a short race is different than for a distance run. The body must be placed at the proper level for the take-off. Another example is how much the knees bend when jumping very high and when jumping over a line on the gym floor. A low crouch is needed to jump high but not to jump over a line.

Movement Quality

The basic elements of quality in movement indicate the different ways in which movement may be released. *Sustained* movement is a moderate release of energy, the movement being slow, steady, and even. *Collapse* movement is a slow, light, relaxation movement towards the floor. It can be done with the arms, the head, or the entire body. *Swinging* movement is a pendular action, either slow or fast, that can involve the arms, legs, the head, or the entire body in a swaying action. *Striking* movement is quick, strong, and percussive. It may be a kick, a hit with the hand, a poke with the fist, or a stamp of the foot on the floor. *Dodging* movement is a quick, light, elusive action used to get away from an opponent or an object.

4
ACTIVITIES FOR BABIES

A child's most important developmental stage occurs in the first three years of life. Experiments have proven that children with experiences in stimulation and development exercises increase their I.Q. more than those not receiving extra training. Family relationships, feeling, moving, belonging, seeing, hearing, and experiences with objects and space all provide opportunities to learn. Interaction with others and the environment help the baby become alert and motivated. Praise, touching and loving help develop security, trust and confidence. The more interaction the child has with its environment, the greater the development potential.

Babies are born with natural drives to move and senses ready to function. These natural movements are referred to as reflexes, and include grasping, placing and walking. Exercises stimulate the baby to learn how to control these movements and learn about the environment. Physical activities also help develop the nervous system and other functions of the body.

It is important to know that the rate of development varies and is unique to each child. Progressive activities depend on the level of the child, not age; therefore, activities should be adapted to the child's development level. There is no danger of overstimulation. Both parents should play with their baby regularly and thus become aware of the baby's developmental level. This will help them choose appropriate activities. It will also help them understand unusual behavior and seek professional advice if necessary.

Teaching Suggestions
- Father and mother should share in the playtime experience.
- There should be a consistent routine established for the exercise period.

- The length of the session depends on how tired the baby gets. When the child gets restless or fussy, it is time for a change.
- You should remain calm, relaxed and smooth throughout the session.
- Be consistent and gentle. Enjoy the baby and make it a fun playtime together.
- Have a special place for the daily lesson and use special equipment for the session. Only one toy should be used at a time.
- Keep distractions away from the area.
- Be positive and give the baby praise for accomplishments.
- Gradually help expand the baby's attention span exploring new experiences.
- Show the baby how to do the desired activity. Imitation is a basic learning method for children.
- Repetition of the skills is good and will increase the baby's attention span. Trial and error are basic to the learning process.
- Provide activities that the child knows as well as skills that are new.
- Choose activities that use all the senses to increase awareness of the child's abilities and the environment. Use talk, song, rhythm, music, etc. to help stimulate learning.
- Talk about what you are doing, using appropriate words and sounds so the child gets used to them.

The activities in this chapter are presented in progressive order. There are four basic developmental stages. As the child progresses in development at one level, select additional activities from the next level. The fourth level includes activities to encourage walking and locomotor activities. For activities beyond this level see Chapter 5, Movement Exploration Activities, and Chapter 6, Perceptual Motor Activities.

PHASE ONE

The following activities are listed in progressive order, beginning with activities for newborn babies. As they become appropriate, include additional activities on the list until the child is ready for phase two activities.

- Change the baby's position in the crib and move the crib in the room so the child experiences different environments, lighting and position.
- During diaper changes, gently move and massage body parts.
- Put a brightly colored toy on the crib in the baby's sight line. Change the toy often, varying colors, sizes and shapes.
- Carry your baby with you to other rooms in the house. Talk and sing, rock, cuddle and hold your child.

ACTIVITIES FOR BABIES

- Play the radio for short periods of time.
- Take your baby outside to experience and make adjustments to noise, light and other environmental factors.
- With the baby on his back:
  A. Gently move arms over the head and back.
  B. Push the legs to a bent-knee position and stretch them to the resting position.
- Put a mobile across the crib.
- Draw attention to a noisy toy by shaking it.
- Let your child track a bright toy with his eyes until it is out of sight.
- Move her hands and feet where she can see them. Move them apart and together.
- Stimulate the child's hearing by putting a bell on his shoe or a rattle in his hand. Take him to listen to the sounds in the house, such as the TV, piano, music box, clock, bells.
- Go for a ride in the car or a walk and talk about what you see and hear.
- Include her in family-centered activities and games.

Exercises

- **Purpose.** General body movement and touch stimulation.
  Procedure. Place the baby on his back. Help him stroke his face and body.
  Suggestion. Use both hands.
- **Purpose.** Arm and leg relaxation.
  Procedure. With the baby on his back, toss the arms and legs gently to get them to relax.
  Suggestion. Gently patting the body parts will also help him to relax.
- **Purpose.** Flexibility and relaxation.
  Procedure. Slowly stretch both arms and move them forward, up, down and across the chest. Stretch the legs and move them apart, up and down, through the normal range of motion.
  Suggestion. When exercising the legs, keep the lower back flat on the surface. Stretch the arms and legs to a completely extended position. Repeat the exercise moving the arms separately, alternating right and left arms. Next, repeat the exercise for the legs, moving one leg at a time.
- **Purpose.** Abdominal strength.
  Procedure. With the baby on his back, trace a line around the navel on the child's stomach with your fingernail. He will pull in the abdominal area.
  Suggestion. Repeat the exercise after he relaxes.
- **Purpose.** Strengthen the abdominals and bowels.
  Procedure. With the baby on his back, place the hand firmly on

the child's abdomen. He will pull in the abdomen. Release the pressure immediately.
Suggestion. Repeat the exercise after he relaxes.
- **Purpose.** Back strength.
Procedure. With the child on his stomach, stroke his back to make him lift his head.
Suggestion. Limit the arch in the back to a slight arc.
- **Purpose.** Back strength.
Procedure. Hold the baby with his back to you. Place one hand on his chest and one on his knees. Lean him forward until he cannot keep his head up.
Suggestion. Allow him to look at a toy or in a mirror.
- **Purpose.** Turning back to stomach.
Procedure. Place the child on his back. Place your right hand under his bent left knee, keeping the right leg straight. Stretch his right arm out and up with your left hand. Flex the left hip and roll him to the right side.
Suggestion. Repeat the exercise several times to reinforce the process and encourage the child to learn control.
- **Purpose.** Turning stomach to back.
Procedure. With the child on his stomach, fold the right arm under the chest and turning will follow automatically.
Suggestion. Support the head until she learns to control her body. Repeat the exercise turning to the other side.

PHASE TWO

When the child is comfortable with the activities in phase one, add activities from the following list to the child's exercise program. Exercise sessions can be longer, and more challenging exercises may be incorporated into the program. Be sure to include activities for all body areas and for stimulation of all the senses.
- Stimulate the body parts with materials of different textures such as silk, terry cloth, feathers, flannel. Name the body parts so your child becomes familiar with terminology. Allow him to handle the materials to study the textures.
- Use toys such as clutch balls, stuffed stockings or yarn balls, which the baby can grasp and release.
- Use a variety of toys that have different textures such as plastic rings, sponge, tape, tissue paper, rubber toys, fluffy animals, etc.
- Put a rattle in his hand. Encourage him to look at it and study it.
- Show her toys near her hand; help her see and grasp them.
- Tie a balloon to his wrist for him to move, feel and watch. Rattles and other objects can be used in a similar way.
- Stimulate her recognition of sounds by rubbing balloons, ringing bells, crumbling paper, and playing the piano.

- Encourage him to use his feet to kick a balloon or other toys.
- Encourage him to hold his bottle.
- Put her on a scooter which will hold her body while she reaches for toys and moves around.
- Hold him under the arms while he jumps and dances to music or your singing.
- Encourage play during her bath, such as kicking, splashing, and playing with toys.
- Go for a walk with the baby in the stroller. Explore outside things such as kitten fur, car noises, friends, grass, etc.
- Let him play and talk with other children.
- Encourage vocal sounds and imitations of your movements, expression, and sounds.

Exercises
- **Purpose.** Back strength.
  Procedure. Lie on your back. Place the baby face down on your abdomen. Hold him under the shoulders and he will lift his back. (Fig. 4-1)
  Precaution. Do not stress the shoulder joint.
  Note. This exercise may be done on a table or bed, also.
- **Purpose.** Back strength.
  Procedure. Place the baby on a table in a prone position with his head and shoulders over the edge of the table. Hold him at the hips and arms or by the hands if baby is insecure. (Fig. 4-2)

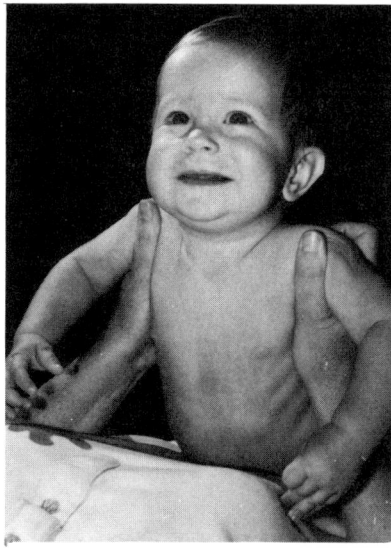

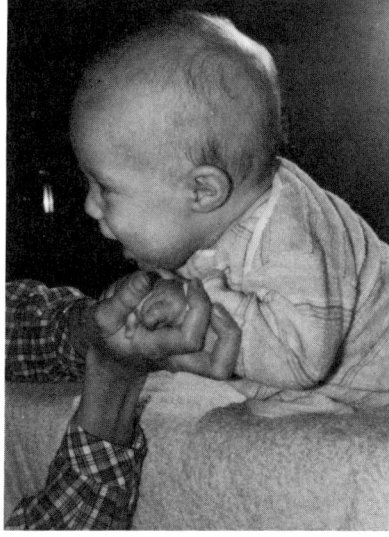

Figure 4-1   **Figure 4-2**

Precaution. Assist the baby as much as is necessary to provide trust and security. (Fig. 4-3)
Note: As the baby gets stronger, gradually remove the support on the arms and move him further off the table.
- **Purpose.** Strengthen hips and lower back.
Procedures. Place the baby with her legs over the edge of the table in a prone position. Pat the lower back to make the legs stretch out. (Fig. 4-4)
Suggestion. Place a toy in front of the baby to keep her attention and provide security.

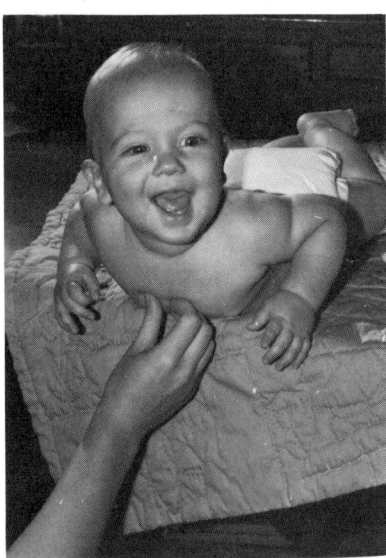

Figure 4-3

- **Purpose.** Arm and shoulder strength.
  Procedure. Place the baby in a push-up position. Support him with one hand on his knees and the other hand under his chest. (Fig. 4-5) Gradually allow him to support more of his body weight.
  Suggestion. Place a toy in front of him to draw his attention.
- **Purpose:** Leg and shoulder strength.
  Procedure. Place the baby on her knees, leaning on a round pillow. (Fig. 4-6) Roll her across the pillow onto her hands. Hold her legs to assist her with the movement.
  Suggestion. Place a toy for her to reach as a goal. This will become a fun activity as the baby becomes secure and develops strength.
- **Purpose.** Arm and abdominal strength.
  Procedure. With his legs bent, assist the baby in raising his head and chest toward you by holding his hands. Have him hold your fingers to encourage using the arms. (Fig. 4-7)
  Suggestion. Use a toy to encourage him to lift his head without your assistance.

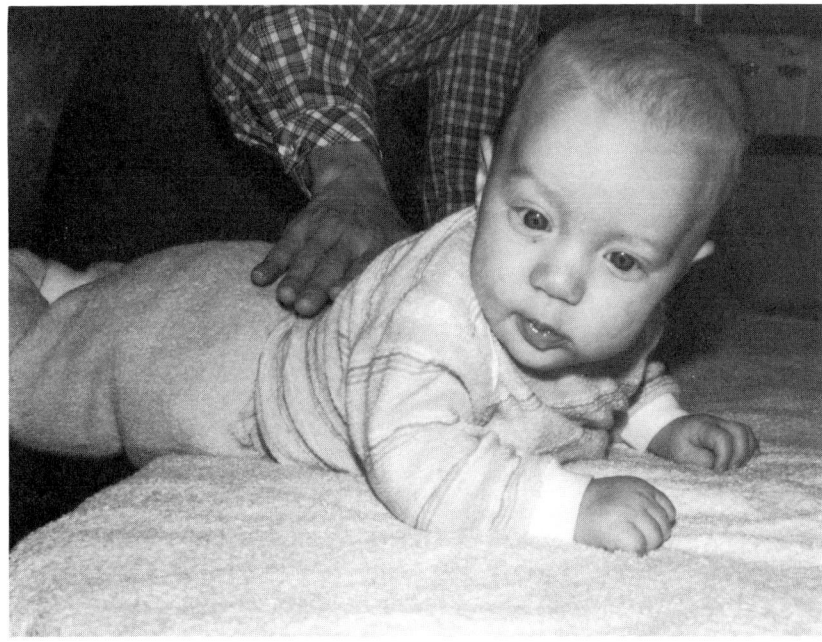

Figure 4-4

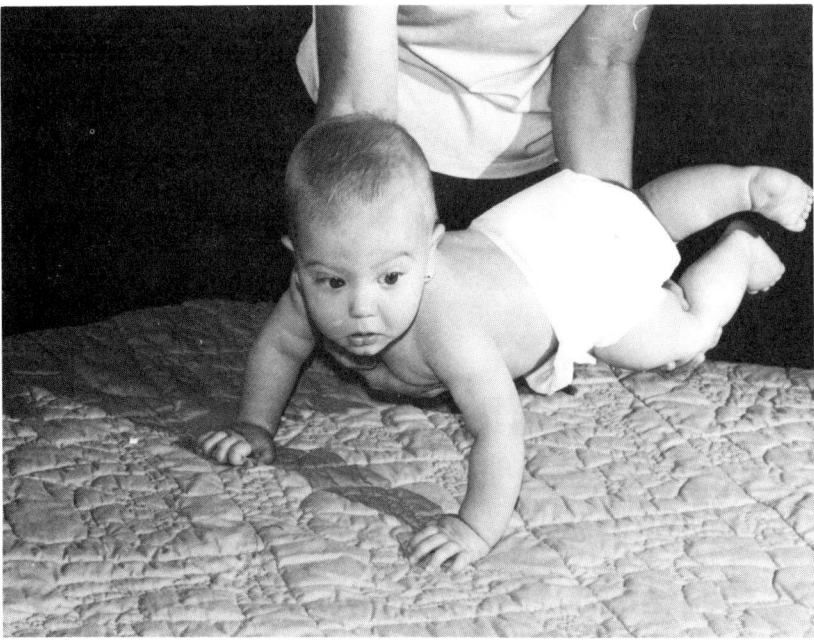

Figure 4-5

Figure 4-6

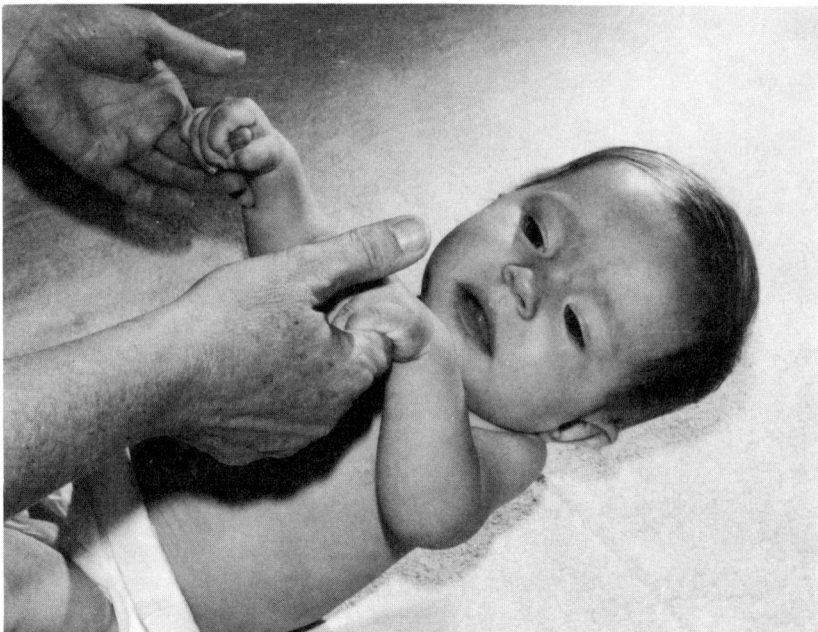

Figure 4-7

- **Purpose.** Leg and lower abdominal strength.
  Procedure. Suspend a toy above the stomach. Hold her arms out and encourage her to play with the toy with her feet. (Fig 4-8)
  Suggestion. A toy with a noise-making ability will stimulate activity.
- **Purpose.** Develop balance and abdominal strength.
  Procedure. Sit the baby on a soft couch or bed and push on the bed around him to cause him to adjust his balance. Support him at the hips. (Fig. 4-9)
  Suggestion. This may also be done while he is lying down to teach awareness and adjustment.
- **Purpose.** Coordination of body parts.
  Procedure. Place her in a supine (lying on back) position. Bend the right leg and hip. Show her a toy to attract her attention and help her roll to her stomach toward it.
  Suggestion. Reverse the process to teach rolling to her back.

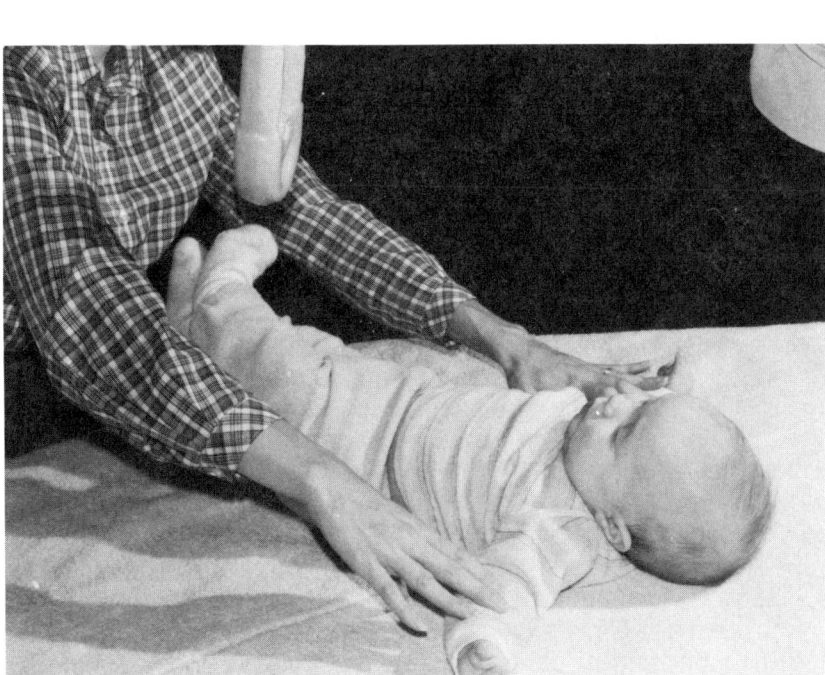

Figure 4-8

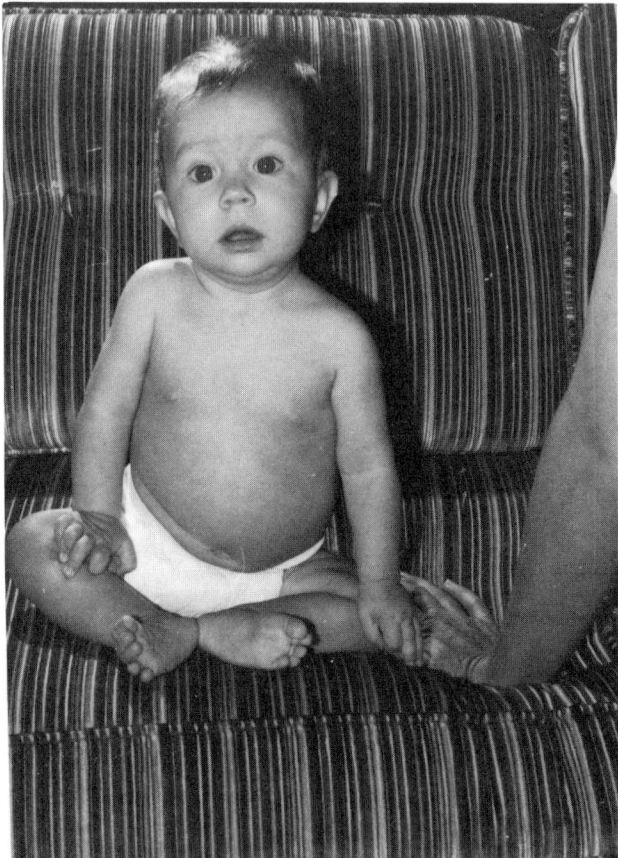

Figure 4-9

PHASE THREE

The child is now more active and is learning to sit alone, likes to touch and explore things and can now make sounds of vowels and consonants. The child is sociable with family members, but can play alone for longer periods of time. He has good coordination for grasping and can handle large toys. Ordinary household items are of interest and make good toys. The exercise period should be lengthened to about a half hour session and there may be two sessions a day. Continue some of the previous activities and add some of the additional activities from the following list.
- Give your child several household objects to play with. Identify the objects by name and demonstrate how to feel them, make noises with them and explore them. Objects such as pans, spoons, a hairbrush, magazines, cards, bottle rings, wooden spoons, mirrors, etc., may be used.

- Place toys in different locations for her to reach and in that way explore her body control. (Toys need not be expensive, but can be blocks of wood of various sizes and shapes.) (Fig. 4-10)
- Encourage him to use both hands by changing toys from one hand to another.
- Put a toy in each hand and encourage her to drop one and reach for a third toy.
- Encourage him to feed himself small pieces of food.
- Help her change toys from hand to hand.
- Normal activities such as "peek-a-boo," waving "bye-bye," and "patty-cake" will teach him body coordination activities such as covering his eyes.
- Encourage rolling and moving by playing with her on the floor.
- Show him books with colorful pictures. An oilcloth picture book is a good quiet time toy.
- Use toys such as squeak toys to help her learn about cause-effect relationships.

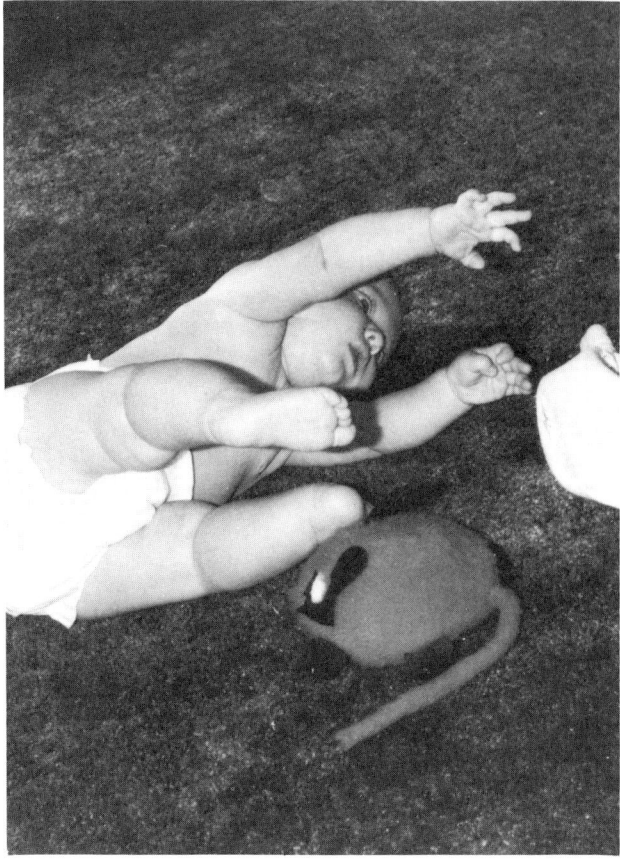

Figure 4-10

Exercises

- ***Purpose.*** Back Strength.
  Procedure. Hold the baby with one hand on the knees and the other on the chest. Lean him forward as much as his strength will allow.
  Suggestion. Gradually give him support and lower your hand off his chest. Let him look into a mirror and play with a toy to stimulate activity in this position. (Fig. 4-11)
- ***Purpose.*** Shoulder strength.
  Procedure. Place the child on a table. Hold his thighs and encourage him to walk on his hands.
  Suggestion. To give him more body weight to support, gradually move your hands toward the lower leg.
- ***Purpose.*** Body awareness.
  Procedure. Stand her on one side of a large round pillow and let her reach for a toy on the other side. (Fig. 4-12)
  Suggestion. Encourage her to explore methods of movement toward the toy.
- ***Purpose.*** Balance and body awareness.
  Procedure. Place the child in a prone position on a round pillow. Make the pillow roll slightly to each side. (Fig. 4-13)
  Suggestion. Use a toy to encourage movement. This same exercise can be done with the child sitting on the pillow.
- ***Purpose.*** Abdominal strength.
  Procedure. Place the child in a sitting position. Lift his legs and allow him to lie down and sit back up.
  Suggestion. Give assistance until he can do it by himself.
- ***Purpose.*** Trunk strength.
  Procedure. Place the child in a sitting position. Support the opposite thigh and encourage her to reach for a toy placed to the side and slightly behind her. (Fig. 4-14) Also, let her reach for toys on the floor in similar position. (Fig. 4-15, Fig. 4-16)
  Suggestion. These exercises can also be done with the child sitting on a small stool.
- ***Purpose.*** Crawling.
  Procedure. Place a toy in front of the baby and encourage him to pull and push toward it. Begin with creeping movements, dragging the hips. Progress to a support position on the hands and knees. (Fig. 4-17)
  Suggestion. Encourage movements in opposition, pulling with the right arm and pushing with the left leg.
- ***Purpose.*** Use of hands and feet.
  Procedure. Place the child on her father's thigh with her weight on the hands and feet. Roll her alternately onto her hands and feet.
  Suggestion. Encourage her to use her hands and feet to make the movement.

Figure 4-11

Figure 4-12

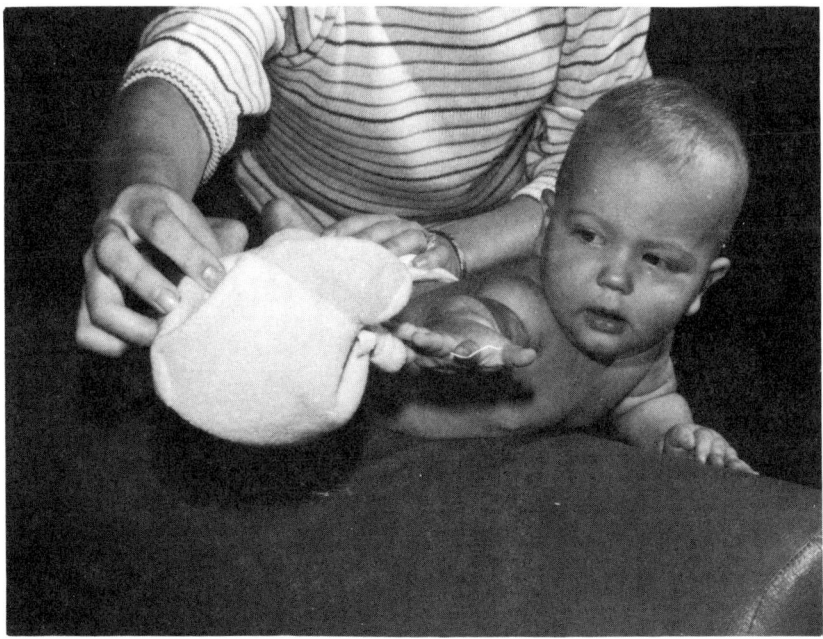

Figure 4-13

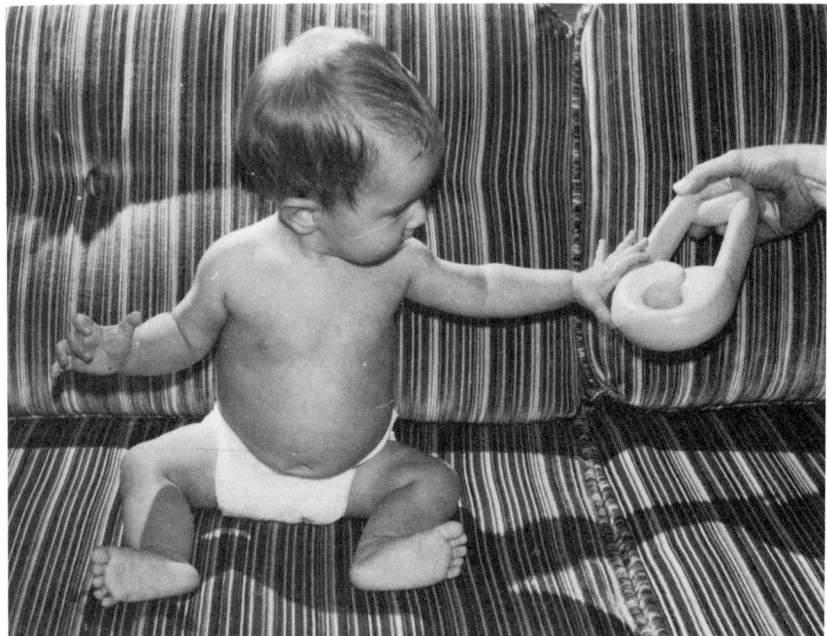

Figure 4-14

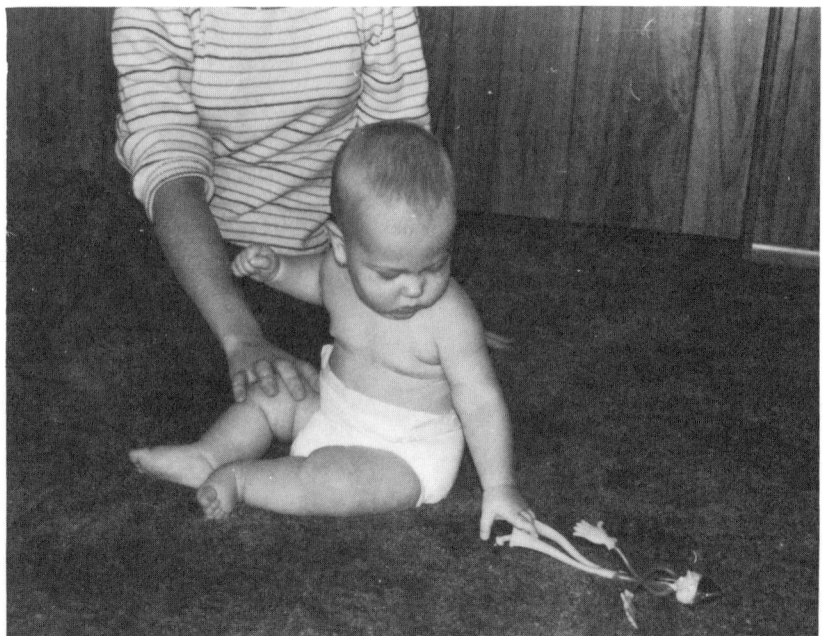

Figure 4-15

Figure 4-16

Figure 4-17

- **Purpose.** Standing position.
- **Procedure.** Stand the child with his hand on a pillow-roll, chair or a parent. Move his support slightly so he will follow it.
  Suggestion. Support him at the hips to give confidence.
- **Purpose.** Standing position.
  Procedure. Let the child sit on your leg or a roll. Move her to a standing position.
  Suggestion. Support the legs and let her use her hands at first.

PHASE FOUR

Skills of sitting and rolling are now fairly easy for the baby. She can pick up smaller objects and likes to use her fingers to explore objects. Sounds start to become simple words like "mamma." Baby can now enjoy most family activities. The play period may be increased to forty-five minutes. Encourage longer attention span by doing a single activity for a longer period. Continue favorite activities from the previous program and add new activities from the following list.
- Assist him to use a spoon during meal time.
- Encourage the giving and receiving of toys, food and other objects. Talk about it as you receive objects and give others back.
- Put some toys in pans, boxes, suitcases, etc., and help her get them out and put them back.
- Start to identify body parts by pointing to them.
- Provide toys that encourage noise-making processes—a toy drum, etc.
- Explore more textures, such as bricks, sand, leaves, etc.
- Explore spaces—under tables, in boxes, and other narrow and low spaces.
- Play with mechanical toys and pull toys.
- Make sounds, such as laughing, panting, blowing, etc.
- Invite other children to play with your child to encourage interaction with others.

Exercises

- **Purpose.** Standing up.
  Procedure. Place a toy on a chair. Encourage her to crawl to the chair and stand up to get the toy. (Fig. 4-18)
  Suggestion. Help the baby grasp the support and stand up.
- **Purpose.** Standing up.
  Procedure. Sit the child on your knee or a chair and help him stand and reach a toy on a chair. (Fig. 4-19)
  Suggestion. Hold him at the chest and hips.

ACTIVITIES FOR BABIES

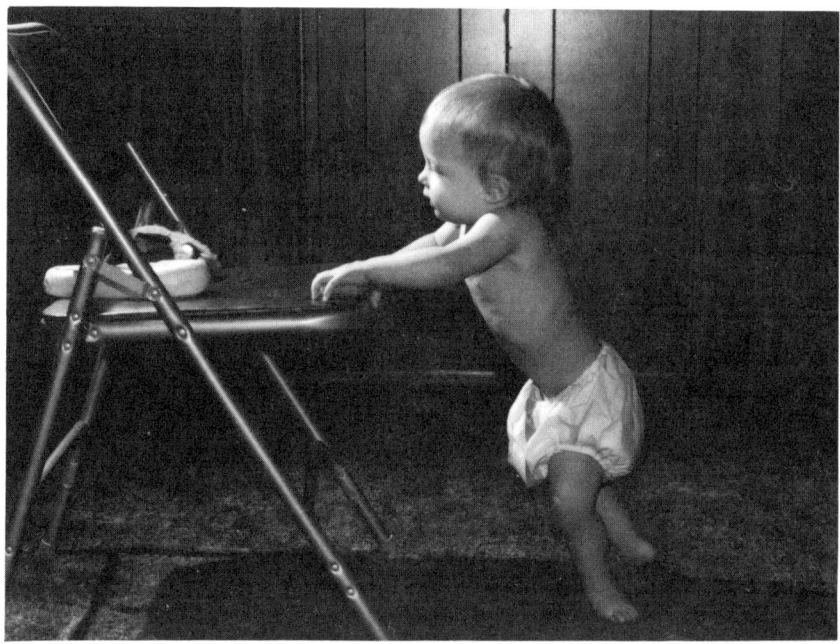

Figure 4-18

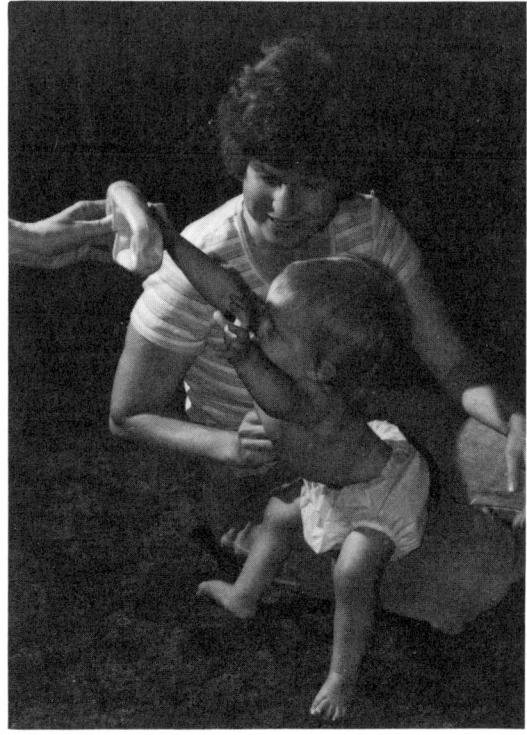

Figure 4-19

- **Purpose.** Balance.
  Procedure. Hold the child in a standing position, supporting her at the hips. Turn her to the right and left to explore balance adjustments.
  Suggestions. This will lead to the first step. After she gains experience, lean her forward slightly.
- **Purpose.** Balance.
  Procedure. Stand her between two wands with her hands holding them. Lean the wands forward and encourage a step. (Fig. 4-20)
  Suggestion. At first, hold her hands on the wand. Then move in front to give her confidence.
- **Purpose.** Balance.
  Procedure. Let the child hold onto a hoop with both hands. Encourage the child to step forward, backward and sideways.
  Suggestion. Soon you can move in a walking rhythm.

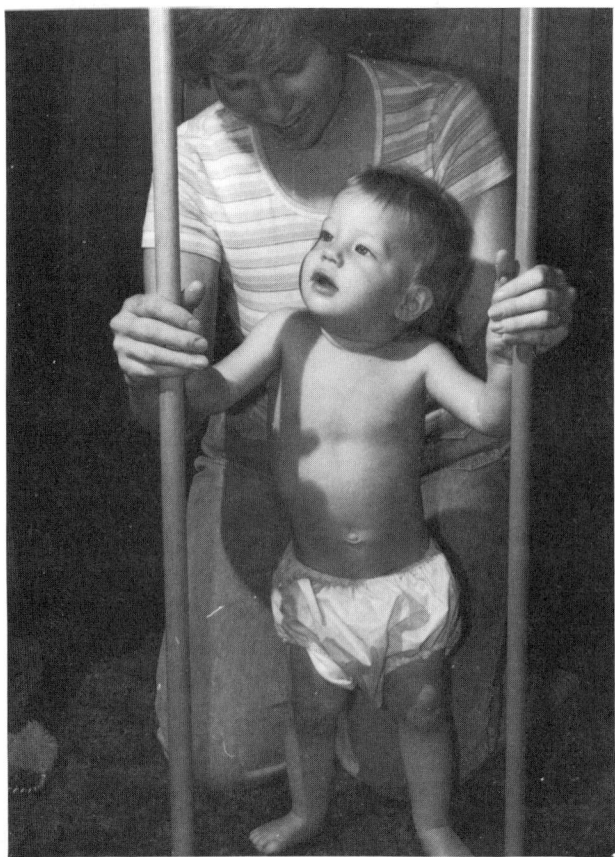

Figure 4-20

5
MOVEMENT EXPLORATION ACTIVITIES

The activities in this chapter are designed to provide experiences for good physical development that will integrate with the many forms of learning needed by retarded children. They provide opportunities for the children to develop many new movement skills; a better body image; the ability to follow direction; and concepts about the use of space, time, direction, dimension, speed, movement quality, rhythm and mood when moving. The activities are presented with a basic approach that will work for most children. There are many opportunities for development, and the procedures used should be varied enough to meet the needs of each individual child.

The chapter has been developed to include activities that progress from experiences in a nonmobile position to locomotor activities requiring much energy and space. The progression is from unilateral movements of one leg or arm to bilateral movements of running and jumping. The development of basic motor skills, good posture, the ability to follow directions with movement, memory practice, and language usage are encouraged and can be developed by using the activities included.

A basic activity, such as walking, is presented. One by one, the elements of the walk are changed until many different variations of walking are developed, providing a basis for learning new movement patterns. This transfer and extension of learning may be difficult for some mentally handicapped children because these children learn only one idea or skill at a time. And yet, learning is based on past experience and can be structured to relate to the individual frame of experience for each child. By designing the movement activities in this manner, a basis for learning the necessary concepts is provided. The involvement of the child in moving provides an additional sense or modality that can aid the child to learn. This sense is called *kinesthetic awareness* and is necessary for efficient performances. The child soon becomes aware of how the body moves and can imitate the teacher or other children, and thus improve personal skill levels.

Movement exploration is a good way to stimulate and motivate a child to learn and progress in development. Everyone can feel successful, with a slight movement of one hand, a vigorous fling of the arm, or a great run down the floor, if the teacher recognizes these as successes. The child can be asked to verbalize the word "up" as he raises his hand, or say "my hand" as his hand is raised. This can increase his ability to speak and to understand his body, as well as his ability to move. Recognition should be given to each child for accomplishments. Cooperation by the child in trying to carry out the activity should always be rewarded by the teacher. Encouragement to use his body to its fullest range of movement, and to associate verbal expression with learned concepts should be a part of recognized success. The child should be rewarded for attempting to do with the body what is requested by the teacher.

For normal children, the usual approach is to present the exploration activity in the form of a problem that is to be solved. The child then proceeds to explore the problem with his body, learning and creating new patterns and understandings. For example, "How many different ways can you move one arm?" For mentally handicapped children, the activity will need to be more structured toward the achievement of the desired goal; "Lift your arm high," "Move your arm to the side" and so on. These activities should be planned to integrate the new learning experience with what has already been learned. This will increase the vocabulary of movement while learning about the body and various movement patterns. Verbal rhythmic noises and words should be encouraged as the movement is made, but the noise and words should be appropriate to the activity. The possibilities for learning, using this method or presentation are unlimited.

The basic skills of movement are the fundamentals of the movement exploration experiences. These basic skills include activities done in place; nonlocomotor skills of bend and stretch, twist and turn, rise and fall, swing and sway, strike and dodge, and push and pull; and locomotor skills of walk, run, leap, jump, hop, skip, slide, and gallop. The confidence required to perform these skills is basic to successful participation in rhythm activities, games, and self-testing activities. The experiences provide the child with opportunities to learn these basic skills in nonstressful, noncompetitive and successful settings that will prepare him to perform activities more complex in nature.

The suggested activities include tasks requiring different levels of involvement. Some are very simple, while others require more ability to understand instructions. The teacher should select the appropriate task for the child and should adjust the movement problems to meet the ability of the child.

Activities in Place

There are many children who are limited extensively in their ability to move. These children are in need of direct physical activity that helps them learn how to use their bodies. The following presentation contains a number of nonlocomotor activities that encourage a variety of movements to be learned. This is not intended to be specifically a prescriptive approach for children with severe motor handicaps, but a presentation of movement activities that may be done by children to provide opportunities for the development of normal physical skills. The activities are listed in progressive order from simple to more complex tasks. These activities listed are only a few of the possible movements and combinations of movements that may encourage children to use their bodies. From these ideas, the teacher may enlarge the list of movements to meet the needs of each individual.

Teaching Suggestions

For presenting nonlocomotor activities:
- The activity should be demonstrated so the child will understand what is to be done.
- The teacher may actually need to move the child through the desired motion before the child understands how to do the activity.
- Time should be allowed for the child to process mentally what is being asked.
- Any degree of success should be recognized and improvement encouraged. This contributes to the child's motivation for participation and better performance.
- Be sure the action continues through the complete range of motion in the body joints. Big and vigorous movements are better than timid, restricted attempts.
- Encourage the child to show what he can do by asking him to perform; for example, "Show me how you can move your arms." This will help the child initiate the activity and show the teacher what actions the child knows. The teacher should then supplement the child's actions with those illustrated by other children.
- The children should be encouraged to name the parts of the body as they are used. Verbal modeling may be necessary.
- Relate concepts learned by the children in their classroom experiences to the activities they are doing. This will help them understand better what the concepts mean as they use them in activities.

Suggested Activities

Back Lying Position—Identification of Body Parts
The teacher may use the following instruction and questions:
- Touch your head.
- Touch your legs.
- Where are your arms?
- Show me your feet and your hands.
- Where is your elbow, knee, ankle?
- Put your hands on your waist.
- Move your fingers.
- Wiggle your thumb.
- Where are your toes and your heels?

Back Lying Position—Movement Problems
- Cross your arms so your elbows touch.
- Move your arms away from your body.
- Move your feet apart.
- Reach toward the ceiling with your hands.
- Press your wrists against the floor and move your arms in an arc until you can clap your hands above your head.
- How far can you reach to your right with your right arm?
- How far can you reach to your left with your left arm?
- Lift your right leg as high as you can.
- Bend your left knee and place your left foot flat on the floor.
- Lift your right arm and your right leg as high as you can.
- Bend your right arm and left leg at the same time.
- Stretch your left arm and right leg.
- Move your arms quickly.
- Show me how big you can be.
- Stretch hard and relax. (Check for relaxation and help the child attain a relaxed position.)

Facedown or Prone Position
- Bend your knees and point your toes toward the ceiling.
- Lift your arms as high as you can.
- Move your feet apart.
- Raise your right leg.
- What can you do with your head?

Lying on Side
- What can you do with your right hand?
- What can you do with your right leg?
- What can you do with your right hand and right leg?
- Show me you can make a circle with your hand and foot.

- Show me how you can roll.
- Change from little to big.

Sitting Position
- What can you do with your feet and legs?
- What can you do with your arms and hands?
- Can you balance on two parts of your body?
- Raise two legs, but don't fall over.

Kneeling Position
- Show me how many parts of your body you can shake.
- Swing your arms.
- Collapse to the floor.
- Look like an angry cat.
- What can you do while you balance on one knee?
- Can you balance on three parts of your body?
- Make a square, diamond, triangle, or circle.
- Show how to crawl like a snake.
- How much space can you use?

Standing Position
- Can you jump in place—with your feet together, with your feet apart, with one foot forward and one foot behind?
- Can you turn around?
- How big can you be?
- How small can you be?
- Can you stand on one foot?
- Can you stand on one foot with your eyes closed?
- Stand on one foot and move your other foot.
- What can you do with one foot and one hand?
- Can you make the letters of the alphabet?
- What kind of shadows can you make? (This will need to be done in the sunlight or with a lamp behind the children.)

NONLOCOMOTOR SKILLS

Bend and Stretch
In bending movements, the body parts flex toward each other (Fig. 5-1). A stretching movement is the extending of the body parts (Fig. 5-2).

Teaching Cues. Stretching and bending activities should include a full range of movement that will facilitate flexibility in the joints. These actions may be done in a sitting, lying, or standing position, according to the child's ability and need for variety.

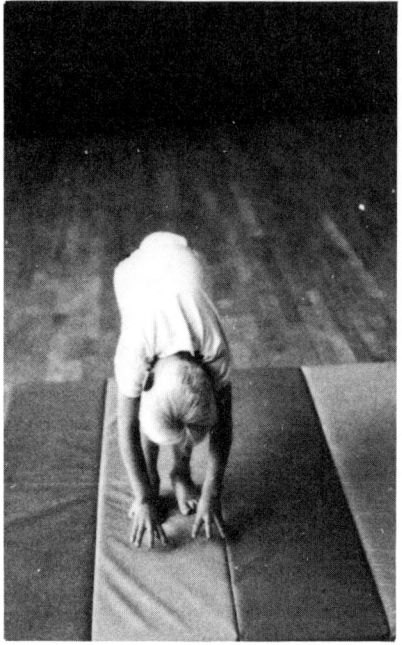 

Figure 5-1   Figure 5-2

Suggested Activities
- How many parts of the body can you bend?
- Bend all parts of the body until you are like a ball.
- Bend the arms and legs toward the body.
- Stretch and become as big as you can.
- Bend and stretch the various parts of your body as they are named—arm, leg, body, neck, elbow, knee, wrist, ankle.
- Can you bend your legs and stretch your arms?
- Bend one arm and stretch the other arm.
- Stretch to see how tall you can be.
- Stretch like a puppy that just woke up.
- How small can you be?

Twist and Turn

In a twisting movement the body or body parts rotates around a stationary base of support (Fig. 5-3). In a turning motion, the base of support rotates with the body (Fig. 5-4).

Teaching Cues. While turning, focus on one spot in front of the area, keeping the eyes on the spot as long as possible and returning the focus of the eyes back to that spot as soon as possible.

Figure 5-3 Figure 5-4

Suggested Activities
- How many parts of the body can you twist?
- Turn and face the side wall.
- Turn and face the wall behind you.
- Do a three-quarter turn.
- Turn all the way around.
- Turn the other way.
- Twist the parts of the body as they are named.
- Turn like a top using one foot.
- Dance "beautifully" with lots of turns.
- Twist your neck like you were a tall giraffe trying to see over the fence at the zoo.

Rise and Fall

Rising is upward motion from a low level (Fig. 5-5). Falling is the downward movement of the body or body parts from a higher level.

Teaching Cues. Any time an individual participates in an activity, there is the possibility of falling. Everyone should be taught to fall correctly to avoid injury. Land on the muscular parts of the body—the shoulders, hips, and thighs. Keep the knees, hands, elbows, and head tucked for protection. Relax and roll in a curled position to absorb the momentum of the fall. Learn the fall and recovery from a low level and progress to an upright position.

Figure 5-5

Note. By using the continuous rolling motion of a fall, one can rise to an upward position and continue the activity. The arms may help in the recovery. Football players use this technique. (Figs. 5-6, 5-7, 5-8, 5-9).

Suggested Activities
- Can you rise from a sitting position to a standing position quickly?
- Show how you get out of bed in the morning.
- From a sitting position, fall to the side by slowly relaxing. Land on the side and shoulder.
- From a kneeling position, gradually fall to the side, rolling from the hip to the shoulder.
- From a standing position, relax and fall to side, rolling from the side of the thigh to the hip and shoulder.
- Fall, roll, and recover to a standing position.
- Pretend you are a seed that grows to be a beautiful flower and then withers and dies in the hot sun.

- Drop dead as if you were a cowboy who had just been shot.
- Show how the sun rises in the morning and sets in the evening.
- Show what a balloon does when you let go of it after you blow it up.
- Burst like a balloon that has just popped.
- Melt like an ice cream cone.

Figure 5-6

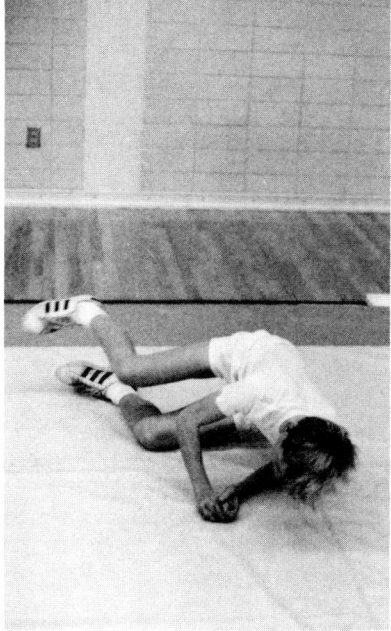

Figure 5-7

Figure 5-8

Figure 5-9

Swing and Sway

A swing is a pendular movement in which the base of support is above the moving body part. In a swaying movement the base of support is below the moving part. (Fig. 5-10)

Suggested Activities
- How many parts of the body can you sway while standing up?
- How many parts of the body can you sway while lying on your back?
- Swing as many parts of the body as you can.
- Show how you swing at a baseball and at a golf ball.
- Sway like a tree does when the breeze blows briskly.
- Swing your arms and see how high you can jump.
- Swing your arms together and in opposition.
- Swing your leg as if you were kicking a football.

Figure 5-10

Figure 5-11

Strike and Dodge

A strike is a percussive movement toward an object. A dodge is an elusive movement away from an object or person. (Fig. 5-11)

Teaching Cues. The children should be encouraged to use the whole body when imparting force to an object. When teaching them how to dodge, remind them to keep their knees bent (thus keeping the center of gravity low), to use the arms for balance, and to push off from the supporting foot or feet. To be able to move in any direction, they should keep the weight on both feet in a good ready position.

Suggested Activities
- Dodge an imaginary ball thrown at your waist.
- How many different ways can you strike a ball?
- Pretend someone is chasing you and dodge him.
- Show how you chop down a tree.
- Play bean-bag.
- Slash your way through a forest.
- Run through an obstacle course without touching anything.
- Duck to dodge an object.
- Jump to dodge an object.

Push and Pull
Pushing is directing force away from the body (Fig. 5-12). Pulling is directing force toward the body (Fig. 5-13).

Figure 5-12

MOVEMENT EXPLORATION ACTIVITIES

Precaution. When pushing or pulling an object or another person, it is important to lower the center of gravity by bending the knees, and using the leg muscles to direct the force. The body should be on a slight incline in the direction of the force.

Suggested Activities
- Grasp right hands with a partner and pull him across a line.
- Grasp left hands with a partner and pull him across a line.
- Use a two-hand grip and try to pull a partner across a line.
- Stand back-to-back with a partner and try to push him until he moves his feet.
- Place your hands on your partner's back and push until one of you moves your feet.
- Have a tug-of-war with the class. Use correct pulling technique.
- Pull a wagon with several items in it.
- Push an object. Use the correct technique.
- Sit down back-to-back with a partner. Try to push him over a line.
- Grasp right hands with a partner. Push and pull without moving your feet until he moves his feet.

Figure 5-13

LOCOMOTOR SKILLS

Walk

A walk is a transfer of weight from one foot to the other foot, with one foot always in contact with the floor (Fig. 5-14).

Teaching Cues. In moving through space, the child should use good walking technique, assume good posture with the head erect and the chest lifted, point the feet forward, use proper transfer of weight from the heel along the outside of the foot and across the ball of the foot, and push off with the toes.

Suggested Activities

- Walk forward, backward, to the right, to the left, and on a diagonal.
- Walk and freeze on the signal. Keep your balance.
- Walk heavily, lightly, quietly, and noisily.
- Walk low, and on your tip toes; change position on the signal.
- Walk with big steps, giant steps, and small steps.
- Show how you walk when you are happy, angry, afraid, tired, on ice, in the wind, and in the rain.
- How many body parts can you move while you are walking?
- Walk like an elephant, a tiger, a horse, and so forth.
- Walk quickly, and then slowly.
- Have a walking race. (Be sure the children walk, not run.)
- Walk through the space without touching anyone else. The area will gradually get smaller. Remember correct procedures for dodging.

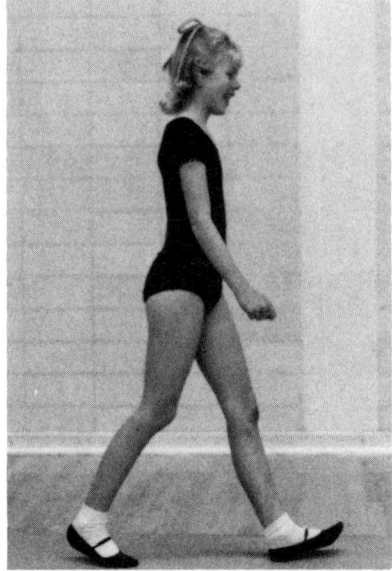

Figure 5-14

Run

The movement of a run is a walk, except there is a time when both feet are off the floor (Fig. 5-15).

Teaching Cues. All movements should be toward the direction of the run, usually forward. Sideward movement should be discouraged. Look forward with the head up.

All body parts should contribute to the desired movement. A slight body lean forward will help move the body weight forward. The body lean should increase when more speed is desired. The arms, with the elbows bent, should move forward so the hands are shoulder high and backward until the hands are next to the hip.

The leg action is initiated from the hip. The knee lift depends on the speed of the run. When jogging, little knee lift is needed. When running for speed, a high knee lift is used.

Land on the balls of the feet and "toe down" to the heel.

Note. Some children with restricted movement run with a flat foot. These children can be taught to run correctly by progressing from walk on the toes, with a "toe down" action using the ankle, to a run landing lightly on the balls of the feet.

Figure 5-15

Suggested Activities
- Jog around the area.
- Run and stop on signal. Use only two steps to stop.
- Run in the area without touching anyone. The area will become smaller.
- Run with a long stride or big steps.
- Run with short, quick steps.
- Keep running and change direction as the command is given to go forward, backward, to the right, to the left, and reverse.
- Run low and gradually get higher and higher.
- Run through an obstacle course without touching anything.
- Run like you are trying to hide.
- Run as fast as you can and as slowly as you can.

Leap

The leap is a movement through space with a transfer of weight from one foot to the other, during which the body is elevated and suspended in the air for an extended length of time (Fig. 5-16). It is an extended run.

Teaching Cues. The arms should help lift and reach in opposition (right arm and left leg forward) to help sustain the movement.

Figure 5-16

Suggested Activities
- How far can you leap?
- How high can you leap
- Leap five times in a row.
- Leap with the left leg leading.
- Leap with the right leg leading.
- Run two steps and leap.
- Run with a partner and leap together.
- Leap and reach as high as you can.
- Can you do several leaps quickly?
- Use as much space as you can as you leap.

Jump
A jump is a simultaneous transfer of weight from one or both feet.

Teaching Cues. Bend the ankles, knees, and hips in preparation for the jump. Swing the arms from behind the hips upward in the direction of the jump. This will help move the body. When landing, bend the hips, knees, and ankles to absorb the movement.

Suggested Activities
- Can you jump high and land lightly?
- Can you jump and turn around?
- Jump and reach as high as you can.
- Jump forward, backward, and sideward.
- Run several steps and jump.
- How far can you jump?
- Jump like a kangaroo.
- Can you jump several times quickly?
- Jump as high as you can.

Hop
A hop is a lifting of weight into the air from one foot and landing on the same foot (Fig. 5-17).

Teaching Cues. Swing the arms to gain more momentum. When landing, give with the knee and ankle. Keep the free foot off the floor.

Suggested Activities
- Hop on the right foot.
- Hop on the left foot.
- How high can you hop?
- How far can you hop?
- Can you hop and turn around?
- Hop forward, backward, and to the right and left.
- Hop three times on the left foot and three times on the right foot.

- Hop as quickly as you can.
- Hop and swing the arms.
- Take as few hops as possible to cover twenty feet.

Skip

A skip is a combination of a walk and a hop, with an uneven rhythm and elevation (Fig. 5-18). The foot pattern is a step right, hop right, step left, hop left. The rhythm is a slow (step), quick (hop) uneven pattern.

Figure 5-17

Figure 5-18

Teaching Cues. Swing the arms in opposition. Also, the mood while skipping is usually one of joy or happiness. Land lightly.

Suggested Activities
- Skip high.
- Skip low.
- Skip fast.
- Skip and turn around.
- Be as big as you can while you skip.
- Skip foward, backward, to the right, and to the left.
- Move as many parts of your body as you can while you skip.
- Skip and make a circle, a square, or a diamond.
- Skip quietly and then loudly.
- Take as few steps as possible to go from one line to another line.

Slide

In order to slide, step to the side, move the other foot to meet the supporting foot, and transfer weight to take another step. The movement is an uneven one—slow (step), quick (leap to the free foot).

Teaching Cues. Use the arms to help by swinging them slightly during the transfer of weight. Land lightly.

Suggested Activities
- Slide with a long step.
- How high can you go while you slide?
- Can you slide down low?
- Make a triangle while you slide in your own area.
- Do something new while you slide.
- Slide with a partner, face-to-face and back-to-back.
- Be as big as you can while you slide.
- Slide forward, backward, and to the side.
- Slide as quickly as you can from one line to another line.
- In a circle holding hands with the group, slide eight steps to the right and eight steps to the left. Slide four steps to the right and four steps to the left. Slide two steps to the right and two steps to the left. Continue to slide two steps to the right and two steps to the left and turn to face the direction of the slide. The group is now doing a polka—hop, step close step.

Gallop

A gallop is a movement like a slide and is done while moving forward. The pattern of the movement is as follows: a step forward on one foot, move the other foot to meet the supporting foot, and transfer the weight to the back foot with a leap.

Teaching Cues. The same leg always leads the movement, and the rhythm is an uneven movement—slow (step), quick (transfer to the back foot). Land lightly.

Suggested Activities
- Gallop forward.
- Gallop as fast as you can.
- Gallop as high as you can.
- Gallop like a pony.
- Gallop like a prancing circus horse.
- While you gallop, do tricks with your arms.
- Gallop like an old mule.
- Gallop like a work horse.
- Gallop in a circle.
- Gallop and jump a ditch.

MOVEMENT EXPLORATION ACTIVITIES

Space Exploration
- Explore your own space, always keeping one foot or one hand on the ground. How big is it? How high is it?
- Explore two objects in the area and return to your own spot.
- Hop to a corner in the room and skip back to your spot.
- How fast can you run around the area and return to your spot?
- Explore the ceiling and the walls and report what you saw to the teacher.

Partner Activities
- Jump over your partner.
- Be a seesaw with your partner and rise and fall in opposition.
- Make a bridge so your partner can go under and over it.
- Do different locomotor movements with your partner.
- Ask your partner to count while you hop five times on each foot.

Group Activities
- Follow the leader, who will do the various locomotor and nonlocomotor skills.
- Form a circle. Skip ten steps away from the circle and run back to the circle.
- Every other person in the circle weave in and out of the remaining members of the circle. Walk at first, then run.
- Slide in a circle and then gallop.
- As a group, make the various geometric shapes.

Action Words and Pictures

- Do the actions shown in the pictures. (Show pictures of children running, playing ball, riding horses, and so forth.)
- Mimic the actions of the objects in the pictures. (Show pictures of airplanes, trains, birds, elephants, Indians dancing, and so on.)
- Do the actions of the words on the flash cards. (Use words like "vibrate," "ouch," "crash," "shake," "sigh," "laugh," "oh," "fall." These words may need to be illustrated on the card for some children.)
- Make the shape shown on the picture. (The cards may have numbers, letters, or geometric shapes.)
- As the teacher tells the story, every time you hear the action words or key words, do the action and then listen to the story for another action word. (Tell a story like "Going Through the Jungle." The action words should be repeated often in the story. "Fall," "shiver," "crash," and so on are good action words.)

Drama Activities

- Show how you feel when it is raining on you.
- How does the sun make you feel?
- What does the color green make you do?
- Show how grandmother walks.
- Are you sad or happy? Show me.
- What do you do when you are angry?
- How do you feel after a race?
- Show what your favorite baseball star or football star can do.
- Can you dance like a ballerina?
- Can you roll like a ball or wheel? Can you push like a bulldozer?
- Do pantomimes and see if the class can guess what you are doing.
- Use only your actions and expressions to tell a story.
- Be a circus performer.
- What do you do on New Year's Day?

6
PERCEPTUAL MOTOR ACTIVITIES

Our physical senses—visual, auditory, and kinesthetic—provide the tools that we use in perceiving the world around us. It is important that a child's perceptual abilities be developed through activities, games, and experiences that are planned and designed with this as an objective. These abilities do not develop by chance and do not develop just because the child gets older. Through participation in physical education activities, these senses may be practiced and improved.

An individual can perform mental tasks efficiently only if he feels well physically. If health and physical fitness do not provide the energy to participate, the child is not going to apply enough effort to the academic pursuits demanded by the school. Likewise, if he has no confidence in his ability, he will be at a disadvantage. It is important, therefore, that a child have a good image of himself and of his ability to succeed when performing many and varied motor skills. Success in performing physical skills and games helps the child approach all tasks more willingly.

Physical education activities provide the child with opportunities for immediate feedback about success. This feedback is definite—he hit the target or he missed it. Perceptual motor physical education activities extend the opportunity for the development of the necessary perceptual skills in a more accepting and less stressful setting than either regular playground or gymnasium activity. The child learns about himself as a result of being aware of his performance. This awareness is accomplished by the perceptual abilities which a child possesses. The more acute and sharp his perceptual abilities, the better prepared he will be for learning complex motor skills, and the more readily he will achieve academic success.

Perceptual motor activities in physical education activities are divided or separated into their fundamental parts and are practiced as individual tasks. Specific objectives for performing each part are often separate from and in addition to the general objectives of physical education. These specific objectives are established, and the child is encouraged to concentrate in depth upon the skill and upon the specific goal of the activity. The activity should be organized and structured so the child will always succeed when performing— thus, giving the child a sense of accomplishment, improving his feeling of self worth, and developing a good self image. These positive feelings can then manifest themselves in his academic work as well as in his skill performance.

The activities presented in the following section were created with the development of perceptual skills as their specific purpose. Color, size, auditory and visual discrimination as well as kinesthetic awareness are included. They are examples of elementary perceptual motor activities, and are basic to more complex activities that follow. For example, visual perception is practiced in activities such as rope jumping, ball handling, bean bag activities and equipment exploration; the activities included here are fundamental to more demanding activities such as stunts and tumbling, described elsewhere in the text. They demonstrate how many common physical education activities can be adapted to meet the need for perceptual-motor skills.

Teaching Suggestions

Following are some suggestions for teaching perceptual-motor skills:
- Encourage the child to verbalize the color, shape, or size of the object he uses.
- Repeat the task several times to reinforce the learned concept. Then vary the pattern as to size, shape, or color.
- Do not combine the various attributes, such as numbers or colors, until each concept is well learned.

Color Discrimination
- Place several colored patches of oil cloth, a variety of sizes, around the room. Tell the children to go to a blue patch, red patch, and so on until all the colors have been used.
- Place several colored targets on the walls. On command, direct the children to go to each color and touch it.
- Ask the children to throw a ball at a colored target and verbally indicate the color of the target.
- Each child selects a ball from a box of colored balls and throws it at the target which is the same color as the ball he selected.
- Place a set of patches of different colors in a row before a line of children. A colored block to match each patch is placed on the starting line. Each child, in turn, takes one block and places it on

the matching patch. The task may be changed so the children place the colored blocks on different colored patches as the teacher names them.
- Call out a color and direct the children to stand on a design of that color.

Size Differentiation

Preparation. Place before the children an oil-cloth chart or charts on which diamonds, rectangles, triangles and circles have been painted (Fig. 6-1). There should be several of each shape, with each having a different number, size, and color than the others of the same shape. The children should have a set of patches to match the shapes, colors, sizes, and numbers on the chart.

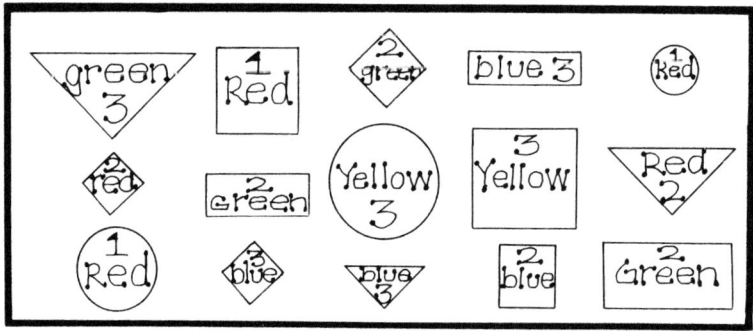

Figure 6-1

- Each child, in turn, runs from a starting line to the chart with a patch in his hand and places the patch on the chart so the shapes match.
- Ask the children to hop to the chart with a patch and match the shape and size of the patch with the same design on the chart.
- As the children jump to the chart, name the shape on which the children should stand.
- Each child, in turn, runs to the maze, stands on a design and names the shape on which he is standing.
- Direct the children to throw the big balls at the big targets and the small balls at the small targets.
- Ask the children to match the size, shape, and color of the patches with a design on the chart.
- Tell the children to match the number on the patch with the number on the chart.
- The children match the shape and number of a patch with the proper design on the chart.
- Each child places a patch on the chart so the size, shape, color or number match.

- Place the patches in scattered formation on the floor. As the teacher names the shape, size, number and/or color, the children run to the appropriate patch.
- As a class, the children play follow-the-leader and make the different geometric shapes, with the class members forming the designs.
- Each child makes a design with his body while lying on the floor.
- The children crawl through boxes in which the holes are cut in the various geometric shapes.

Auditory Differentiation

- As the children are running freely in the area, give a command or blow a whistle at which the children "freeze" immediately.
- Play a series of recorded sounds which represent those typical in the child's environment. Help the children recognize the sound and imitate the activity which the sound represents, such as a train, a dog, or a soldier.
- Beat a drum to various rhythms to which the children hop, walk, and so forth.
- As the instruments make the various sounds, the children imitate the movements represented by the sounds, such as tambourine—dance, shakers—shake, tuning fork—vibrate, and so on.
- With the children's eyes closed, tap a beat pattern and tell the children to hop out the pattern.

Visual Discrimination and Kinesthetic Awareness

- Instruct the children to mirror the activity of the teacher. Start with gross movements, such as running in place, and progress to fine motor movements, such as finger patterns.
- Set up a circuit with stations around the area. As the whistle blows, the children progress to the next station and carry out the exercise which is drawn on the chart until the whistle blows again.
- The children close their eyes and touch the parts of their body as they are named.
- Each child walks on a line.
- The children walk in the area *without* stepping on a line or crack.
- The children mirror a position demonstrated by the teacher—a scarecrow and so forth. Next, they close their eyes and assume the same position.
- The children throw a ball at a target with their eyes closed.
- Direct the children to jump over taped lines approximately two feet apart. Repeat the task with closed eyes.
- Instruct the children to do different locomotor movements through mazes placed on the floor (Fig. 6-2).
- Use the hopscotch maze on the playground at school and design a movement pattern for the children to follow (Fig. 6-3).
- Play hopscotch.

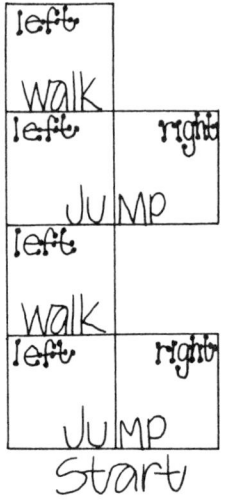  

Figure 6-2

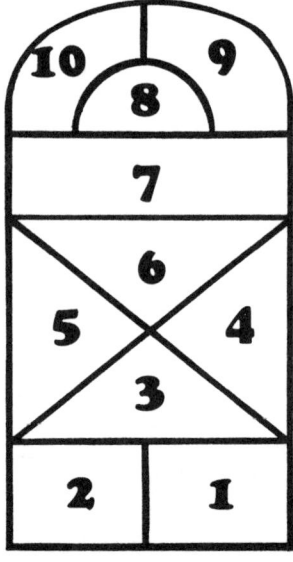

Figure 6-3

7
RHYTHM AND DANCE

Most children have an innate sense of rhythm, and most children love to move to music, to the beat of a drum, or to the clap of hands. This sense of rhythm will be more developed if the child has had opportunities to express himself in movement experiences. Children are eager for opportunities to be involved in the free movement expression allowed in most rhythm and dance activities. Rhythm, basically, is movement, and rhythm provides the form, the language, the action of the driving force that is the music. When a child moves to a rhythm or to the music, he is being uniquely himself, and his body, mind, and spirit are all working to produce the action. As he becomes confident and is more free and willing to move, he develops a sense of achievement. This recognition of his own accomplishment will manifest itself in his smile, in the shine of his eyes, in his relationship with other children, and in his relationship with his teachers and other adults.

The approach a teacher can use to rhythm and dance activities is to present the movement idea with a strong beat; allow the children to explore the idea with movement by giving tasks with a movement objective; and then together, the teacher and the children give the movement shape, pattern, and organization.

Through participation in dance activities, a child can
- learn to relate to his surroundings,
- function as an individual while being a part of a group,
- understand how the body works when it moves,
- learn how a group works together,
- develop good posture,
- feel good about what he is doing,
- feel good about himself and
- develop good social values while taking part in exercise activities in dance.

The specific objectives of a rhythm and dance program are to:
- Provide opportunities for self expression.
- Develop a greater sense of rhythm through movement activities.
- Develop acceptable social behaviors and ease in social situations.
- Provide opportunities for individual recognition.
- Provide understanding of and appreciation for all cultures.
- Understand how the body moves and what the body can do.
- Recognize that one stops and starts when the music or drum starts and stops.
- Recognize one's own space and function in that space.

Teaching Suggestions

Dance is an activity which a regular classroom teacher might feel insecure in her ability to teach. Possibly that confidence in the ability to teach dance activities can be gained by taking a class in which dance for children is taught, by listening to music, by moving freely to the music, by joining a beginning dance group, and by attending dance concerts. Gradually, the teacher will look forward with real enthusiasm to directing dance activities.

Some teaching suggestions are:
- Remember that the participants are children first and dancers second.
- Assume that all children are creative, because in their own way they all are.
- Plan specific movement suggestions for each part of the lesson. Have in mind several different qualities to bring the children to a deeper depth of involvement and to some refining of movements.
- Allow for individuality—creativity—but give the children some specific objective to get them started at the beginning of the activity.
- In each lesson provide both locomotor and nonlocomotor activities relating to the specific objective of the lesson.
- Encourage the children to give their own interpretations of the lesson theme, but help them to stay with the idea of the lesson.
- Guide the activity by giving praise and encouragement rather than criticism.
- Remember that children like to move and will respond to movement challenges.
- Select several children to demonstrate a performance, not just one child. Through the series of lessons each child should have a turn.
- Keep the accompaniment simple and remember that it should aid and not control the activity.
- Allow time to talk about and reflect upon the activities of the lesson.
- Create a satisfying conclusion for each lesson involving all the activities that have just been performed.
- Place emphasis upon participation by the children, with technical accuracy and artistic values later.
- Have a happy time.

Creative Dance

Creative dance is the language of the body, and its goal is to communicate ideas through movement. Creative dance provides the child with freedom that no other activity allows. There are few rules and many correct movements in creative dance. A teacher can bring any child into the activity because individual skill is developed as the child participates. A child may need to copy or imitate other children before she feels free and confident in her own ability. The teacher should allow this, but as soon as the child is moving freely without help, she should be recognized for her own accomplishments.

The primary problem in teaching creative dance is selecting ideas for creative movement that are image provoking and can result in movements usable in a dance practice exercise. Ideas such as taking a cold shower, children on the ball field, or a child blowing up a balloon, all can help a child create his own movement patterns. Rather than trying to *be* an animal, we should deal, in dance, with how we (or the child) relate to the animal. We pet it, we feed it and we hug it, but we cannot become the animal.

Movement Objectives and Activities

Following are some examples of movement objectives and some suggestions of how the teacher can help the children explore each objective. The teacher can use these examples as a start, and then expand upon the idea for complete lesson organizations.

- **Objective—SHAPES**

  The teacher will ask the children to imitate her position. She will then move to another position. The children will copy her several times. Retarded children may need help to be able to copy the teacher positions. They should be helped as much as is necessary. The different shapes should be at various levels. The teacher will tell the children to walk around as a drum beats; when it stops, they are to stop in a shape different from their previous one. The teacher can make suggestions to vary the shapes. The shapes can be bent, twisted, and stretched. They can be high or low to the floor, limp or very strong, upside down, slanted, on one leg or two. The teacher then will direct the children to run and make shapes, to run and stop and twist and turn. To leap into the air and create a shape while in the air can challenge the most active child. To jump and land with the feet together, crossed, or apart will add variety. The hop, skip, gallop, and slide can be used to explore the lesson objective.

- **Objective—PERSONAL SPACE**

  The children should be instructed to select a spot on the floor to be their own. They should look at it so they will recognize their own space. The children will be told to leave their space, and on the drum signal return to that space. They should feel the inside of their own space—defining how high, how wide, how low, how round it is. The children can walk, skip, hop, run, and leap around the outside of their own space. Movement should be encouraged to include the exploration of space with bending, stretching, twisting, and turning in their space. The tempo can be varied to include both fast and slow movements.

- **Objective—DIRECTIONS**
  Walk forward to a space and back away from the space. Move sideways and return to your own space. Run, hop, skip, slide forward, sideways, and backward. Always return to your own space. Run, walk, hop, etc. slowly. Then fast. Combine fast and slow with the walk and run. Move around other moving people. The teacher can give a different signal to direct some children to stop and others to keep moving around and between them. Many different ways of following directions and moving in specific directions can be given.

- **Objective—MUSCLES**
  The children get into the same shape as the teacher. Tighten body muscles to the count of one to ten, and loosen muscles as the count is done backwards. Change position by tightening and loosening muscles. The teacher will not always count all the way to ten, but will count up or down in order to get the children to change shapes. The objective, *muscles*, can also be explored by telling the children to walk, then freeze in a position that takes the strong use of muscles to hold. Poses and balances also require specific strength to maintain. The run and skip can be used to vary the freezes and balances that use strong muscles.

- **Objective—LEVELS**
  The teacher instructs the children to drop to the floor and hold the shape in which they landed. Repeat the fall and hold a different shape. Melt to the floor slowly and hold the shape. Add a jump, and then fall, add a fall and roll. A routine can be developed with a jump, melt, shape, roll, rise, and jump and fall.

- **Objective—BODY PARTS**
  Start the lesson by shaking the whole body. Then shake the individual parts of the body—head, arms, legs, and hands. The individual body parts should stretch, bend, twist, swing, and collapse. Let the children explore while doing the arm duets (both arms follow the same action), head solos, hand duets or solos, arm and head duets (shake the arm and head at the same time), leg solos or duets, hand and head duets, head and arm trios using both arms and their head while twisting, stretching, and shaking.

- **Objective—BIG AND LITTLE**
  Start the lesson by moving through the biggest space. Move high through the biggest space and low through the biggest space. Walk, run, skip forward, backward, and circling through the big

space. Change to tiny space, do runs, walks, and skips in tiny spaces. Do big walks and tiny walks in big and little spaces.

Folk Dancing

Folk dances are traditional dances that have been handed down from generation to generation in the manner of all traditions. They are structured and have specific and unique steps and formations typical of the culture they represent. There has been little or no effort to make changes in the steps or formations from generation to generation. Folk dances are often stories expressed in dance steps. They can communicate human feelings, fears and hopes, or depict religious ceremonies, traditions, and manner of worship. They show challenges of feats of skill and bravery; important events like weddings, births, and deaths; everyday events like crop planting and harvesting; and daily work chores of cooking and hunting. They truly reflect the history and progress of the culture represented by the dance.

Folk dance in the school physical education program provides the student with opportunities to appreciate people of other cultures, to develop physical fitness through dance activities, to provide feelings of accomplishment for all who participate, to develop favorable attitudes toward the opposite sex, and to recognize social satisfaction from moving together in a group with a partner to the music.

Children must have experience in locomotor movement activities, creative dance, and basic rhythmic activities before folk dance activities can be meaningful. Folk dancing can aid learning if the dance activities are considered part of the school program, and are conducted in a meaningful and educational manner. It can also be part of the recreational program, but the dances will need to be taught in the school instructional program. The dances should be accurate in form and pattern as they are presented, and should be conducted to be vigorous, meaningful, and social experiences for the children. The children will try to perform in an accurate manner, but the teacher should not insist on the dance being perfect.

Teaching Suggestions

- Repetition of the steps and their combinations is necessary.
- The teacher must be enthusiastic.
- The dance should be satisfying to perform.
- Progress from the simple step and patterns to the difficult steps and patterns in each dance:

listen to the music;
clap hands to the rhythm of the music;
walk to the music;
teacher demonstrates the first step or pattern;
let the students perform the first steps or pattern;
do the steps and pattern with the music;

demonstrate the next step or pattern;
let the students perform the next step or pattern;
repeat from the beginning;
proceed through all of the steps and patterns of the dance;
add styling to the patterns;
repeat often enough so the children feel comfortable with the sequences of the dance.
- Teach only one dance in a class period. Repeat already familiar dances to complete the lesson.
- Change pace often—fast dance and then a slow dance—in order to keep the class period interesting and lively.
- Plan for a time for the children to *show off* the dances that have been learned. This could be a program or a party for parents and siblings.

8

MOVEMENT EXPLORATION USING EQUIPMENT

Using Equipment

Movement exploration using various pieces of equipment allows freedom of expression often never dreamed of by the manufacturers of the equipment. Children are always ready to experiment, imitate, and make up new activities for toys or complex pieces of equipment. At first a retarded child may need to experience a more structured activity program than would a normal child, and he will want and need more suggestions. But the child will eventually feel so confident and familiar with the equipment that he will create, experiment, and even be able to show and teach other children new and different ways to use it. He then will be benefiting in a creative way from participating in the activity, and will be thinking, acting, and enjoying the experience.

Initially, the teacher should plan to teach the children how to use the equipment. Demonstrations need be given for some activities with the equipment before the children are encouraged to experiment with their own ideas. The teacher should stay in the group as an active member and should not turn the class over to the children, remaining in charge of the activities at all times. S/he can say, "Let's all do what John is doing," or "Show the class, Sue, what you can do."

The equipment described in this chapter is inexpensive and readily available. Some of the activities are group activities and some are individual. Exploration of the equipment can be a lesson in itself or the exploration can be a pace changer at the end of another lesson in physical education. When the children are familiar with the equipment, some of the activities can be used as a special treat—a reward for something very special that has been performed by the class members. The activities presented are suggested to get the task started and the list is not to be considered complete.

Parachutes

Activities using parachutes provide children with opportunities for group experiences. The entire class must work together toward the common goal of various stunts or games. Parachutes come in many bright colors and are interesting and appealing to the children. The parachutes should be stored in a bag or large box so that they will not become dirty or faded.

Activities using the Parachute:

- The children take a two-hand hold around the edge of the parachute. On the signal "up," all the children lift the parachute by pulling up and allowing the chute to billow upward (Fig. 8-1). On the signal "down" all the children pull the chute down toward the floor. Keep repeating "up" and "down" in a rhythm so the children will become used to working together for a common purpose.
- Lift the chute and on the signal "down," the children all step under the chute and let it fall on top of them. This is a good activity for ending the lesson, because the children get really excited and it is good to end with a happy feeling.
- One child sits in the center of the chute. The others, with no signal other than "go," shake the parachute up and down rapidly. The chute tends to surround the child who is sitting in the center (Fig. 8-2). The teacher should make certain each child has a turn in the center.
- On the signal "down," the children all let go of the chute and let it drift down like a cloud.
- The children take a two-hand hold around the edge of the parachute. Everyone pulls out on the parachute and leans back. This will level the chute and the children hold it taut (Fig. 8-3). The children on one side of the chute lift and then lower while the children on the other side are lowering and lifting.
- While the children repeatedly raise and lower the chute, place a ball in the center. The ball will roll around the chute as it is lowered. The goal is to keep the ball rolling.
- The children raise the chute with a ball placed in the center. The ball is to be snapped into the air by pulling the chute; falls back to the chute and is snapped again.
- Before the children raise the parachute, the teacher selects those who are to exchange places. When the chute is almost full of air, the teacher calls the names of those children. When the chute is filled with air, the children exchange positions by running under the parachute before it falls to the floor (Fig. 8-4). Again, the children should be selected *before* the chute is raised because retarded children frequently do not respond quickly to their names being called.

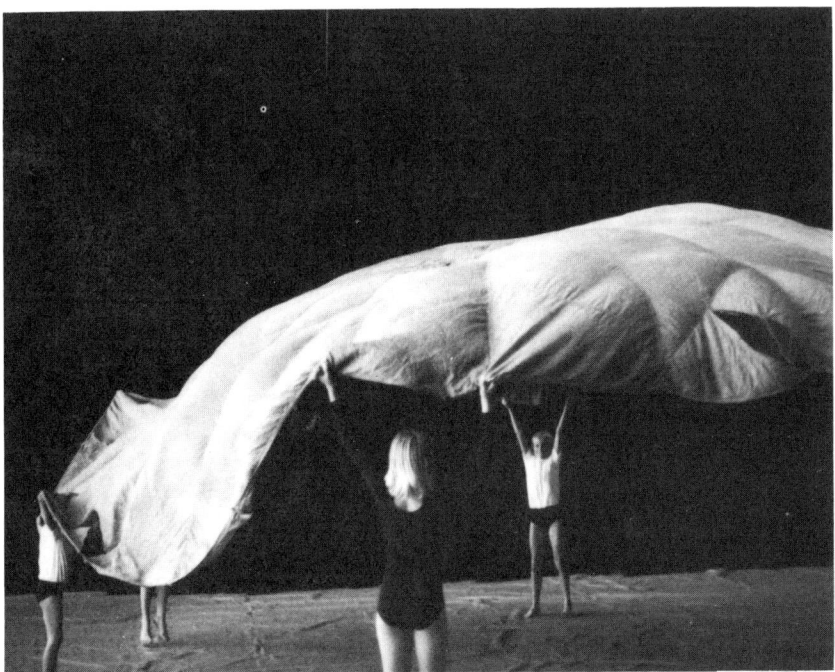

Figure 8-1

Figure 8-2

Figure 8-3

Figure 8-4

- The children are placed boy, girl, boy, girl around the parachute edge. They raise the chute and all the boys run under and to the other side of the parachute. The game is repeated with all the girls running under the chute to the other side.
- The children raise the chute. Two children at a time are selected to get under it. As the chute begins to lower, the children on the outside force the chute to the floor. The children under the chute attempt to get out from under the chute while the children on the outside try to keep them in (Fig. 8-5).
- If the chute is multicolored, all the children who are holding on to one color can exchange places.
- The children sit on the floor with the parachute across their legs. They do curl ups in unison, alternating with the children on the opposite side of the parachute.
- Let the children decide what other activities can be done with the parachute.

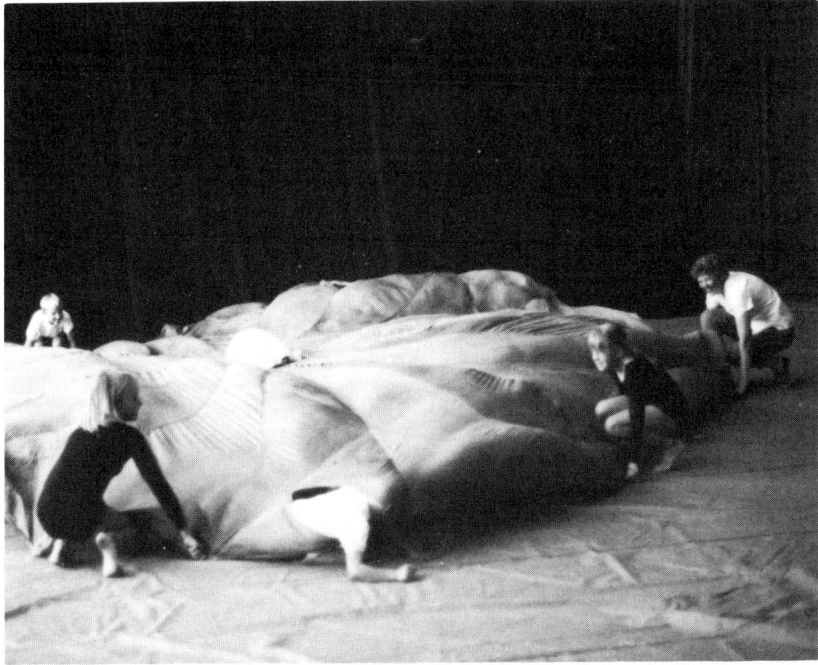

Figure 8-5

Hoops

The hoop has been a toy of childhood through history. A hoop made of brightly colored plastic is inexpensive and available in any toy store. Activities with the hoop offer experiments in combining tumbling, jumping, crawling, rolling, throwing, catching, and spinning.

Activities using the hoop:

- Children jump the hoop like a jump rope (Fig. 8-6).
- One child rolls the hoop to a partner and the partner returns it.
- One child rolls the hoop to a partner and a third child rolls a ball through the hoop to another partner. The children change places.
- One child, or the teacher, puts a backspin on the hoop; at the moment the hoop starts to roll back, a child crawls through it (Fig. 8-7).
- Children each hold a hoop and form a circle—child, hoop, child, hoop. Another child runs in and out the windows by running through the hoops into and out of the circle (Fig. 8 8).
- Using the hoop-circle, play a tag game with two children participating; the children will benefit from a competitive experience.
- The children spin the hoop on various parts of the body—leg, arm, neck, waist, or knees (Fig. 8-9).

Figure 8-6

Figure 8-7

MOVEMENT EXPLORATION USING EQUIPMENT

Figure 8-8

Figure 8-9

Tires

Activities using automobile tires provide a strenuous, rugged type of experience. Football players workout, doing some exercises with tires. Tires are available from garage and service station owners and managers. The tires should be scrubbed, dried, and then painted bright colors.

Activities with Automobile Tires:
- **Leg Strength Run.** Lay the tires down in two adjacent and touching rows. The child runs down the rows, placing one foot in each tire. The child should run slowly at first to get used to the feeling of lifting the feet and knees high enough so the feet will clear the tires.
- **Leapfrog.** The child stands behind the tire with his hands on the top of the tire. He rolls the tire toward him, straddle jumps over it and lets it roll behind him to another child.
- **Jump Over.** One child rolls the tire to another, who jumps over the tire as it rolls toward him.
- **Walk Around.** The child stands on the tire, facing the center, and walks around the edge of the tire by taking small side-steps. This can be carried out as a partner activity with two children standing on the tire, holding hands, and side-stepping around the tire.
- **Target.** The tires can be used as targets into which beanbags are thrown.
- **Tunnel.** Stand the tires on end, side by side, to form a tunnel. The children are the train cars and crawl through the tunnel.

Balls

Exploration activities using balls of all sizes offer limitless opportunities. Activities that are included in other sections of the book will not be repeated here.

Activities using balls:
The children should be directed by the teacher to observe and experiment with the following:
- See how high the ball can bounce.
- See how many times the ball bounces before it stops bouncing.
- Listen to how loud the ball sounds when it bounces.
- See how quietly you can make the ball bounce.
- See if you can spin the ball (Fig. 8-10).
- See if you can roll the ball down your arm (Fig. 8-11).
- See what you can do with a great big ball (Fig. 8-12, 8-13).

MOVEMENT EXPLORATION USING EQUIPMENT 89

Figure 8-10

Figure 8-11

Figure 8-12

Figure 8-13

Elastic Bands

Elastic bands are made from two yards of elastic braid with the ends sewn together to form a ring. The activities are exercise in nature, yet they allow a freedom of movement that is not readily available in a formal exercise program. The elastic bands help the children reach the full stretch that is beneficial in the activity.

Activities with the elastic bands:

- The child sits with legs straight, the elastic bands around both ankles. The child separates the feet, keeping the legs straight and stretching the elastic (Fig. 8-14).
- The child is in a sitting position, legs straight, with the elastic bands around both wrists. The child separates the hands, keeping the arms straight and stretching the elastic (Fig. 8-15).
- The child is in a sitting position with the elastic band around one ankle and the wrist on the same side. The child raises the arm and stretches the elastic (Fig. 8-16). Do exercise on the other side.
- The child is in a sitting position with the elastic around one ankle and the opposite wrist. The child raises the arm and twists, stretching the body (Fig. 8-17).
- The child is in a sitting position with the elastic around both ankles. The child attempts to stand up without the elastic band falling off the ankles (Fig. 8-18).
- The child is in a sitting position with the elastic band around one ankle and one wrist. The child attempts to stand without the elastic band falling off (Fig. 8-19).

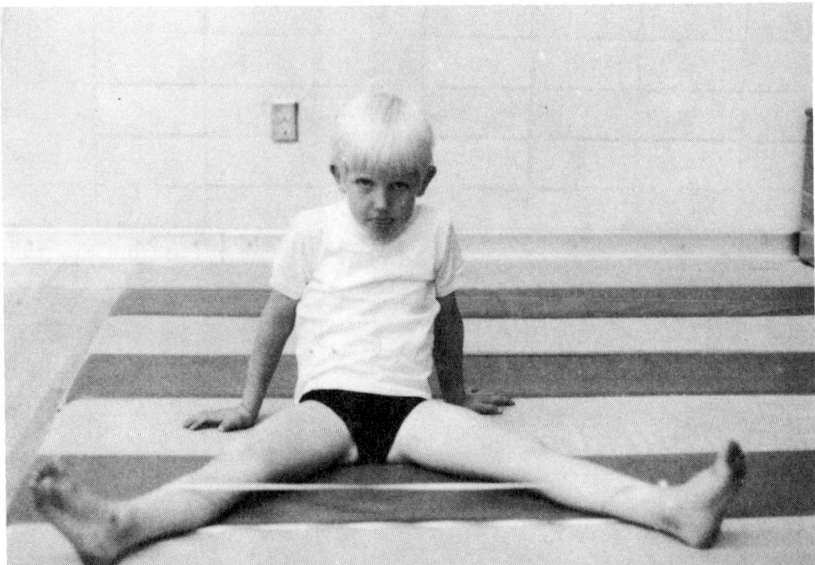

Figure 8-14

Figure 8-15

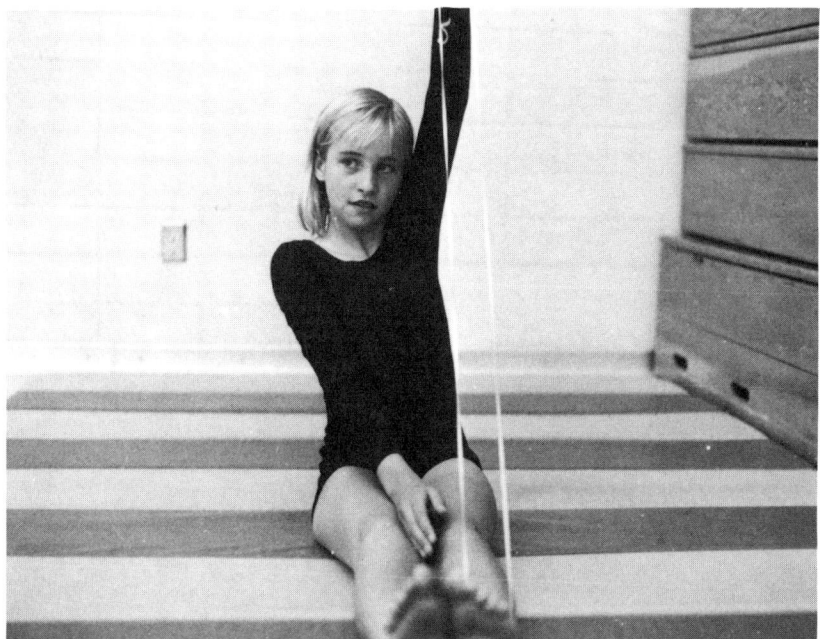

Figure 8-16

Figure 8-17

Figure 8-18

MOVEMENT EXPLORATION USING EQUIPMENT

Figure 8-19

Tricycles

Riding a tricycle is a skill that all children want to know. When a child can ride a tricycle, he has mastered a series of skills. These three wheeled and pedaled vehicles can help to normalize some of the activities of a retarded child's playtime. A child must learn how to climb on, to sit erect, to hold on to the handlegrips, to keep his feet in constant contact with the pedals, to push with one foot at a time, to turn the handle bars in order to guide the tricycle, and to learn the rules of the road. These are all important skills of riding, and all must be learned, even if they are learned one skill at a time.

Tricycles come in many sizes, so it is not difficult to purchase one to fit the child who will be using it. It is also possible to adjust the height of the seat and the handle bars to accommodate the child as he grows. The child should be able to reach the pedals with the foot when the pedal is at the bottom of the pedal circle. The knees should clear the handle bars at the top of the pedal circle. The seat should be large enough so the child can sit safely and still move his legs as the pedals go around.

The tricycle should be of steel construction for long years of active use. The wheels should be sturdy and the axle made of steel. The seat should be steel and of the right width and depth to fit the child. The handlegrips should fit tightly onto the handlebars, and the handlebars should be only wide enough so the child reaches forward, not out to the side, to hold onto them.

Some special features of tricycles and accessories for children with special needs are: shock absorber seats with special springs, recurved and upright handlebars for children who have difficulty gripping in the regular position, metal or leather stirrups that hold the feet to the pedals, lateral torso support braces for a second rider who cannot stand alone, shoe support blocks to shorten the distance to the pedals, and low-slung style models for additional, nontipping stability.

In a class situation, the teacher often will not be able to allow the children to ride freely around the playground or gymnasium. There is always the need for activity organization to keep the children together. While the children are riding they must be safe. Riding should be a learning experience, not just a recreational period. Some activities that can be carried out while the children are riding the tricycles are:

- The children ride around in a large circle formation, all going the same direction and following one another. They can all turn into the circle to turn around, and go the other direction around the circle.
- The children ride around the circle, moving in and out between marker cones that are placed a few yards apart. When the children are skilled, the cones can be placed closer together to make the activity more demanding.
- The children can ride in a line through the hallways of the school. They learn to follow one another and to start and to stop.
- Lines can be taped to the floor so the children can practice riding the tricycles along the lines.
- Children can learn to follow directions by obeying commands to "Get on the tricycles," "Ready go," "Get off," and "Park."
- Roadways can be designed that will include straightways, curves, parking places, turn around spots, and ramps so the children can practice starting, turning, backing, guiding, and parking the tricycles.

Obstacle Courses

Obstacle courses can provide a child with experience in remembering what comes next, with a variety of movement activities, and can be challenging activity for most children. There is a feeling of accomplishment that all children experience by going through the course. There is no need to make the completion of the course into a race. Older children and teenagers can design their own courses and speed may be an objective if this is appropriate. Obstacle courses can be an enriching addition to the physical education program and they can combine many activities using various pieces of equipment in a creative manner (Fig. 8-20).

Roller Skating

The popularity of roller skating seems to come and go, but the value of this activity for the retarded child remains steady. A retarded child should learn to skate for a variety of reasons:
- Skating is an activity that normal children do.
- Skating is an activity that families can practice together.
- Skating can be as strenuous or as passive as the child can handle.
- Skating is an excellent way for a child to get exercise as a free time activity.
- Skating will increase a child's motor coordination and general balance.
- Skating can increase a child's feeling of self worth.
- Skating requires courage on the part of the child.
- Skating can be enjoyed at school, at home, on tennis courts, and on sidewalks.
- Skating is fun.

Skates for children come in a wide range of prices. It is recommended that children use clamp-on skates, not shoe skates, because of the cost and the fact that children grow so rapidly. Skates can be purchased with clamps that are for either leather shoes or for sneakers. The wheels should be urethane or a rubber-like plastic (not steel) in order to provide a softer and smoother ride when the skater is on rough surfaces. The precision bearings should be sealed so dirt and grime will not get into the wheels. The skate should be adjustable lengthwise, so its use is adaptable to more than one skater.

Activities for using roller skates. The parent and the teacher should use good spotting techniques with young skaters. These techniques, which should be provided for as long as the skater needs the assistance, are:
- Hold the child under the arms while standing behind him.
- Hold the child's hands and give support while facing the child and walking backward.

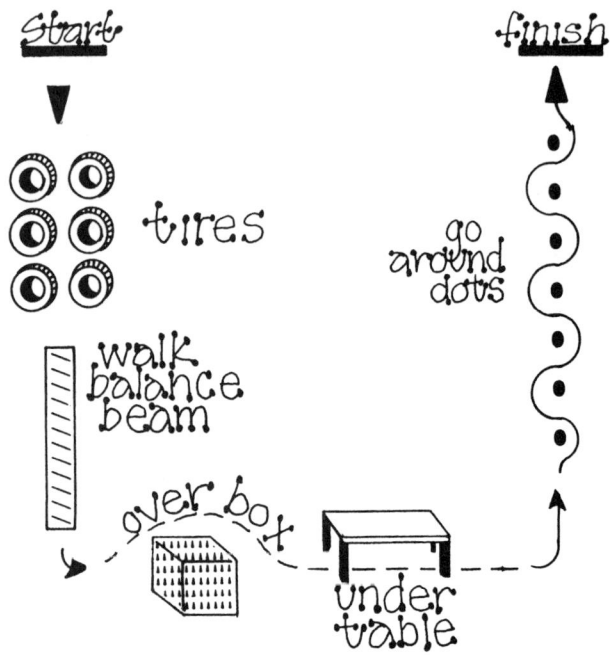
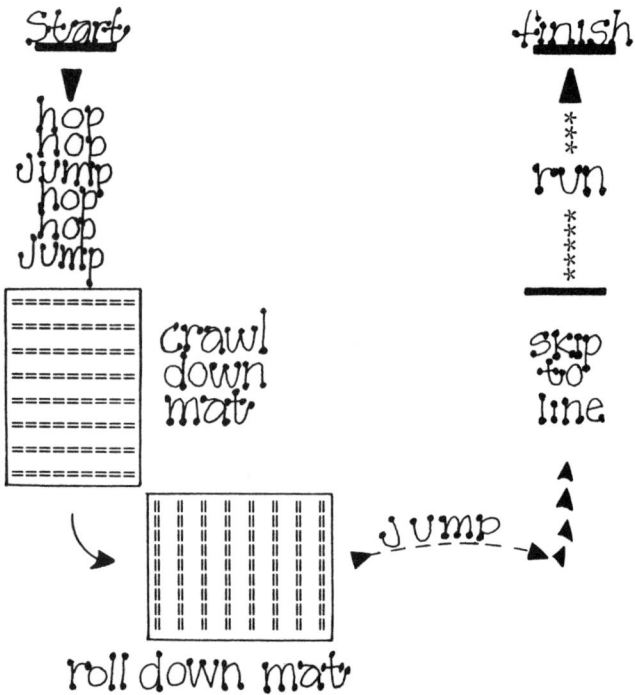

Figure 8-20

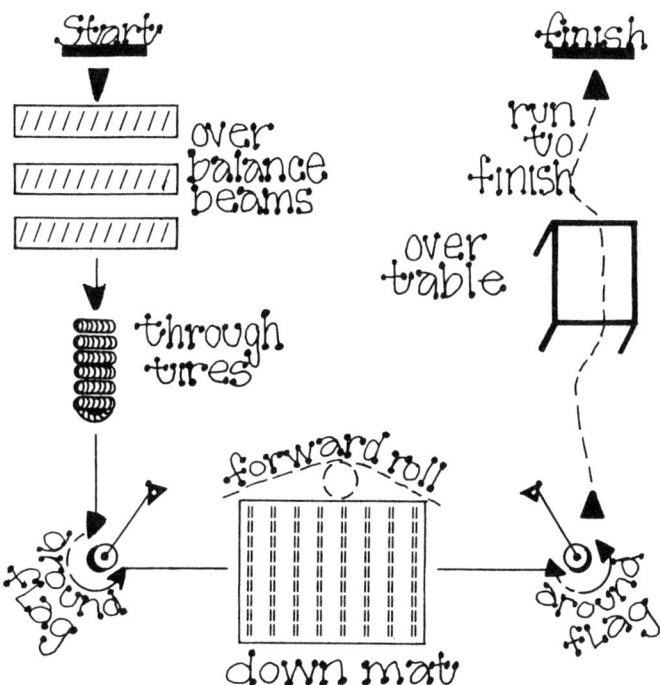

- Hold one of the child's hands while standing to one side and walk as the child skates.
- Hold one of the child's hands and skate side by side with the child.
  On a carpeted surface:
- Allow the child to wear one skate and walk-skate around the carpet.
- Let the child wear both skates and walk-skate around the carpet.
- Let the child sit down while wearing both skates and stand up and regain balance.
- Allow the child to practice walk-skating around the carpet until the balance required has been established.
- Direct the children to start and stop at a signal.
- Skate to a chair, go around the chair, and return to the start. Everyone in the group can do this at once.
- Skate to a chair, turn around and skate back to the next skater.
  On a wooden or vinyl floor:
- Review the activities that were practiced on the carpet.
- Provide a spotter as long as necessary.
- Direct the child to skate around the room, pushing a chair that will slide easily.
- Encourage the child to learn to push off and glide with each foot. The push off should be strong enough to result in a long glide.
- The skater can now skate, and should learn to perform more advanced skills of skating backwards, making turns smoothly, and skating safely with a partner.

9
EXERCISE THEORY AND PRACTICE

Handicapped children have the same needs for exercise as other children. The qualities of enthusiasm and ambition necessary for success depend greatly on the vigor and energy that the physical condition of the body provides. It is through use that the physiological systems of the body function efficiently. Lack of strength, poor circulation, sluggish reflexes, general tenseness, fatigue and general poor health may be the results of inactivity. In some cases, physical handicaps such as poor posture and weak muscle development may result from a lack of physical activity.

To the mentally retarded child, who may not be allowed to participate freely in after-school sports and dance programs, a good exercise program in the home as well as the school is essential. An individual program for each child should be designed so the program meets the needs of that child and so the child will benefit specifically. Such a program can provide activities and experiences that can help the child gain the strength, endurance, flexibility, balance and coordination needed in all activities in the physical education curriculum.

The following presentation incorporates the theory of an exercise program, and includes several exercises to select when designing a program. The exercises have been designed in terms of the type of physical development expected and the area of the body for which the exercise is constructed.

COMPONENTS OF PHYSICAL FITNESS

Physical fitness is the ability to meet everyday occurrences successfully with a reserve of energy for an emergency or recreational pursuit. In order to understand better what physical fitness really is and how it is obtained and retained, it is necessary to know the various components and those activities which can develop each of them.

Flexibility. The range of motion in the body joints indicates the degree of flexibility in each area of the body. Flexibility is also called stretching. Exercises to obtain and maintain the normal range of motion are necessary to keep the body parts functioning efficiently and to insure good posture. Muscles stretch better when they are warm. Some general warm-up movements, such as jogging or other large muscle activity, should precede stretching exercises. Flexibility exercises should be performed before a strenuous activity in order to prepare the muscle for movement. Toe touches, knee to chest pulls, and side stretches are examples of exercises that improve flexibility.

Strength. The muscular power to resist force or move against force is termed strength. To increase strength, the degree of resistance applied to the working muscle must be increased. This may be done by adding an external weight or by a change of body position, thereby increasing the body weight to be moved in the exercise. Specific exercises like curl ups, push ups and trunk raises are examples of exercises that increase strength in the muscles being used.

Endurance. Muscular endurance is the ability of a muscle to continue to perform a task. Cardiorespiratory endurance is the ability of the respiratory and circulatory systems of the body to function efficiently and without stress in providing the muscles with the energy necessary to work. Increased breathing rate and heartbeat rate are responses to the energy needs of the working body parts. In a conditioned person the heart beat is slower, the circulation is better, the lungs have greater capacity, and the heart is more efficient. Therefore, they can be more effective in meeting the demands of the working areas of the body. Endurance exercises are usually performed near the end of an exercise period after the body is really warmed up. Distance running, wind sprints and jumping jacks are examples of endurance activities.

Coordination The ability to move body parts willfully and efficiently toward a common goal is termed coordination. Coordination is grace and smoothness of movement without extraneous motion. Practice of coordinated body movements enhances the ability to use learned motor patterns and to learn new movement patterns.

Agility. Agility is the ability to change body positions with grace and ease. Movement through various body positions as a practice exercise will help develop effective, coordinated body movements. Obstacle courses, circuits, and dance routines are activities that require agility.

Balance. Balance is the ability to maintain a stable posture in various positions. Through practice, adjustment in body positions to maintain balance while moving through space can be learned. Gymnastic stunts, bicycle riding and dance activities all require balance.

EXERCISE PROGRAMMING

In constructing a fitness exercise program, exercises designed to develop each of the components of physical fitness should be selected for the various areas of the body. The repetitions of each exercise performed will also depend on the purpose of the exercise. Strength exercises are usually performed a maximum of ten times. The work load or the resistance of the exercise is then changed to increase the strength required. As the work load is changed for an exercise, it becomes a new progression of the same exercise. When an exercise program is started, strength exercises should be repeated three times the first day, five times the second day, seven times the third day and ten times from there on until the progression is changed. This gradual approach will prevent extensive stiffness. Endurance exercises should become gradually more demanding by continually increasing the number of repetitions until the desired level of fitness is attained. Each day the cardiorespiratory system should be overloaded, thus gradually increasing the capacity and efficiency of the heart and lungs.

The exercises presented in this chapter have been selected for their known contribution to physical fitness. The major contribution of each exercise and the general body area for which it is designed is designated. These exercises are "isotonic" or moving type exercises. For most exercises, a basic four count is used to move into position, providing continuous smooth movement. Each exercise should be held four counts, and four counts are used to return to the starting position. Strength exercises should be performed slowly and in a controlled manner. Endurance exercises can be done quickly and vigorously. Care should be taken to encourage a full range of motion in all exercises.

Isometric exercises provide variety in an exercise program. An isometric exercise is done by pushing vigorously against an external force in a static contraction for a six-second count. The various positions for isotonic exercises may be adapted to isometric exercises. The force may be one's own body part against another body part, a partner's resistance, or activities of resistance such as a tug-of-war.

Exercises

- **Toe Touch (Standing Position)**
  Purpose. Low-back and hamstring flexibility.
  Procedure. Stand with the knees straight. Bend forward and hang the head and hands toward the toes. Stretch gently until a slight stretch pain is felt (Fig. 9-1).
  Precaution. Do not bounce. Keep the knees straight.

EXERCISE THEORY AND PRACTICE 101

Figure 9-1

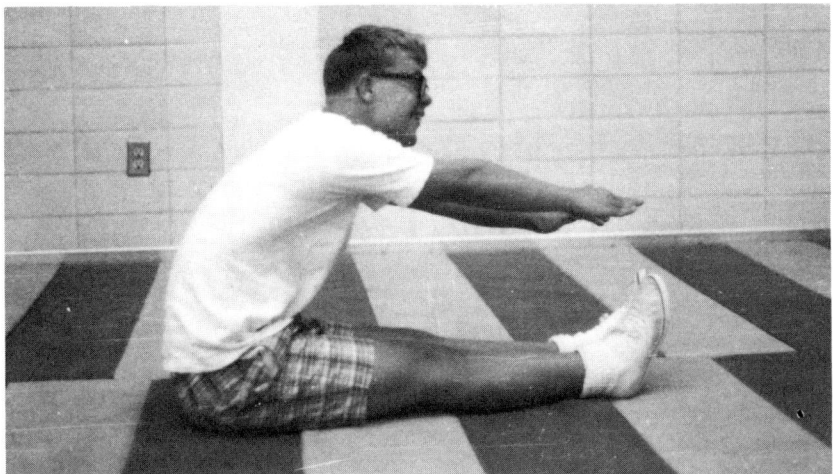

Figure 9-2

- **Toe Touch (Sitting Position)**

  Purpose. Hamstring flexibility.

  Procedure. Sit with the legs extended forward and the knees straight, the toes pointed and the arms forward. Reach the fingers toward the toes (Fig. 9-2), hold, and return to the starting position.

  Precaution. Keep the knees straight. Do not bounce.

- **Airplane**

  Purpose. Low-back and hamstring flexibility.

  Procedure. Stand with the feet shoulder-width apart. Hold the arms up and straight at shoulder level. On count one, twist the upper body to the left and bend forward, reaching the right hand toward the left foot (Fig. 9-3). On count two return to the starting position. Repeat the exercise to the right.

  Precaution. As the head reaches for the foot, be sure to rotate the trunk.

Figure 9-3

- **Shoulder Stretch**

    Purpose. Shoulder flexibility.

    Procedure. Hold a three-foot rope, wand, or towel near the ends. With the arms straight, move the towel from in front up over the head, and behind the back (Fig. 9-4). Return back over the head to the starting position.

    Precaution. Keep the arms straight. Move the hands closer together to provide more stretch.

- **Heel Cord Stretch**

    Purpose. Lower-leg and ankle flexibility.

    Procedure. Stand facing the wall, approximately two feet away. Place the hands on the wall at shoulder level. With the body straight, lean toward the wall and keep the heels on the floor (Fig. 9-5). For a greater stretch, stand further from the wall.

    Precaution. Keep the hips and waist straight.

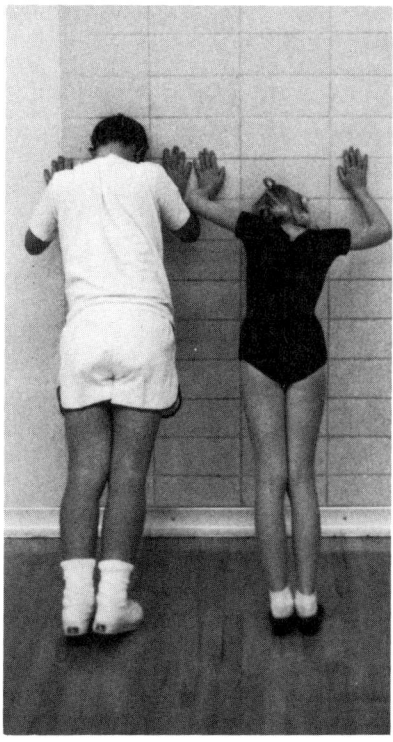

Figure 9-4

Figure 9-5

- **Arm Circles**

    Purpose. Shoulder strength and flexibility.

    Procedure. Hold the arms shoulder high and to the sides, palms upward (Fig. 9-6). Rotate the arms backward, making a circle with the arms. Make small circles, progressing to large circles in which the arms go backward and forward as far as possible.

    Precaution. Keep the arms and back straight and the head erect.

- **Hands and Knees**

    Purpose. Abdominal strength.

    Procedure. Kneel on the hands and knees with the knees directly under the hips and the hands under the shoulders. Relax the abdominal wall so that the back is arched and the head is up (Fig. 9-7). Make a hump with the lower back by dropping the head and contracting the abdominal muscles (Fig. 9-8). After holding this position for three to five seconds, relax the abdominal muscles, lift the head, and return to the starting position.

    Precaution. Keep the arms straight and breathe normally.

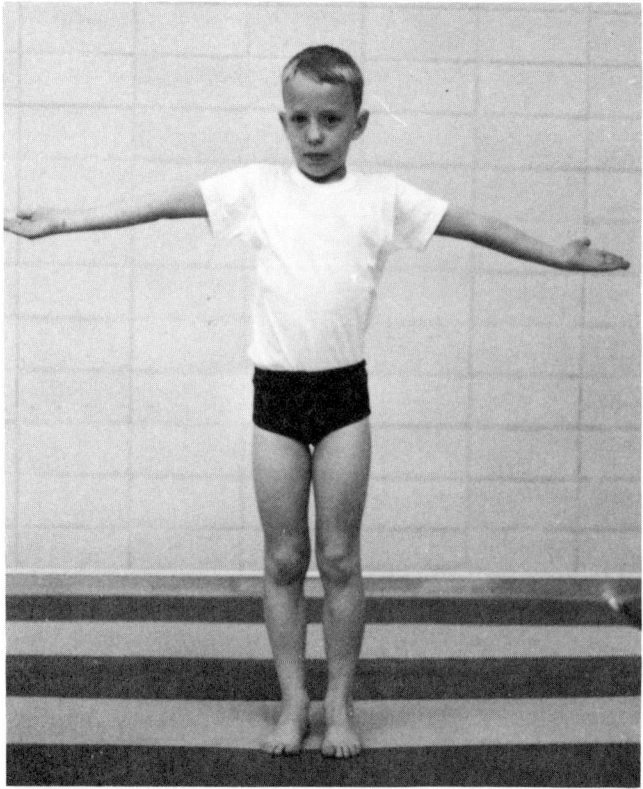

Figure 9-6

EXERCISE THEORY AND PRACTICE

Figure 9-7

Figure 9-8

- **Curl**

    Purpose. Abdominal strength.

    Procedure. While lying on the back (supine) with knees bent and the feet on the floor, place the hands forward. Rotate the hips so that the small of the back touches the floor. Lift the head and place the chin on the chest (Fig. 9-9). Slowly and smoothly lift the upper trunk in a curling motion until a sitting position is reached. Curl back down slowly. Second progression: With the knees bent, the feet flat on the floor and the arms folded across the chest, curl to a sitting position in the manner described above. Third progression: Lace the fingers behind the head, and with the knees bent curl to a sitting position (Fig. 9-10).

    Precaution. Keep the back rounded. Do not jerk up. Each progression should be performed ten times smoothly before proceeding to the next exercise position.

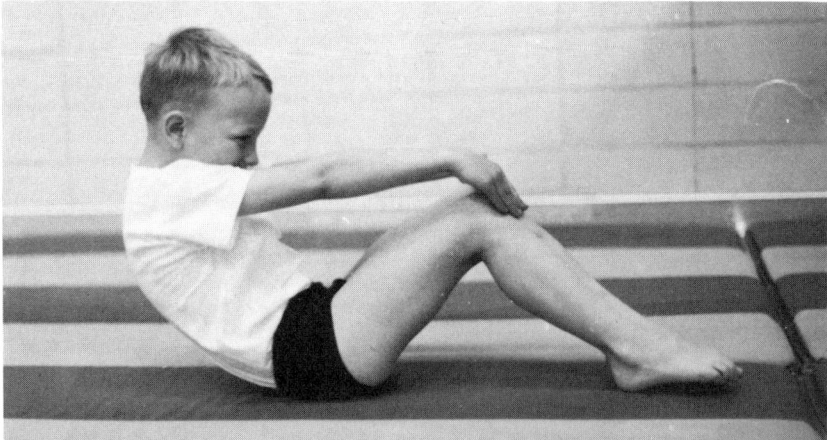

Figure 9-9

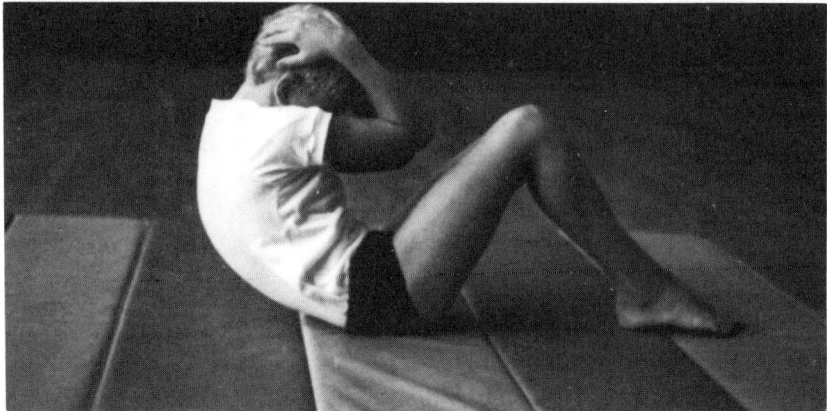

Figure 9-10

- **Rotation Curl**

    Purpose. Abdominal strength.

    Procedure. Begin the curl from a supine position with one arm folded across the chest. As the upward curling motion begins, rotate by reaching toward the opposite knee with the free hand. Return to the starting position by reversing the action. Alternate sides. The progressions for this exercise are the same as those listed for the curl exercise. When this exercise can be performed ten times, do the exercise as described in the second repetition of the curl with a rotation. Use the same procedure for the third and fourth progressions.

    Precaution. Do not roll to the side. Lift and rotate smoothly.

- **Bent Knee Leg Lifts**

    Purpose. Lower-abdominal strength.

    Procedure. From a supine position with the small of the back flat on the floor, bend and lift the knees to the chest (Fig. 9-11). Return to the starting position.

    Precaution. Bend the knees before lifting them to the chest.

- **Modified Push-ups**

    Purpose. Arm and shoulder strength.

    Procedure. Assume a straight-arm support position with the weight on the hands and the knees (Fig. 9-12). Lower the body until the chest touches the floor. Return to the starting position.

    Precaution. Keep the body in a straight line by contracting the trunk and hip muscles. Do not arch the back. Keep the elbows in close to the body.

- **Push-ups**

    Purpose. Arm and shoulder strength.

    Procedure. Assume a straight-arm support position with the weight on the toes and the hands. Lower the body until the chest touches the floor (Fig. 9-13). Return the starting position.

    Precaution. Keep the body in a straight line by contracting the trunk and hip muscles. Do not arch the back. Keep the elbows in close to the body.

- **Trunk Lifts**

    Purpose. Upper back strength.

    Procedure. In a prone position, with the arms extended, clasp the hands together behind the lower back. Beginning with the head, lift the upper body off the floor as high as possible (Fig. 9-14). Hold the position four counts and return to the starting position.

    Precaution. Keep the feet on the floor. Do not rotate or jerk.

Figure 9-11

Figure 9-12

EXERCISE THEORY AND PRACTICE

Figure 9-13

Figure 9-14

- **Leg Lifts**

    Purpose. Hip strength.

    Procedure. From a prone position, tighten the muscles in the hip area and while keeping the hip bone on the floor, lift the left leg as high as possible (Fig. 9-15). Hold this position four counts and return to the starting position. Repeat the exercise with the right leg.

    Precaution. Keep the legs straight. Do not lift the hip off the floor.

    Note. An alternate position for this exercise is to bend the leg at the knee and keep the toes pointed upward.

- **Arm Lifts**

    Purpose. Shoulder strength.

    Procedure. From a prone position with the arms extended outward at shoulder level, pinch the shoulder blades together and lift the arms upward as high as possible (Fig. 9-16). Hold this position four counts and return to the starting position. Second progression: Bend the arms at the elbow and perform the exercise in the same manner (Fig. 9-18). Perform the exercise in the same manner. Fourth progression: Place the arms directly over the head and perform the exercise in the same manner (Fig. 9-19). Each position is a progression of the original exercise and should not be attempted until ten repetitions of the previous progression can be done.

    Precaution. Pull the shoulder blades together before lifting the arms. Keep the head and trunk on the floor. Maintain the original arm position throughout the exercise.

Figure 9-15

Figure 9-16

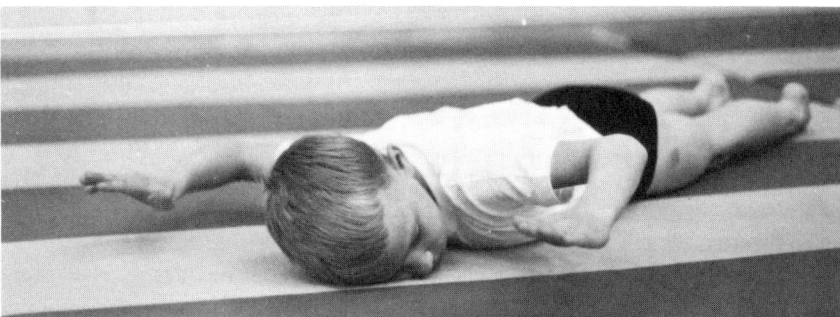
Figure 9-17

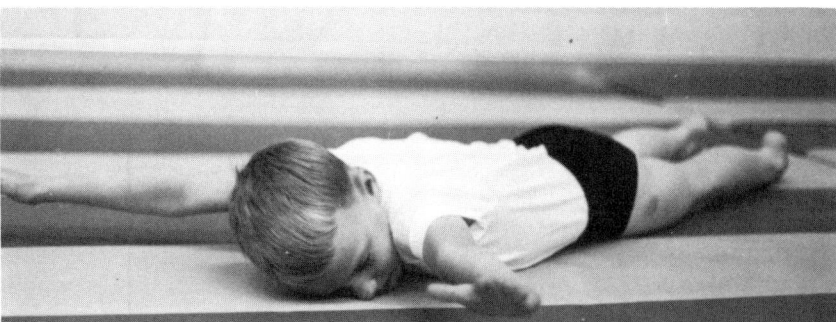
Figure 9-18

Figure 9-19

- **Partial Knee Bends**

    Purpose. Leg strength.

    Procedure. From a standing position, rise to the toes on count one (Fig. 9-20). On count two, bend the knees to a semisquat position (Fig. 9-21). On count three return to the straight-leg position with the weight still on the toes. On count four return to a flat-foot position.

    Precaution. Do not bounce into a full squat position. Keep the trunk straight.

- **Arm Patterns**

    Purpose. Coordination and shoulder strength.

    Procedure. Assume a standing position with the arms at the sides of the body. Move the hands up over the head and clap them (Fig. 9-22). Return the arms to the side with a slap on the side of the thighs (Fig. 9-23). Clap the hands in front, shoulder high (Fig. 9-24). Clap the hands behind the back (Fig. 9-25). Repeat the exercise ten times. Increase five repetitions each exercise period until twenty-five is reached.

    Precaution. Keep the shoulders and back straight.

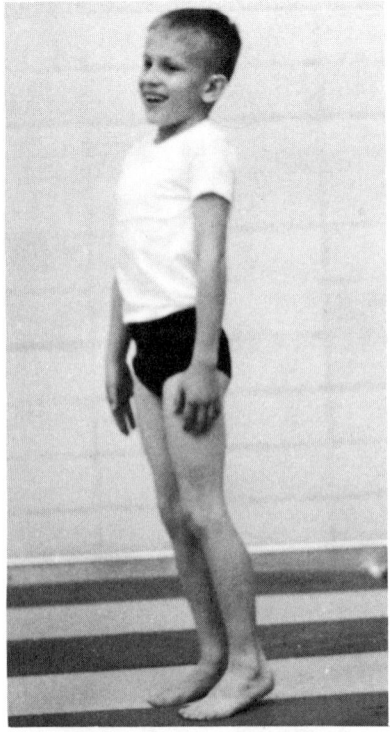

Figure 9-20

Figure 9-21

- **Passive Hang**

  Purpose. Arm, shoulder, and head flexibility and strength.
  Procedure. Hang by the hands from a horizontal bar. Stretch to become as long as possible (Fig. 9-29). Hold this position five seconds.
  Precaution. Grip firmly.

- **Active Hang**

  Purpose. Arm, shoulder, and hand flexibility and strength.
  Procedure. Hang by the hands from a horizontal bar and twist, turn, and kick (Fig. 9-30).
  Precaution. Grip firmly. Dismount lightly with the knees slightly bent.

Figure 9-29

Figure 9-30

- **Running**

    Purpose. General body conditioning and endurance.

    Procedure. Running may be done in various forms. Each form requires a little different muscle action and energy output. Jogging is a moderate run used for endurance conditioning. Running in place using a high knee action is good cardiovascular conditioning and will help slenderize the abdominal area. Dashes require a complete output in a short time and are excellent for general body conditioning and leg strength. Running activities should be a basic part of each day's conditioning program and may be done in many different ways: relays, races, games, circuit training, or as a jogging club program.

    Precaution. In each form of running, care should be taken to land on the balls of the feet with a slight knee bend to absorb the force of the movement and prevent injury to the legs and back.

- **Squat Thrusts**

    Purpose. General body conditioning, coordination, and agility.

    Procedure. Start from a standing position with the arms at the sides. Move through the partial knee-bend position to a front-lean position with the trunk bent and the weight on the hands and feet. Extend the legs to a straight body-lean position (Fig. 9-28). Return to the hand and foot support position and subsequently to a strength standing position.

    Precaution. Go through the complete range of motion in each position. Do not bounce to a full-squat position.

Figure 9-28

- **Foot Patterns**

    Purpose. Coordination and leg strength.

    Procedure. Stand in an erect position with the feet together. On count one, jump to a side-stride position with the feet shoulder-width apart (Fig. 9-26). Return to the starting position on count two. On count three, jump to a forward-stride position with one foot forward and the other foot backward (Fig. 9-27). Return to the starting position on count four. After the movement pattern is learned, alternate the right and left foot in the forward position of the forward stride. Repeat the exercise ten times. Increase five repetitions each exercise period until twenty-five is reached.

    Precaution. Land lightly on the balls of the feet with the knees slightly bent.

- **Jumping Jacks**

    Purpose. Cardiovascular endurance and general body conditioning.

    Procedure. From a standing position, jump to a side-stride position and simultaneously clap the hands together over the head. Jump and return to the starting position. Repeat the exercise ten times. Increase five repetitions each exercise period until fifty is reached.

    Precaution. Perform the exercise smoothly.

Figure 9-26   **Figure 9-27**

EXERCISE THEORY AND PRACTICE

113

Figure 9-22

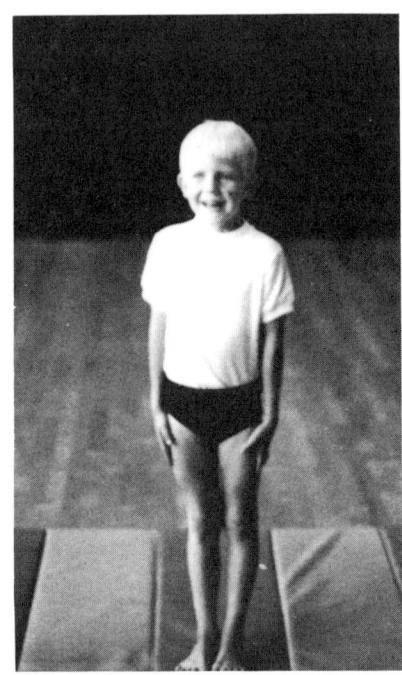

Figure 9-23

Figure 9-24

Figure 9-25

- **Chin Up**

    Purpose. Arm, shoulder, and hand strength.

    Procedure. Grip the horizontal bar with the palms toward the performer. From a stationary hanging position, pull to a position with the chin on top of the bar (Fig. 9-31). Return to a straight hanging position. Note: If the child is unable to begin this exercise, a modified chin-up may be done from a backward leaning position with the bar approximately shoulder high and the feet parallel, supporting the body weight.

    Precaution. Grip firmly.

- **Pull-up**

    Purpose. Arm, shoulder, and hand strength.

    Procedure. Grip the horizontal bar with the palms turned away from the performer. From a stationary position, pull to a position with the chin on top of the bar (Fig. 9-32). Return to a straight hanging position. Note: A modified pull-up may be done in the same manner described for the modified chin-up.

    Precaution. Grip firmly.

 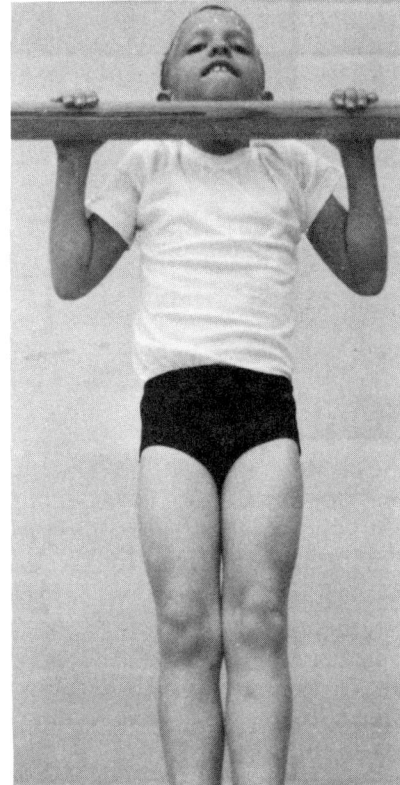

Figure 9-31   **Figure 9-32**

- **Knee Tuck**

    Purpose. Abdominal strength.

    Procedure. While hanging by the hands from a horizontal bar, lift the knees to the chest. Hold this position for five seconds and return to the starting position.

    Precaution. Do not swing the knees up.

- **L-Hang**

    Purpose. Abdominal strength.

    Procedure. While hanging by the hands from a horizontal bar, lift the legs to a horizontal position, parallel to the floor (Fig. 9-33). Hold the position for five seconds and return to a straight hanging position.

    Precaution. Keep the legs straight.

Figure 9-33

- **Bench Steps**

    Purpose. Leg strength, endurance, and coordination.

    Procedure. Stand in an erect position facing a bench approximately eighteen inches high. Step onto the bench with the right foot, bring the left foot onto the bench, and come to an erect standing position with the knees straight. Step down to the floor with the right foot, bring the left foot to the floor, and assume the starting position for the next repetition. Repeat the exercise ten times with the right foot leading and ten times with the left foot leading. For endurance, do additional repetitions by adding sets of ten.

    Precaution. Come to a complete erect position on the bench with the knees straight. Do the exercise to a four-count rhythmical pattern.

Circuit Training

Circuit training is an approach to the exercise program that can provide a creative experience. Circuit training consists of a series of stations placed throughout the gymnasium or exercise area with specific exercises outlined for each station. The directions of the circuit may be to do the required exercise at each station and to complete the entire circuit in the shortest amount of time possible. The objective of this type of circuit is to develop cardiovascular endurance, or as it is commonly called, physical fitness. The directions of another circuit may be to follow instructions at each station and to do the exercises as directed with no emphasis placed upon time for completing the circuit. The objective of this type of circuit would be the strengthening of specific muscle groups, coordination, or a combination that could also include physical fitness development.

The circuit-training approach should be used only after the children are thoroughly familiar with the exercises and have been carefully instructed concerning what to do. Small groups of children can function well on a circuit course if a leader is present to read the directions and to help each child perform the required exercises. Retarded children may need encouragement in the form of cheering and clapping in order to score well if the time it takes to do the circuit is being recorded. Once the circuit course is set and the children are in the process of learning the sequence of exercises, care should be taken not to change the order of the stations or the sequence of the prescribed exercises at each station. One of the associated benefits of the circuit-training experience is improving the child's ability to remember directions and to follow instructions. The directions for each station can be printed on cards of different colors, and reference can be made to specific exercise groups by referring to the color of the cards. The children will soon make the station, exercise, and color association.

The entire circuit should not be presented at once. Each station should be presented to and learned by the children before advancing to the next station. After the entire sequence has been learned, the circuit-training experience will start to have meaning and the child will begin to benefit.

Examples of the circuit-training stations with exercises that place emphasis upon physical fitness are listed below:

Station 1. Twenty-five jumping jacks. Run to the next station.

Station 2. Ten bent-leg sit-ups. Roll to the next station.

Station 3. Five full push-ups. Run to the next station.

Station 4. Crawl under five chairs. Run to the next station.

Station 5. Run in place for thirty counts. Count one each time each foot touches the floor. Run backwards to the next station.

Station 6. Do stride-together-stride-together in a pattern. Run to end of course.

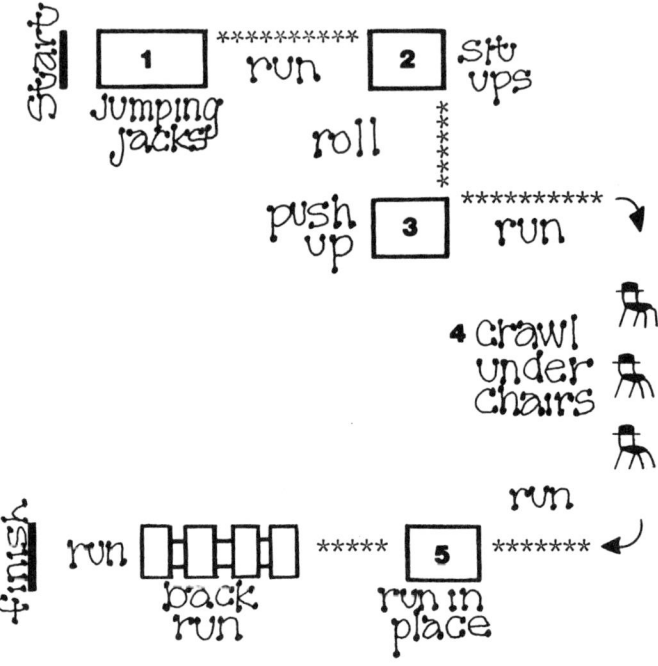

Figure 9-34

Examples of circuit-training station exercises with emphasis upon strengthening specific muscle groups and physical fitness are:

Station 1. Abdominal strength.
1. Ten bent-leg sit-ups.
2. Ten hand and knee cat contractions.
3. Ten diagonal sit-ups, five to each side.

Station 2. Shoulder strength.
1. Isometric hand presses, three positions (Fig. 9-35, 9-36, 9-37).
2. Five arm raises, three positions.
3. Three bent-leg push-ups.

Station 3. Leg and hip strength and slenderizing.
1. Five leg raises from prone position.
2. Five side leg lifts on each side (Fig. 9-38).
3. Hip walk, ten counts forward and ten counts backwards (Fig. 9-39).

Station 4. Back strength.
1. Upper-body raises, five straight.
2. Upper-body raises, five to each side.

Station 5. Foot strength.
  1. Towel gathering (Fig. 9-40).
  2. Marble pick-up. (Fig. 9-41).

Station 6. Endurance.
  1. Two-minute run around the room as fast as possible.

The students can function as one group with everyone doing the exercises together, or the class can be divided into squads with each squad starting at different stations and going through the entire circuit.

Figure 9-35

Figure 9-36

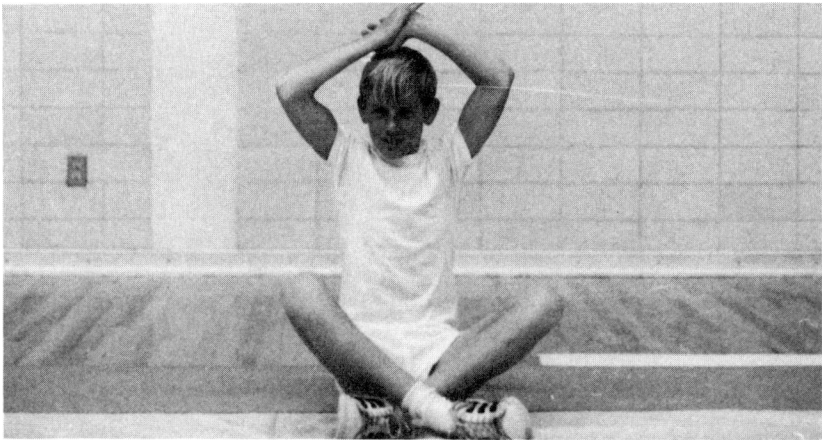

Figure 9-37

Figure 9-38

Figure 9-39

EXERCISE THEORY AND PRACTICE 123

Figure 9-40

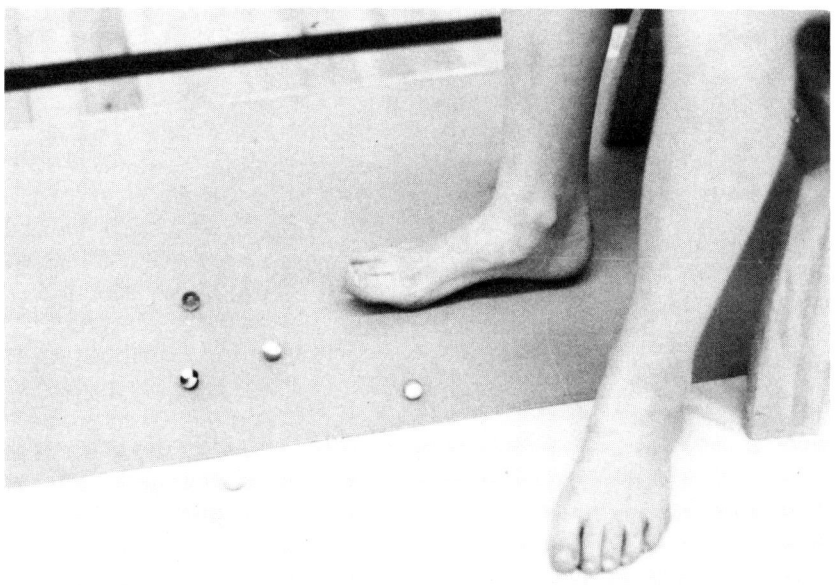

Figure 9-41

10 LOW-ORGANIZATIONAL GAMES

The benefits to the mentally retarded child from being a member of a group cannot be overrated. Frequently the retarded child is isolated and not included in family or neighborhood group experiences. There are many reasons why he is left out of these activities; nevertheless, he needs group experiences in order to develop to his full potential. We hear mothers of normal children talk about how important it is for their children to play with others, to learn about sharing from these other children. Mothers often go to great lengths to arrange for children to meet in groups for this needed growth experience. The retarded child has equal needs for group association experiences. Games of low organization can help serve this need. Group games for all children can teach them to get along with one another without argument, to cooperate, to have fun in a group, and to be an accepted member of a group or team. The retardate will benefit from association with normal children as well as association with other retarded children. A mixed group of retardates and normal children will be a structured group, especially set up for teaching the normal children to be understanding and compassionate. They all can function together in this situation.

Games included in this section are specially selected to be easily understood with uncomplicated rules and low excitement levels. The retarded or emotionally disturbed child often cannot participate in active, exciting games of chasing or throwing. Many of the games included here require verbalization by the children. This type of game should be encouraged so the child becomes accustomed to responding. These games can be used at birthday parties, family group outings and in school setting.

Cat and Mouse
Formation. Children seated in a circle.
Equipment. Two bean bags, different colors.
Number of Players. Small group, six to eight children.
Game. One bean bag is called the mouse and is passed around the circle. The other bean bag is called the cat and is passed around the circle in the same direction. When the cat catches the mouse, the game is over.

Circus
Formation. Single circle with one child in the center.
Equipment. None.
Number of Players. Six to eight children.
Game. The child in the center is the ringmaster and moves around the inside of the circle calling out names of animals. The circle children imitate the sounds of the animals. The leader calls out, "Join the parade." All the children march around behind the ringmaster while acting like animals.

Duck Duck Goose
Formation. Single circle with children seated. One child is standing outside the circle.
Equipment. None.
Number of Players. Six to eight children.
Game. The child (It) runs around outside the circle, touches one child and says "Duck," touches another child and says "Duck," touches a third child and says "Goose." The "Goose" gets up and chases "It" around the circle to the "Goose's" original position in the circle. If "It" is tagged before he sits down, he is "It" again. If "It" gets there, he sits down and the "Goose" becomes "It."

Objects Go Around
Formation. Single circle with children seated.
Equipment. Three or four different-shaped objects and a record player or piano.
Number of Players. Eight to ten children.
Game. Objects are distributed around the circle. Music starts and the players pass the objects around the circle in the same direction. The point of the game is not to have an object in your possession when the music stops.

Ball Counting
Formation. Single circle with the children seated.
Equipment. Large playground ball.
Number of Players. Eight to ten children.

Game. The teacher rolls the ball across the circle; a child catches it and says "one." He then rolls the ball across the circle to another child, who says "two." The object of the game is for the group to count as high as it can. If rolling the ball is too easy, the children should be standing and the ball may be thrown.

The leader should make certain that no child is left out.

Go, Go, Go, Stop

Formation. Children standing in a single line with a leader twenty feet in front, his back to the group.

Equipment. None.

Number of Players. Eight to ten children.

Game. Leader says "Go, go, go" and continues saying "Go" as the children advance toward the leader. The leader says "Stop" and turns around. The children all stop. If any child is moving after "Stop," that child goes back to the starting line.

The teacher may need to be the leader for this game.

Jump the Brook

Formation. Single line of children. Two chalk lines are drawn in front of the children. Increase the width of the lines gradually.

Equipment. None.

Number of Players. Eight to ten children.

Game. Each child looks over the brook and decides where he can safely run and jump across without getting his feet wet. When all the children are over, they jump again. The children should be encouraged to jump at a wider spot each time.

Jump the Shot

Formation. Single circle with a leader in the center.

Equipment. A long rope with a towel, sock, or boxing glove tied to one end.

Number of Players. Eight to ten children.

Game. Leader swings the rope so that the "shot" is close to the floor and swings around the circle. The children jump over the shot as it comes close to them. If they miss, it is only a miss; no one is eliminated from the game. At the end of the game, all children who did not miss are honored.

Bowling

Formation. Single circle.

Equipment. Three bowling pins, empty milk cartons or plastic bottles, and two small playground balls.

Number of Players. Three or four children.

Game. Players take turns trying to knock over the pins by rolling the balls. One ball is rolled at the three pins. The second ball is rolled at any pins left standing. Each child retrieves his own balls and sets up the pins for the next bowler.

Cut the Cake
Formation. Single circle with one child in the center.
Equipment. None.
Number of Players. Eight to ten children.
Game. The children in the circle join hands. The child in the center raises his hand over his head (the knife). He *gently* brings his hand down over the joined hands of two circle players (cuts the cake). The two children run in opposite directions around the outside of the circle. The first one back into place is the new knife and the game continues.

Other games played on the playground or in the gymnasium can be taught to mentally retarded children. By teaching the retardate the same games that are being played by the normal children in his neighborhood, his chances of being accepted by the group are increased. Some of these games played by children everywhere are "Red Rover," "Red Light, Green Light," "Here Comes a Jolly Butcher Boy," and "I Have a Little Dog and He Won't Bite You."

Teaching Suggestions
The following suggestions should be useful:
- The leader should play an active role in the game. He should be a part of the game by leading or by helping each child take his part. As soon as a child can take the leadership position, he should be encouraged to do so.
- The leader should place the children in the formation to be used for the game before any explanation or demonstration is given.
- The leader should talk to each child as his turn comes. He should encourage him to be ready and assist him to succeed.
- The leader should let the class play the game only as long as the interest level is high. A child's attention span can be increased through games, and this can carry over into other learning situations.

11
SPORT SKILLS

A major concern for parents and teachers of retarded children is to help the children learn to live with their families and to function in society as well as possible. Participation in sports is part of life in our society. Family recreation activities usually involve sport skills and related games and most neighborhood play centers around these same types of games. It is for the child with learning disabilities that the following approach toward sequential development of sport skills is designed. The handicapped child needs to learn the skills that normal children know if he is to associate with them. What is more important to a normal child than to be able to throw and catch a ball and participate in the neighborhood games? It is equally important to the handicapped child!

The slow learner is mainly self-centered. His self-image and what he thinks others think of him dictate to a great extent his potential for learning and his participation in activity. The special child wants to increase his own ability so he can participate with the normal children and in his own peer group. When he learns a skill he gains confidence, especially if he learns a skill normal children use. He may not do it as well, but he still can say, "I can do it." He may be able to make only one out of twenty-five shots at the basket, but he can make that one.

The sequential approach for teaching the basic sport skills is to simplify the skills, to provide games of a simple nature which can be used to practice these skills, and to provide gradual involvement leading up to sport games and the sport games themselves. The main concern is with simplification of the skills and the beginning aspects of game involvement.

Analyzing and breaking down a skill will vary according to the characteristics of the child or group. It should be individualized to meet each child's needs. A basic premise to remember when teaching skills to the slow learner is to plan for guaranteed successes. Start at the point at which the participant is successful, then reinforce this success and progress to the next step. All activities need to be adapted to the potential of the individual. He needs to feel success and be motivated to continue to improve his ability.

Satisfaction is a primary factor in motivation and it is especially necessary for the handicapped. Because of the short attention span, satisfaction needs to come early. Praise from parents is particularly appreciated. Retarded children are *object bound*—problems or games involving success with objects are particularly effective motivators for them. A good example of this is the popularity of bowling as an activity among the retarded.

Imitation is one of the most effective means of teaching the retarded. A good mental image is necessary for any student to learn a skill; therefore a demonstration of the activity is needed. This would suggest the use of audio-visual aids, exploration, and sound-teaching techniques.

Incidental learning is low among the retarded. They cannot surmise for themselves that a good follow-through will give force and direction to an overhand throw. All the basic principles of a movement need to be observed in practice and reinforced to provide for good skill performance. It is imperative for the retarded child to learn the skill correctly so re-learning it is not necessary.

One of the typical problems is to convince the handicapped to use all body parts in the movement. Many retarded students, particularly the trainable, tire easily and therefore expend as little energy as possible. Others have not been encouraged to use their bodies, but rather have been encouraged to sit quietly and not be a disturbance. These children use as little motion as possible. A throw for a retarded youngster usually involves the use of the arm only. As a result the power and distance of the throw is limited.

Other teaching suggestions which may be helpful:
- Begin by using large balls and gradually reduce the size of the ball used.
- Teach a ready position to be used to catch, dodge, or chase.
- Most skills will be performed more efficiently when opposition in the movement is stressed. For example, "Step out with the foot opposite the throwing hand."
- For the handicapped the ability to exert force is difficult to develop. Poor timing of movement, muscular strength, and momentum are factors to utilize where force is lacking. Proper timing is movement at the correct moment; for example, "Step as you throw." Momentum is developed by increasing the distance of the preparatory movement, such as rotation in a throw. Force can be increased by increasing the speed of the movement.

- The follow-through is also important in the action. If movement stops too soon, speed is reduced and less momentum is imparted to the object. Lack of follow-through will also affect the direction of the action or the ball.
- Focus on the object of the action; for example, "Keep your eye on the ball."
- Change the rules and equipment to fit the situation; for example, a deflated ball is easier to handle than a fully inflated one.
- Try to make the situation and practice as much like the regular game as possible so the child will be able to participate in a normal activity.
- The interest span of these children is short; therefore activities should be changed often.
- The retarded child lacks a knowledge of basic skills, such as a pivot or a dodge, so these need to be taught specifically.

The following ball handling skills are presented with a brief description of the skill, a progressive list of practice drills, several simple games for each skill, and games which are enjoyed by normal children. The beginning drills and skill games are for those children who have not had any experience with ball handling activities. Children who have played games in their neighborhood or who have had school experiences would be ready for more advanced practice drills. Other children may be more advanced and may be ready to participate in the activities of normal school children. Learning concepts from other areas of the curriculum, such as communication, have been incorporated into the skill game as an example of an integrated learning situation.

BEAN BAG SKILLS

Skill Progression
- Using an underhand toss, throw a bean bag to a partner.
- Using an underhand toss, throw a bean bag into the air and catch it. Gradually toss it higher.
- Toss a bean bag into the air, clap hands together, and catch the bean bag.
- Toss a bean bag so it lands in a circle on the floor eight or ten feet away.
- Toss a bean bag into a wastebasket.
- Using two bean bags, toss one bean bag to partner and catch the one the partner has thrown.
- Using an underhand toss, throw a bean bag at a small target (bowling pin on a chair).
- Throw a bean bag (overhand) to a partner.
- Throw a bean bag as far as possible. Run and pick it up.
- Toss the bean bag into the air, turn around, and catch it.

- Throw a bean bag so it lands in a circle twenty feet distant.
- Throw a bean bag at a target fifteen feet away.

Teaching Suggestions
- A bean bag, a stuffed stocking, or a yarn ball is easier to catch and throw than a ball; therefore, it is wise to begin practice in throwing and catching with one of these items. This will also provide more practice in throwing and catching since a missed bean bag does not roll away.
- Beginning players will usually use two hands.
- Do not be too concerned with the mechanics of the throw at first, but emphasize catching with both hands; let the children become familiar with the bean bag and the action.
- After some experience, most children will begin to use a dominant hand instead of both hands.
- When the majority of the participants are using one hand, emphasize correct stance and action.

Bean Bag Skill Games

Kitten in a Basket
Formation. Semicircle at the starting line. Place a wastebasket or box six feet in front of each team.

Equipment. Five stuffed stockings (kittens) and one box or wastebasket for each team.

Number of Players. Five or six on each team.

Game. Each child is given five consecutive throws at the basket. Each time the kitten lands in the basket the children all repeat together "One kitten in the basket" or "Two kittens in the basket" and so on. After each player completes his last throw he collects the kittens, gives them to the next player, and returns to his position in the semicircle. The player or team with the highest number of kittens in the basket wins.

Teaching Suggestions. As skill improves use bean bags and increase the distance or make the basket smaller.

Kitten on the Fence
Formation. A column formation behind the throwing line.

Equipment. A stool or balance beam with a stuffed stocking or stuffed kitten on it. One bean bag for each player.

Number of Players. Five of six in each group.

Game. Each child is given one throw at the kitten. If he succeeds in knocking the kitten off the fence, he runs up and places it back on the fence and returns with his bean bag. Each child must run up, get his bean bag, and return to the end of the column before the next player may throw. The child or the team with the most hits wins the game.

Teaching Suggestions. To simplify the game one kitten for each child may be placed on the fence. The bean bags may stay on the floor until the game is over to avoid confusion.

BALL EXERCISES
- Reach up high while holding the ball.
- Hold the ball at arm's length and twist from side to side.
- Place a ball by the toes and pick it up. Keep the legs straight.
- Roll a ball around the feet.
- Make a figure eight by rolling a ball in and out of feet.
- Run while carrying the ball.
- Sit up while a ball is held in different positions.
- Jump over a stationary ball.

BALL ROLLING SKILLS

Two-Hand Front Roll, Sitting. Partners sit on the floor facing each other and roll the ball back and forth, using both hands to push and catch the ball.

Two-Hand Front Roll, Standing. Partners roll the ball back and forth while in a standing position. The ball should be held with the fingertips, one hand on each side of the ball. The back-swing goes between the legs. The action is forward toward the partner. Release the ball near the floor. Follow through toward the partner.

Two-Hand Side Roll, Right Side. Stand with the left foot forward in a front-stride position. The ball is held in both hands. The ball is brought back on the right side and forward toward the partner, releasing the ball near the floor.

Two-Hand Side Roll, Left Side. Stand with the right foot forward in a front-stride position. The ball is brought back on the left side and forward toward the partner, releasing the ball near the floor.

One-Hand Roll. Place the left foot forward, knees bent; hold the ball in the right hand in front of the body. Swing the arm backward and forward, stepping with the left foot as the ball comes forward. Release the ball near the ground and follow through toward the target.

Ball Rolling Progression and Drills
- While sitting with the legs spread, roll the ball to a partner.
- While seated, roll the ball against the wall.
- While standing, roll the ball forward, run after and stop it.
- Roll the ball through a partner's legs.
- Roll the ball at partner's foot (Fig. 11-1).

SPORT SKILLS

Figure 11-1

- Roll the ball along a painted line.
- Roll the ball into a box.
- Roll the ball at a pin six to fifteen feet away.
- Roll the ball backwards through the legs.
- Do a two-hand side roll on the right side.
- Do a two-hand side roll on the left side.
- Do a one-hand roll.
- Roll the ball, run and jump over it.
- Roll the ball for distance.

Ball Rolling Skill Games

Roll Call

Formation. Fan Formation.

Equipment. Utility ball (9 or 13 inches).
Number of Players. Four to six in each group.
Game. One child is chosen to be "It" for each group. He assumes a position fifteen feet in front of the group. "It" rolls the ball in front of the group, calling one of his group by name. The called player runs forward and catches the ball in front of the group. After catching the ball, the called player rolls the ball back to "It." The game continues until all the children's names have been called by "It," or until the teacher designates a time limit. Each child is given an opportunity to be "It."

Teaching Suggestions. The instructor should be "It" until the children understand the game.

The child who is "It" may need help in remembering all the children's names. Also, the other children may need to have their names called before the ball is rolled to them to get their attention.

Leader Ball

Formation. Fan Formation.

Equipment. Utility ball (9 or 13 inches).
Number of Players. Six to ten in each group.
Game. One child is chosen to be the "Leader." He stands fifteen feet in front of the group. The "Leader" rolls the ball to the player at the head of the line, who stops the ball and rolls it back to the "Leader." The "Leader" repeats the action to each player. The last player stops the ball and runs with the ball to become the new "Leader," while all the children call his name and say, for example, "Randy is the new Leader."

Circle Ball

Formation. Single circle with children facing the center.
Equipment. Utility ball (9 or 13 inches).
Number of Players. Eight to twelve.
Game. Players take a kneeling or stooping position in the circle. To start the game, the teacher rolls a ball into the circle. When the ball rolls to a player, he stops it and tries to roll it between two other circle players. If the ball rolls out of the circle, the player who rolled the ball performs a stunt related to the classroom activity of the day.
Teaching Suggestion. Integrate the subject matter into the game, such as a rhyme or chant to reinforce learning and encourage verbalization.

Break the Circle

Formation. Single circle with children facing the center.
Equipment. Utility ball (9 or 13 inches).
Number of Players. Ten to twelve.
Game. One child is chosen "It." He assumes a position in the center of the circle. The children in the circle assume a stride position with the outer edges of their feet touching the player's next to them. "It" attempts to "break the circle" by rolling the ball between the legs of any circle player or between any two players. If the circle player can catch the ball, he becomes "It."
Teaching Suggestion. Tell the children to face away from the circle. The ball must be rolled through the legs.

Roll Dodge Ball

Formation. Single circle with children facing the center.
Equipment. Utility ball (9 or 13 inches).
Number of Players. Ten to twelve.
Game. One child is chosen to be "It." He assumes a position in the center of the circle. The children in the circle try to roll the ball at the feet of the player who is "It." "It" must stay within a two-foot circle. He may jump or slide within the circle to avoid being hit.

Circle players may enter the circle to retrieve the ball; however, they may not throw at any opponent until they return to the edge of the circle. If the circle player can hit "It," he then becomes "It" and the former "It" joins the circle.
Teaching Suggestion. If the circle players have difficulty hitting "It," use two or more balls.

King's Guard

Formation. Single circle with the children facing the center.
Equipment. Bowling pin and ball.
Number of Players. Eight to twelve.
Game. Place the bowling pin in the center of the circle. One child is chosen to be the "King's Guard." Circle players roll the ball and attempt to knock down the bowling pin while the "King's Guard" may stop the ball by knocking it with his legs or catching it. If the "King's Guard" accidently knocks down the "King Pin" or the ball knocks the "King Pin," the circle player who last threw the ball becomes the "King's Guard."
Teaching Suggestions. A circle drawn on the floor for the pin will help to keep it centered. A circle on the floor for the circle players will help them maintain the proper size of the circle.

Three-Pin Bowling

Formation. The class is in a column behind the starting line.

XXXX .... o o
                                                        o
                                                        o

Equipment. Three bowling pins and a utility ball or a rubber bowling ball.
Number of Players. Four to six in each group.
Game. Two children are chosen to set the pins and return the balls. Each child is given two attempts to knock the pins down. Each child adds his pin total on the blackboard after each turn. The child with the highest total after ten turns is the winner.

The children take turns setting up the pins and returning the balls.
Teaching Suggestions. Circles drawn on the floor for the bowling pins will help the children to place them in a proper triangle shape. The ball should be rolled from the side of the body.

Ten Pin Bowling

Adapt official rules to meet the situation. Use a large space.

BALL BOUNCING SKILLS

Two-Hand Bounce. Hold the ball in the finger tips. Extend the arms downward and slightly forward and push the ball with the fingertips. The hands meet the ball on the rebound and give with the ball as it comes up. The fingertips serve as a cushion as the ball rebounds and is pushed down.

One-Hand Bounce. Hold the ball in the left hand with the right hand on top of the ball. The weight is on both feet with the knees slightly bent. Extend the forearm downward and slightly forward and push the ball toward the floor with the fingertips. As the ball rebounds, the fingertips, wrist, and elbow give. The cushion is ready to rebound the ball back to the floor with a pumping action from the elbow (Fig. 11-2).

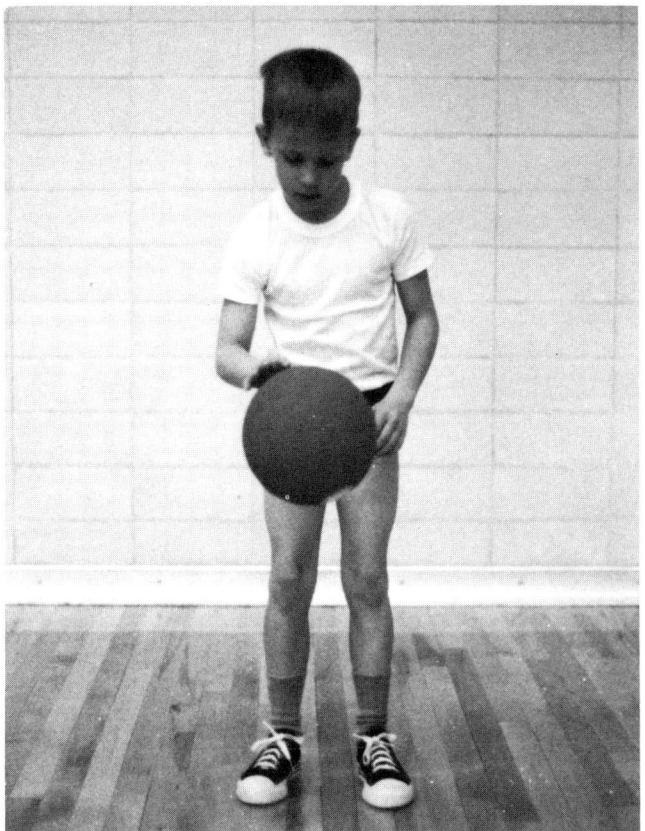

Figure 11-2

Ball Bouncing Progression and Drills
- Using two hands, bounce the ball to yourself and catch it.
- Using two hands, bounce the ball two or three times and catch it.
- Using two hands, bounce the ball to a partner.
- Still using both hands, bounce the ball hard and catch it as it comes down.
- Bounce the ball with one hand.
- Bounce the ball with the other hand.
- Bounce the ball several times with one hand.
- Bounce the ball several times using one hand and two hands alternately.

- Bounce the ball while walking.
- Bounce the ball while running.
- Bounce the ball, clap the hands, and catch the ball.
- Bounce the ball in rhythm.
- Bounce the ball, turn around, and catch the ball.
- Bounce the ball in a circle so it rebounds to a partner.
- Bounce the ball in a target several times (hopscotch maze).
- While bouncing the ball, swing one leg over the ball (Fig. 11-3).
- Bounce the ball around, behind, and back to the front and catch the ball (Fig. 11-4).
- Bounce the ball several times on the right side, bounce to the left side, and bounce the ball several times on the left side without stopping.
- Keep the ball bouncing while assuming a sitting position (Fig. 11-5), then a lying position. Return to standing position.

Figure 11-3

Figure 11-4

Ball Bouncing Skill Games

Circle Bounce Ball

Formation. Single circle with the children facing the center.
Equipment. Utility ball (9 or 13 inches).
Number of Players. Six to twelve.
Game. One child is chosen to be in the center of the circle. The center player bounces the ball to a circle player, who returns it with a bounce pass also. The center player continues to bounce the ball

SPORT SKILLS 139

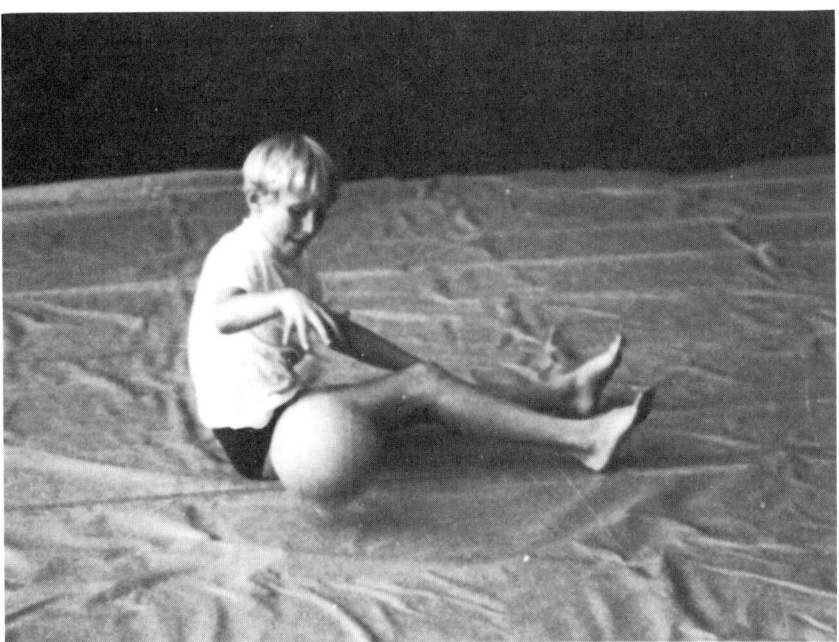

Figure 11-5

around the circle until all circle players have had a turn. After completing his turn in the circle, the circle player chooses a new center player.

Teaching Suggestion. All players should have a turn in the center of the circle. Also, two balls and two center players may be used for more advanced children.

Fifteen Bounces

Formation. Single circle with the children facing the center.
Equipment. Utility ball (9 or 13 inches).
Number of Players. Four to eight per group.
Game. One player stands in the circle with the ball. The center player attempts to bounce the ball fifteen times in succession. If the center player misses the ball before completing fifteen times in succession, the child in the circle who retrieves the ball goes to the center and attempts to complete fifteen bounces. If the center player completes fifteen bounces, he selects the next child to become the center player.

All the children in the circle count the bounces for the center player.

Teaching Suggestions. All players should have a turn in the center of the circle. Encourage all children to count, too.

Use all available balls.

Bouncing Ball

Formation. Single circle with the children facing the center.
Equipment. Utility ball (9 or 13 inches).
Number of Players. Five to ten.
Game. One child is selected to start the game in the center of the circle. The center player begins the game by bouncing the ball several times. While bouncing the ball, he calls the name of a circle player. The child called runs to the center of the circle and, without losing the bounce, keeps the ball bouncing. If the center child loses control of the ball, he catches the ball, returns to the center of the circle and starts the ball bouncing again. Play continues until all children have had a turn bouncing the ball. Try to decrease the number of errors each time the game is played.

Teaching Suggestion. The first time the children play the game, let them use two hands. Gradually progress toward using only one hand to hit the ball.

Number Bounce

Formation. Single column behind the starting line.

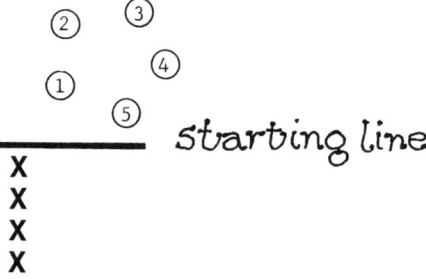

Equipment. Utility ball (9 or 13 inches).
Number of Players. Four to eight.
Game. The first player in the column walks to circle number one, bounces the ball once, catches the ball, and walks to circle two and bounces the ball twice. He continues through all five circles. The second player begins when the first player finishes. The first player goes to the end of the column. Play continues until all children have finished the maze. The children who complete the maze without a mistake write their names on the blackboard or lead the class in a rhyme or song.

Teaching Suggestion. The children should help the performer count in each square.

Target Bouncing

Formation. Single circle with children facing the center.
Equipment. Utility ball (9 or 13 inches).
Number of Players. Six to twelve in each group

Game. A three-foot circle is drawn in the center of each circle of children. Using a two-hand pass, the children in the circle attempt to bounce the ball into the center circle on the floor. One point is earned each time the ball lands in the center circle. The group with the most points after a designated time limit wins.

Teaching Suggestion. Points can be counted for each child rather than group competition. The group could compete against itself by attempting to improve the group score each time the game is played.

CATCHING SKILLS

Catching with Arms and Body. The arms are held in front of the body in a partially bent position. The fingers are spread and curved. The arms and body make a "basket." As the ball approaches, line up with the ball so it lands in the "basket." Give with all parts of the body and bring the ball to the body as it is caught (Fig. 11-6).

Catching with Hands and Body. The hands are cupped with the palms up. The fingers are spread and the arms partially extended. Grasp the ball with the hands and pull the ball to the body. Give with the ball as it is caught. The ball remains largely in the hands (Fig. 11-7).

Catching with Hands. The fingers are curved and slightly relaxed. The hands and arms extend to meet the ball. Give with the

Figure 11-6

ball as it is caught. If the ball is chest high or higher, the thumbs are together, the fingers spread, and the palms are turned away from the body (Fig. 11-8). If the ball is waist high or below, the little fingers are together with the palms up.

Figure 11-7

Figure 11-8

Catching Skill Progression
- With the arms and body, catch a simple toss from a partner.
- Toss the ball to yourself and catch it with the arms and body.
- Using the hands and body, catch a toss from a partner.
- Using the hands, catch a toss from a partner.
- Toss the ball high and catch the ball after it bounces.
- Catch a toss with the hands.
- Using the hands, catch a throw from a partner.
- Catch a bouncing ball.
- Catch a moving bouncing ball.
- Catch a long pass.
- Catch a pass while moving.

Catching Skill Games
Circle Pass
Formation. Single circle with the children facing the ball.
Equipment. Utility ball (9 or 13 inches).
Number of Players. Six to ten.
Game. Each child faces the ball. The player with the ball passes it to the player on his right. After catching the ball, each player faces the player on his right and passes the ball to the next player. Play continues until the ball reaches the starting point.
Teaching Suggestions. Change direction after completing the circle. Time the group and try to improve the length of time it takes the group to complete the circle.

Circle Call Ball
Formation. Single circle with children facing the center.
Equipment. Utility ball (9 or 13 inches).
Number of Players. Ten to twelve.
Game. One child is chosen to be "It." "It" tosses the ball in the air and simultaneously calls the name of a circle player. The circle player must catch the ball while it is in the circle. If the circle player catches the ball, he becomes "It." If the circle player fails to catch the ball, "It" remains in the circle and calls another name as he tosses the ball.
Teaching Suggestion. As the players improve their catching ability, require them to catch it after one or two bounces. Progress until the children are able to catch it before it bounces.

Leader Call Ball
Formation. Single circle with the children facing the center of the circle.
Equipment. Utility ball (9 or 13 inches).

Number of Players. Eight to twelve.

Game. The leader is in the center of the circle. The leader tosses the ball into the air and calls the name of one player. The called player attempts to catch the ball after one bounce. After catching the ball, the called player throws it back to the leader.

Teaching Suggestions. As the skill of the players improves, (a) the children should attempt to catch the ball before it bounces and (b) allow the child who caught the ball to be "It."

THROWING SKILLS

Two-Hand Underhand Throw (Toss). Weight is on both feet with the knees slightly bent. The feet are spread. The ball is held by the fingers with both hands slightly under the ball. The throw begins with a backswing between the legs and continues forward and upward as the arms extend. The follow-through is in the direction of the throw (Fig. 11-9).

Two-Hand Side Throw. Stand with the left foot forward. The ball is held by the fingers of both hands. The ball is held in front of the body. The throw begins with a backswing to the right side as the weight is transferred to the right foot. The action continues forward. As the arms extend toward the target, the weight is transferred to the left foot (Fig. 11-10).

Two-Hand Chest Throw. Stand with the feet apart and one foot slightly forward. The ball is held by the fingers at chest level. Elbows are bent and close to the sides. Thumbs are behind the ball with fingers spread. Move the weight forward as the arms extend forward toward the target. Snap the wrists (Fig. 11-11).

One-Hand Shoulder Throw. The left foot is forward. The ball is held by the fingers in front of the body. Bring the arms back, transferring the ball to the right hand when it is above the right shoulder and behind the ear. The body rotates to the right. Shift the weight to the right foot. Rotate the body forward and whip the arm forward, shifting the body weight forward. Release the ball with a wrist snap (Fig. 11-12).

Underhand Throw (Pitching). Hold the ball by the fingers in front of the body with both hands. The throw begins with a backswing downward and backward, transferring the ball to the right hand. The body rotates to the right. Swing the right arm foward, rotate the shoulders forward, and step forward on the left foot. Follow through in the direction of the ball (Fig. 11-13).

Overhand Throw. Stand with the left foot forward. Hold the ball by the fingers in front of the body. Twist the body to the right as the ball is brought backward and upward behind the ear in the right hand. Swing right arm forward toward the target as shoulders rotate forward. Step on the left foot as the action continues forward. Release the ball off the fingers with a wrist snap (Fig. 11-14).

SPORT SKILLS 145

Figure 11-9

Figure 11-10

Figure 11-11   **Figure 11-12**

Throwing Skill Progression
- Two-hand underhand throw to partner.
- Two-hand underhand throw to self.
- Underhand throw into a box six feet away.
- Underhand throw at a target on the wall six to thirteen feet away.
- Underhand throw into the air, clap hands, and catch.
- Underhand throw into the air, turn around, and catch.
- Two-hand side throw on right side to partner.
- Two-hand side throw on left side to partner.
- Two-hand chest throw to partner.
- One-hand shoulder throw to partner.
- Underhand throw to partner.
- Overhand throw to partner.
- Throw to wall and catch the ball.
- Count the number of consecutive throws and catches without an error.
- Throw at a target on the wall.
- Combine a bounce with all types of throws while throwing to a partner.
- Throw the ball for distance.
- Throw to a moving target.

SPORT SKILLS 147

Figure 11-13

Figure 11-14

Throwing Skill Games
Circle Toss Ball
Formation. Single circle with the children facing the center of the circle.
Equipment. Utility ball.
Number of Players. Six to ten.
Game. The ball is tossed across the circle from child to child. Encourage throws across the circle rather than around the circle. Count the number of passes without a miss. The count starts over after each miss. Keep a record of the group's performance and try to improve their score each time the game is played.
Teaching Suggestions. Begin by using an underhand throw. As the skill of the group improves, use other types of throws.

Target Ball
Formation. Single circle with the children facing the center of the circle.
Equipment. Two utility balls of different colors.
Number of Players. Eight to twelve.
Game. One ball is placed on a box in the center of the circle. The circle players throw the other ball at the "target" ball, attempting to knock it off the box. When a player knocks the ball off the box, he runs around the circle once while the teacher or a helper replaces the ball on the box.
Make provision for equal turns for each child.
Teaching Suggestions. Allow those children who have difficulty in hitting the target to help in replacing the ball on the box.
Begin by using an underhand throw. As the skill of the group improves, use other types of throws.

Hit the Star
Formation. Column behind the throwing line.
Equipment. Utility ball and a star wall target.
Number of Players. Five to six per group.
Game. Each child is given one throw at the target each turn. Each time a child hits the target he is given a star to paste by his name on an achievement chart. Each child should have at least three tries before the game ends.
Teaching Suggestion. Start with an underhand throw. As the skill of the group improves, use other types of throws.

One-Base Throw
Formation. One person with the ball at home base while the rest of the class is in the field around first base, fifteen to twenty feet from home base.

Equipment. Utility ball and two bases.
Number of Players. Six to ten.
Game. The player at home base throws the ball with a two-handed side throw into the playing area nad runs to first base and back home. The players in the field attempt to get the ball and run home with it before the runner returns home. If the fielder tags home base before the runner returns home, the runner becomes a fielder. A fielder who has not had a turn becomes the thrower at home base.
Teaching Suggestion. If the child at home base is more skilled than the other players, let him throw the ball under his leg before running.

Pin Guard

Formation. Single circle with the children facing the center of the circle.
Equipment. Bowling pin and a utility ball.
Number of Players. Eight to twelve.
Game. One child stands in the center to guard the pin. The circle players attempt to knock the pin down by hitting it with the ball. If the circle player knocks the pin over, he becomes the "pin guard." The guard may use his hands, feet, legs, or body in protecting the pin. If the guard knocks the pin over while attempting to protect it, he changes places with the circle player who threw the last ball.
Teaching Suggestion. Begin by using an underhand throw. As the skill of the group improves, use different types of throws.

One-Man Dodge Ball

Formation. Single circle with the children facing the center of the circle.
Equipment. Utility ball.
Number of Players. Six to ten.
Game. One player is selected to be "It." He assumes a position in the center of the circle. The players in the circle attempt to hit "It" below the shoulders. If the circle player is successful and hits "It," the circle player then becomes "It." After the children become familiar with the game, count the number of throws the circle player requires to hit "It."
Teaching Suggestion. Begin by using an underhand throw. As the skill of the group improves, use different types of throws.

Three-Man Dodge Ball

Formation. One third of the class stands on each outside line and the other third of the class on the center line.

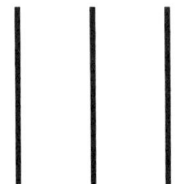

Equipment. One utility ball for each set of three players.
Number of Players. Three to thirty.
Game. Group an inside line player from each side with a center-line player. Each group of three should be at least five feet from the next group. The two outside line players in the group of three throw the ball at the center-line player, attempting to hit him below the waist. When an outside line player succeeds in hitting the center-line player, he then becomes the center-line player and the center-line player goes to the outside.

Teaching Suggestion. Begin by using underhand throw and progress to an overhand throw.

Players staying on the center-line the longest may move to the top of the line and be regrouped, thus equalizing the competition.

Goal-Line Ball

Formation. Rectangular area with a center line drawn width-wise. Children are divided into two groups on each side of the area.
Equipment. Utility ball.
Number of Players. Six to twelve.
Game. Players stand one step in front of their own goal line. The players try to throw the ball over their opponents' goal line. The ball is throw from the place where it is caught.

The ball must bounce at least once before crossing the opponents' goal line. One point is awarded each time the ball crosses the goal line.

Teaching Suggestions. Children with a weak throw may go to the center line to throw the ball. Advanced players may use two balls.

Circle Pass

Formation. Single circle with the children facing the center of the circle.
Equipment. Utility ball.
Number of Players. Six to ten.
Game. The ball is passed across the circle using a chest pass or throw. All the players in the group count the number of passes

their group can make in one minute. If a ball is missed, the count continues on the next throw.

Each time the game is played, try to improve the group's score.

Teaching Suggestion. Other types of passes may be used.

Circuit Ball

Formation. Children equally distributed at each skill station.

Equipment. Six balls, a barrel or box, ten bowling pins, two wall targets, a floor maze, and an obstacle course.

Number of Players. Ten to fifteen.

Game. Each child is placed at a skill station in the gym. The children perform the skill at the station until the whistle is blown. At the whistle each child replaces the equipment and moves to the next station, where he performs the specified skill. Stations may change as new skills are taught.

A sample circuit might include the following:
- Wall target for a short throw for speed.
- A large wall target for a distance throw.
- Barrel toss for accuracy.
- Ten pins in a line for a rolling target.
- Bouncing maze.
- Dribble obstacle course.

Teaching Suggestions. A score card may be used for children who are able to understand and record scores. Also, adjust the circuit to the ability of the children.

KICKING SKILLS

Kicking a Stationary Ball. Stand with the left foot to the side of the ball. The right leg is in back and up, with the toes pointing down. Swing the right leg downward and forward and contact the ball with the instep. Follow through forward after contact is made (Fig. 11-15).

Kicking a Moving Ball. The foot is placed near the ball as it hits the floor or at the desired contact point. Weight is placed on the left foot. The right leg makes contact with the ball right after the left foot is placed. Contact the ball with the instep and follow through (Fig. 11-16).

Dribbling. Move right foot forward and push ball forward and slightly to the left, using the inside of the foot. Step on the right foot and repeat the action with the left foot, pushing the ball forward and slightly to the right. Keep the ball close. A skip step or short running steps between contacts helps to cover distance and maintain balance (Fig. 11-17).

Figure 11-15

Figure 11-16

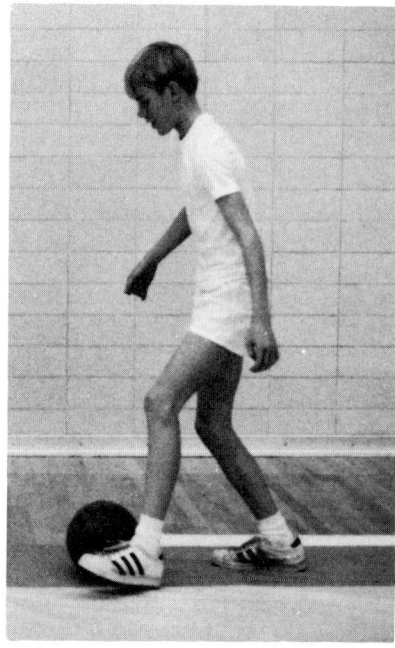

Figure 11-17

Figure 11-18

Punting. The ball is held in both hands. The arms are extended and parallel to the ground. Step forward left, right, left. Bring the right leg forward as the ball is released. Extend the kicking leg and contact the ball on the top of the foot. Follow through upward (Fig. 11-18).

Kicking Skill Progression
- Kick a stationary ball.
- Kick a stationary ball at a target.
- Kick a stationary ball for distance.
- Kick a moving ball.
- Kick a moving ball at a target.
- Kick a moving ball for distance.
- Kick the ball with the inside of the foot.
- Kick the ball with the outside of the foot.
- Dribble the ball fifteen yards.
- Punt a round ball.
- Punt a football.

Kicking Skill Games
Target Kicking
Formation. One column behind the kicking line. Kicking line is twenty feet from target.

3	3	blue
2	2	white
1	1	red
kicking line		

Equipment. Soccer or utility ball.
Number of Players. Four to six in each group.
Game. The first child in the column places the ball on the kicking line and kicks the stationary ball to the target. A ball hitting the red area is one point, the white area two points, and the blue area three points. Each child records his score on the blackboard.
Each child is given five kicks. The child with the highest total is the winner.
Teaching Suggestion. Increase the distance as the kicking skill of the children improves.

Yard Club

Formation. Column formation behind the starting line.

```
_____25 yd._____
_____20 yd._____
_____15 yd._____
_____10 yd._____
       kicking line
       Starting line
```

Equipment. Utility or soccer balls.
Number of Players. Four to six in each group.
Skill. Kicking a stationary ball.
Game. The ball is given to one team on the fifteen-yard line. The ball is placed on the fifteen-yard line. One team member kicks the stationary ball. The opposing team catches the ball as close to their opponents' goal line as possible. The ball is placed on the ground at the point where it was caught. The new kicking team now attempts to kick the ball toward their opponents' goal. The point is declared when one team is forced to catch the ball behind the goal line which they are defending. The team with the most points at the end of the game period is the winner.

Teaching Suggestions. Give all children an opportunity to catch and kick the ball. If the game is slow, award the team five steps toward their opponents' goal line each time the ball is caught. Change the distance between goals to challenge participants.

Kicking Games

Note. New skills not already taught in ball handling would need to be learned before they are used in the games.

One-Base Kick Ball

Formation. Children lined up behind home plate with several children in the field.
Equipment. One home plate, one base, one kick ball.
Number of Players. Six to twelve.
Game. All the children run from home plate to first base to establish the running path. Children who understand how to field the ball or the teacher's assistant will be the fielders. In the beginning, the teacher is the pitcher.

The first player kicks a ball rolled by the pitcher and runs to first base, where he remains until the next player kicks the ball. The second player kicks the ball and runs to first base while the runner on first runs home. The player can be put out by touching the base with the ball or with the foot while in possession of the ball before the base runner reaches the base. After his turn at bat, each player goes to the end of the line at home base.

As the children become familiar with the procedure of the game, appoint the child who is put out to become the pitcher until the next runner is out. Then appoint the child who is put out to become the first baseman until the next runner is put out. He then progresses to be pitcher

Teaching Suggestions. As the children learn the concept of playing fielder's position, change the game by adding fielders and play a game of "work-up."

At first children will need to be reminded what they are to do when the ball is kicked. To help the children to determine the difference between being a base runner at first and the first baseman, teach the runner to crouch for a running start and the first baseman to put one foot on the base and reach toward the pitcher. This symbolism will help them to remember their responsibilities.

Long-Base Kick Ball

Formation. One half the children line up behind home plate, with the other half in the field.

Equipment. One home plate, one base, one kick ball.

Number of Players. Six to twelve.

Game. The first kicker kicks a ball rolled by the pitcher. The kicker runs around first base and home. The fielders attempt to get the kicker out by hitting him with the ball or throwing the ball to home plate before the kicker returns. All the players on the kicking team take their turn kicking the ball, then change with the team in the field. The team with the most runs wins. A run is a successful trip from home to first and back to home before the ball reaches home base or the kicker is hit with the ball.

Teaching Suggestions. The teacher may need to help the fielding team by being the catcher.

Lineup Kick Ball

Formation. One half the children line up behind a restraining line drawn across the field at the point where second base would be. The rest of the children line up in a dugout behind home base.

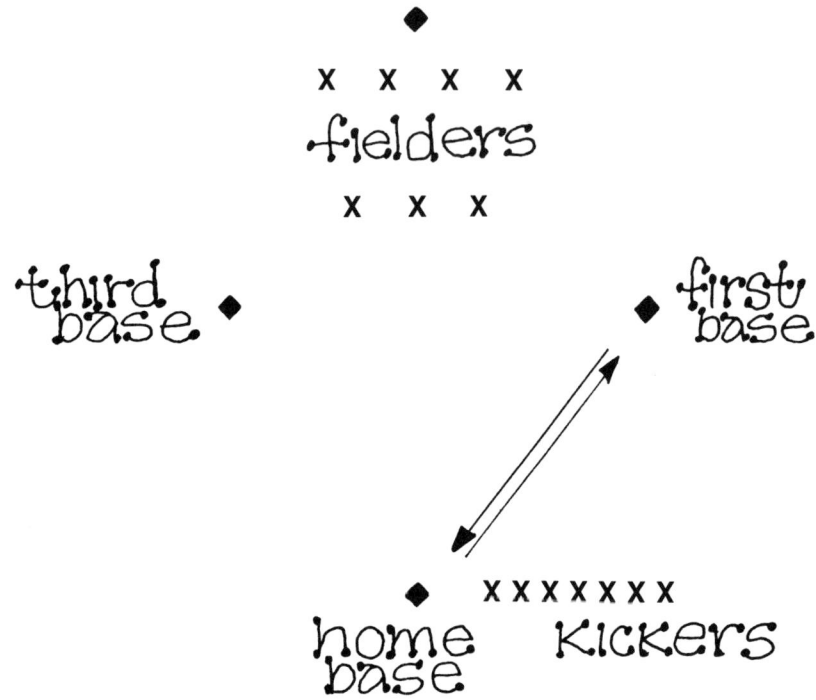

Equipment. One home plate, two bases, and a kick ball.
Number of Players. Six to twelve on each team.
Game. The children in the field should be spaced behind the restraining line in order to field any ball hit into the field between first and third bases. The first kicker kicks a stationary ball off home plate into the field and runs around first base and back to home plate. The player closest to the ball fields the ball and stands on the spot where he gains control of the ball while his teammates run and line up behind him.

If the fielding team should catch a fly ball or if their team lines up before the runner crosses home plate, the fielding team is awarded one point. If the kicker crosses home plate before the fielding team gets lined up, the kicking team is awarded one point. If a foul ball is kicked, the kicker may try again until he is able to kick a fair ball. After everyone on the kicking team has had a turn kicking the ball, the teams change places.

Teaching Suggestions. Traffic cones or bean bags may be used as substitutes for bases.

Encourage the children to line up behind the players rather than crowding onto the line.

Only the player closest to the ball should field it. Running in front of another player to field the ball should be discouraged. The distance of the bases may be varied according to the player's ability.

SPORT SKILLS

Danish Rounders

Formation. One half the children line up behind a restraining line twenty-five to thirty feet from home base. The restraining line should be about eighty feet in length. The rest of the children line up in the dugout behind home plate.

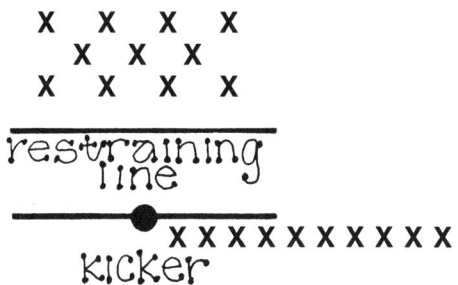

Equipment. One home plate, markers for the restraining line, and a kick ball.

Number of Players. Six to twelve on each team.

Game. The children in the field should be spaced behind the restraining line in order to field any ball hit into the field between the markers. The kicking team should be lined up to the right of home plate.

The first kicker kicks a stationary ball off home plate into the field and runs around his teammates. The kicking team counts loudly the number of times the runner is able to run completely around his team before the other team calls "Danish Rounders."

The player closest to the ball fields the ball and stands on the spot where he gains control of the ball while his teammates run and line up behind him. The fielder immediately begins passing the ball under his legs. Each fielder must receive and pass the ball until the last player on the team receives it. He runs with the ball to the front of the line and calls "Danish Rounders."

The kicking team receives one point for each time the kicker runs completely around his own team before "Danish Rounders" is called. If the fielding team catches a fly ball, the kicker is immediately out. If a foul ball is kicked, the kicker may try again until he is able to kick a fair ball. After everyone on the kicking team has had a turn kicking the ball, the teams change places.

Teaching Suggestions. See those for line-up kickball.

Beat Ball

Formation. One half the children line up in the dugout well behind home base. The other team assumes normal fielding positions for softball or kick ball.

Equipment. Three bases, a home plate, and a kick ball.
Number of Players. Eight to twelve on each team.
Game. The pitcher rolls the ball to the first kicker, who kicks it into the field. The kicker runs around the outside of the bases until he crosses home plate. The fielder closest to the kicked ball fields the ball and throws it to first base.

The first baseman catches the ball and touches first base while in possession of the ball, and then throws the ball to second base. The second and third basemen receive the ball and proceed as the first baseman did. The catcher at home base receives the ball and touches home plate.

If the catcher touches home base while in possession of the ball before the runner crosses home plate, the runner is out. If the runner crosses home base before the catcher touches home base with the ball, the kicking team receives one point. If the fielding team catches a fly ball, the kicker is out. If the kicker kicks a foul ball, he may try again until he is able to kick a fair ball. The kicker may not cross home base before the ball is kicked.

After everyone on the kicking team has had a turn kicking the ball, the teams change places.

Teaching Suggestions. The pitcher should roll the ball, not bounce it.

Encourage the basemen to play on the inside corner of their bases so the runner will not interfere with the ball while running around the bases.

Rotate the players so all children have a turn playing bases.

Stunt Ball

Formation. Same formation as that used for beat ball or softball.
Equipment. Three bases, a kick ball, two basketballs, two bowling pins, and two short jump ropes.
Number of Players. Eight to twelve on each team.
Game. The game is played like Beat Ball with the exception that at each base the runner and the baseman must perform either a skill or a novelty stunt.

After kicking the ball fairly into the field, the kicker runs around the bases, stopping long enough to perform a stunt at each base. The fielders must throw the ball to first, second, third, and home in that order. Upon receiving the ball each baseman must also perform the stunt and touch the base before throwing the ball to the next base.

A run is scored if (a) the runner reaches home plate before the ball or (b) an opponent interferes with the runner while he is running the bases or performing a stunt. A runner is out if (a) the ball reaches home first, (b) a fly ball is caught, or (c) a runner interferes with the fielding of a ball or the completing of a stunt. If the kicker kicks a foul ball, he may try again until he is able to kick a fair ball. The kicker may not cross home base before the ball is kicked.

After everyone on the kicking team has had a turn kicking the ball, the teams change places.

Possible stunts may be jump-the-rope three times, five jumping jacks, a forward roll, Indian sit-down, make a basket, knock down a bowling pin and reset it using the feet, jump-the-rope backwards, three push-ups, or stunts from the stunts unit.

Teaching Suggestions. Change basemen often.

Wastebaskets may be used for baskets.

All stunts should be done correctly; if they are done incorrectly, they should be repeated.

Kick Ball

Formation. Assume fielding positions used for softball for one team. The other team should line up in the dugout in a safe area behind home base.

Equipment. Three bases, a home plate, a kickball, and a pitcher's plate.

Number of Players. Eight to twelve on each team.

Game. The rules are the same as for softball, with a few exceptions: (a) the pitcher rolls the ball, and (b) the kicker kicks the ball to put the ball into play. Also, the kicker may not cross home base before the ball is kicked, and, when a soft playground ball is used, the runner may be put out if he is hit below the waist by the ball.

Teaching Suggestions. The pitcher should roll the ball, not bounce it.

Encourage the basemen to play off the base to field balls, and to play the inside of the base to make a forced out or tag out. This provides for better play and causes less interference.

Rotate the players so all children have a turn playing the bases.

Soccer Games

Boundary Ball

Formation. Each team assumes a scattered formation on one half the playing area.

Equipment. One soccer or playground ball.

Number of Players. Ten to fifteen on each team.

Game. The goal line is the end of each team's playing area. The ball is placed in the center of the playing area. A member of each team places one foot on the ball. With the signal to begin, the two players try to pull the ball to their side of the floor. The players on both teams move about in their half of the floor attempting to kick the ball through the opposing team and over their goal line and at the same time prevent the ball from crossing the goal line on their half of the floor. The players may not touch the ball with their hands.

A goal is scored each time the ball crosses the opposing team's goal line. Each goal is one point.

Teaching Suggestions. To prevent an unguarded space and yet allow room to play the ball, encourage the players to play areas on the floor rather than grouping around the ball. The size of the area may be adjusted to provide for more or less play according to the ability and number of the players. For children more advanced in their ability to play, two balls may be used.

Circle Soccer

Formation. Each team forms one half the circle, with approximately two feet between players.

Equipment. One soccer or playground ball.

Number of Players. Eight to ten on each team.

Game. The ball is awarded to one team on the edge of the circle. The team with the ball kicks it toward the opponents, attempting to kick the ball past the opponents through the circle. The defending team attempts to prevent the ball from going outside the circle by blocking and trapping it.

Before kicking the ball across the circle, the attacking team must control the ball by stopping it. If a player used his hands on the ball, the opposing team is awarded a point. If the ball is kicked over the shoulders of the defending team, a point is awarded the defending team. Each goal is worth one point.

Teaching Suggestions. When players are kicking the ball, encourage them to use deception rather than power. For deception, show them how to use the inside and outside of the foot.

Team Circle Soccer

Formation. Each team forms one half the circle, with approximately two feet between players.

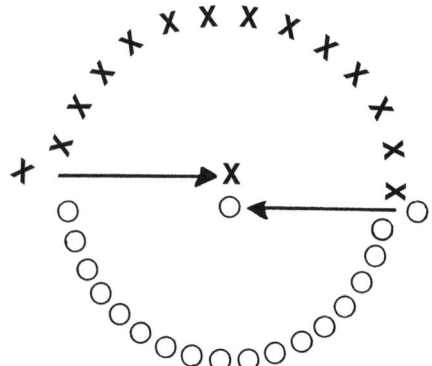

Equipment. One soccer or playground ball.

Number of Players. Eight to fifteen on each team.

Game. One player from each team moves to the center of the circle. The ball is placed in the center of the circle. Then two players in the center of the circle place one foot on the ball while facing the opposing team. With the signal to begin, the two players try to pull the ball free and control the ball. The two center players attempt to keep the ball away from each other by dribbling inside the circle until they can kick the ball past the opponents through the circle for a goal. Each goal counts one point.

The players on the edge of the circle attempt to prevent the ball from going outside the circle by blocking and trapping it. These players should control the ball and pass it strategically to their teammate in the center of the circle. When a teammate on the edge of the circle has the ball, the circle player should move to an open area to receive a pass, dribble, and try to score.

Using the hands on the ball is illegal. Kicking the ball too hard is dangerous and is a foul. Kicking the ball higher than the shoulders is also a foul. For all fouls, the opposing team is given a free kick in the center of the circle by the circle player while the opposing circle player stands at least five yards away. It is also illegal for an opposing player to step between a player who is about to play the ball and the ball. This foul is called obstruction.

After a point had been scored or a time limit called, the players in the center of the circle exit on the opposite side of the circle from which they came onto the floor and all players rotate one position in the circle.

Teaching Suggestions. When kicking the ball, the players should use deception rather than power.

When a teammate on the edge of the circle has the ball, the circle players should move away from the ball to get free for a pass.

In this game players should use passing, dribbling, dodging, and trapping rather than kicking.

When the number of players is sufficient, one player from each team may be assigned to officiate the game. The players rotate in and out of the officiating position in the same manner the players rotate in and out of the center of the circle.

Bombardment

Formation. A rectangle with each team lined up lengthwise on the outside of the area. Eight markers in alternating colors are placed on a line in the center of the area.

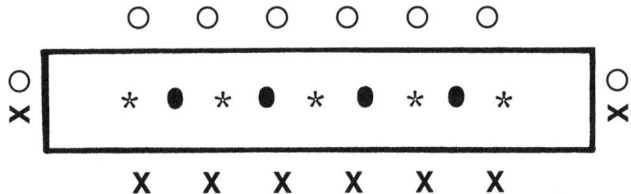

Equipment. A soccer ball or a playground ball and eight markers (traffic cones or liquid containers which tip easily), four of one color and four of another.

Number of Players. Eight to fifteen on each team.

Game. Space the players along the kicking line with one player from each team on the sideline. The ball is awarded to one team on the kicking line. The player by the ball attempts to kick the ball from behind his kicking line and knock down one of his team's markers. The ball should be trapped for the receiving team by the player closest to the ball and kicked at one of his team's markers. If a player should knock down one of his team's markers, the marker stays down and counts as a score for that team.

The sideline players try to prevent the ball from going over the sideline, and kick the ball to their own team behind the kicking line. They may also recover any ball which stops in their quarter of the rectangle.

Using the hands on the ball, dangerous kicking, and stepping over the kicking line are fouls. The penalty for a foul is to award the ball to the opposing team and cancel any score made on that play. Sideline players may not attempt to knock down the center markers.

Teaching Suggestions. Rotate the players after each point or after a predetermined time limit. Also, encourage the players to trap the ball before kicking it at a marker.

Line Soccer

Formation. A rectangle with each team lined up in one half of the court as shown.

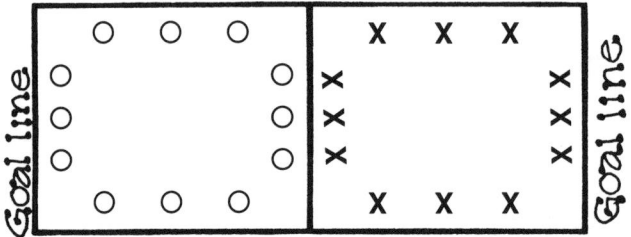

Equipment. One soccer or playground ball and two sets of colored pinnies to distinguish the teams.

Number of Players. Twelve to sixteen on each team.

Game. Each team should space three or four players on the end line, each sideline, and behind the center line, which divides the rectangle in half. The players on the end line are defensive players who protect the goal (which is the end line). The players on the two sidelines prevent the ball from going over the sideline and pass the ball to the active players on the floor.

The game starts with the players in the center spaced on their half of the floor behind the center line. The ball is placed in the center of the rectangle. Two opposing players place one foot on the ball while facing the opposing team. With the signal to begin, the two players try to pull the ball free and pass it to a teammate. The players in the center of the floor may move anywhere within the rectangle to help defend their goal and to control the ball by passing and dribbling until they can score by kicking the ball through the opposing defensive players and over the opponent's goal line. Each goal counts one point.

Using the hands on the ball, dangerous kicking, kicking the ball over the goal line above the shoulders, obstruction, kicking other players, and pushing are fouls. The penalty for a foul is to award the ball to the opposing team for a free kick on the spot where the foul occurred or five yards away from the goal line. No players may be within five yards of the free kick.

After a goal has been scored or a time limit elapsed, rotate each set of three or four players to the next assignment on the floor.

Teaching Suggestions. Encourage the players to use teamwork and play different areas of the floor instead of grouping near the ball. The active players should move to an open area to receive a pass rather than crowd around the ball. Also, the players should try to control the ball instead of kicking it from one end of the area to the other.

Forwards and Backs

Formation. A rectangle with a center line across the middle of the area.

Equipment. One soccer ball or playground ball and two sets of colored pinnies to distinguish the teams.

Number of Players. Twelve to sixteen on each team.

Game. Each team should designate half their players as forwards and half their players as backs. The backs stay on their team's half of the area, defend their goal line (which is the end line of the rectangle), and pass the ball over the center line to their forwards. The forwards stay in their opponent's half of the rectangle and attempt to score by kicking the ball over the opponents' goal line.

The game is started with the ball on the center line. Two opposing forwards place one foot on the ball while facing their defensive players. On the signal to begin, the two players try to pull the ball to their half of the floor and pass it to a teammate.

The players should be assigned to play general areas on the field. This helps them cover the area and provides for more passing room.

Using the hands on the ball, dangerous kicking, kicking the ball over the goal line above the shoulders, obstruction, kicking other players, pushing and crossing the center line are fouls. The penalty for a foul is to award the ball to the opposing team for a free kick on the spot where the foul occurred or five yards away from the goal line. No players may be within five yards of the free kick. The kicker may not play the ball again until it has been played by another player.

Each goal counts one point. After the goal, the team scored against is given possession of the ball on the center line.

If the ball is kicked out of bounds, the ball is awarded to the opposing team for a throw-in with everyone five yards away.

Teaching Suggestions. The players should try to control the ball and get free passes rather than crowding around the ball. At the halfway point in the game, the players should change positions on the team.

Soccer

Children who are able to play the lead-up games are ready to play soccer, an excellent, exciting, and vigorous game. The rules are available in *Soccer Guides* for boys and girls. Most of the basic rules have been incorporated in the lead-up games presented previously. Some variations are:

Scooter Soccer. Regular soccer rules are used with the addition that all participants must play the game on gym scooters.

Crab Soccer. Regular soccer rules are used with the exception that all players assume a crab walk position to play the game.

FOOTBALL

Passing. Stand with the left foot forward. The ball is held toward the end with the fingers on the laces and the thumb on the opposite side of the ball. Move the ball up and back behind the ear, with the shoulder and body rotated away from the target. Rotate the body toward the target and whip the arm forward with the elbow leading, snap the wrist forward, and release the ball off the fingers as the hand draws under the ball. Step into the throw and keep the nose of the ball slightly up (Fig. 11-19).

Centering. Assume a wider stride position and bend down and forward into a crouch position with the hands on the ball (which is slightly in front of the head and shoulders). Grip the ball in the same manner used for a forward pass (Fig. 11-20).

Handoff. To receive the ball, hold the forearms parallel to the ground in front of the body with the palms toward each other and ball-width apart. Lean slightly forward. The ball is placed firmly into the midsection of the receiver by the player with the ball. The receiver holds the ball with both hands. To carry the ball the receiver pulls the ball to the side, away from the opponent, and carries it tucked between the elbow and body with the hand over the nose of the ball.

Figure 11-19

Figure 11-20

Football Games
Punt and Run
Formation. Children in a scatter formation with the kicker facing the group.

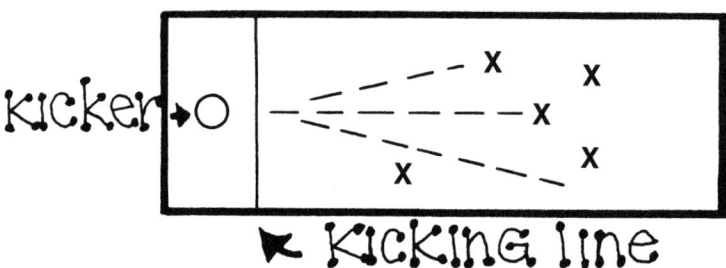

Equipment. One football.
Number of Players. Six to ten.
Game. The kicker punts the ball toward the group. The player closest to the ball catches it and runs to the kicking line. The kicker runs to the catching area with the other children. The process is repeated with the new kicker.

Teaching Suggestions. Encourage the children to carry the ball correctly. Also, provide for all children to have a turn catching the ball.

For children with some experience, a variation may be added in which the kicker tries to touch the ball carrier with a two-hand touch below the waist. If he is successful, he remains in the kicking position.

Punt Back
Formation. Two teams face each other on the field, kicking-distance apart.

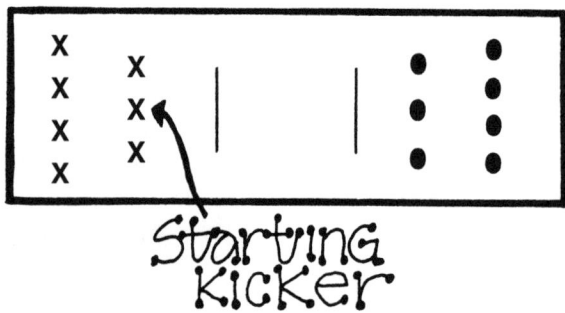

Equipment. One football.
Number of Players. Six to eight on each team.
Game. Each group stands on one half the field facing the other group. The kicker on one team kicks the ball from the middle of their half of the field (or what would be the twenty-five yard line on a football

field). The player on the other team closest to the ball attempts to catch it. If he is successful, he may take five giant steps toward the opponents' goal line and then kick the ball. If the ball bounces, it must be kicked from the spot where the player gained control of it. The process is repeated, with each team trying to force the opposing team backward until they fail to gain control of the ball before it crosses their goal line. When a team fails to gain control of the ball before it crosses their goal line, a touchdown is scored. Each touchdown counts six points.

Teaching Suggestions. Provide for all children to have a turn catching the ball. The best catching technique is to trap the ball against the body and give as the ball is caught.

Field Ball

Formation. Two teams, one on each half of the field.

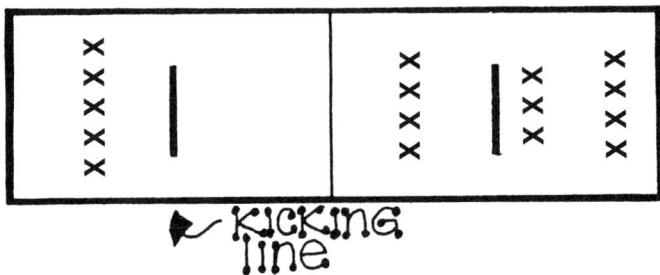

Equipment. One football.
Number of Players. Eight to ten on each team.
Game. The receiving team scatters on their half of the field to receive the kick, either a punt or a place kick, from the opposing team. The kicking team may not cross the center line until the receiving team has gained control of the ball. The receiving team may advance the ball by passing in any direction or running with the ball. Any number of passes is permissible.

The defensive team must tag the ball carrier with a two-hand touch below the waist. There is no body contact in the game other than the touch. When the defensive team makes the touch, they become the offensive team and have one down to move the ball. The offensive team has one down to score a touchdown, which counts six points. An intercepted pass and the return of the kickoff do not count as downs. A ball kicked out of bounds on the kickoff is kicked again.

Holding, blocking, pushing, and tripping are illegal. If the defensive team fouls, the ball is moved forward eight paces from the spot of the foul. If the offensive team fouls, the defensive team is awarded the ball at the spot of the foul. The ball may not be placed closer than five yards to the goal. The ball is dead when it touches the ground.

Teaching Suggestions. For the experienced players, the game may be restricted to only one forward pass and lateral passes. The size of the field also should be adjusted to the ability of the players.

Seven-Man Touch Football

Formation. Two teams, one on each half of a football field.

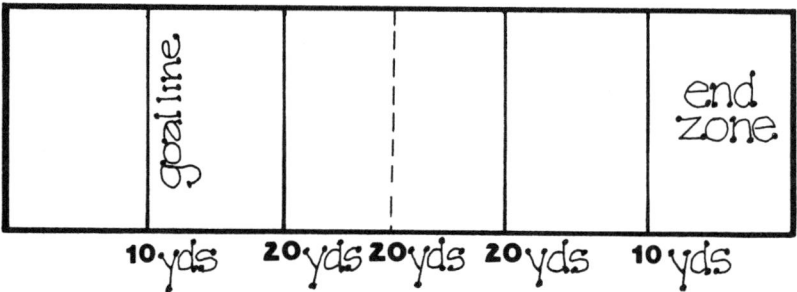

Equipment. One football.

Number of Players. Seven on each team: left end, center, right end, quarterback, fullback, right halfback, and left halfback.

Game. This game is played and scored in the same manner as regular football, with the modifications as listed.

If the kickoff goes out of bounds, the kicking team is given another chance to kick. If this happens a second time, the receiving team puts the ball in play at the fifty-yard line. On all plays the ball is placed at least five yards from the sideline.

When a player with the ball is touched with two hands below the waist by an opponent, the play stops. If the ball is fumbled, the play stops and the team which last had possession puts the ball in play at the spot where the ball hit the ground.

The offensive team has four downs to advance the ball to the next zone on the field or to score a touchdown. A new series of downs is started when a team crosses a zone line.

The offensive team must have three players on the scrimmage line to begin each play.

Any player except the center is an eligible pass receiver.

Body contact is illegal. The only form of blocking which may be used is to place the body in the way of an opponent. Neither team may use the hands when blocking. Both feet must be on the ground. The penalty for infraction of the rules is to award five yards to the non-offending team. For unnecessary roughness or unsportsmanlike conduct, fifteen yards is awarded. The penalty for pass interference is to rule the pass completed. For situations not mentioned, apply regulation football rules.

Teaching Suggestions. Rotate players in each position. Also, adjust the time limit and size of the field to the ability of the players.

Nine-man touch football may be played with the same rules by adding two linemen. In eleven-man touch football, each team has two guards and two tackles in addition to the players used for seven-man touch football.

Flag football may be played with the same rules by using a flag tucked in the belt of each player. When the flag is removed, the ball carrier is stopped.

HITTING SKILLS

Two-Hand Underhand Hit or Volley. Stand with the body bent slightly forward, the knees flexed, and the arms straight forward. The hands are open, with one hand clasped inside the other. One foot is slightly in front of the other. Contact underside of the ball on the forearms and let the ball bounce upward and outward in the direction intended (Fig. 11-21).

One-Hand Underhand Hit. The ball is held in front of the right side by the left hand. The left foot is forward. Weight is on the right foot and the right arm is back, ready to hit. Transfer the weight forward to the left foot as the right arm swings forward. Contact the ball off the left hand with the heel of the hand near the bottom of the ball. Follow through in the direction of the ball. This technique may be used to hit a low ball by reaching under the ball and letting it rebound off the arm and hand (Fig. 11-22).

Figure 11-21 **Figure 11-22**

One-Hand Side Hit. Stand with the left side toward the target. Hold the ball in the left hand in front of the left leg. The right arm moves backward and forward simultaneously with a weight transfer in the same direction. Contact the ball with the heel of the hand behind and slightly under the ball.

Overhand Hit or Volley. Bend the knees. The elbows are bent and to the sides. The fingers are spread and curved, with the thumbs and forefingers together and the palms upward. Contact the ball above the head and extend the fingers, arms, and body upward. Complete the follow-through in the intended direction of the hit. Hit from a stationary position under the ball, facing the intended direction of the ball (Fig. 11-23).

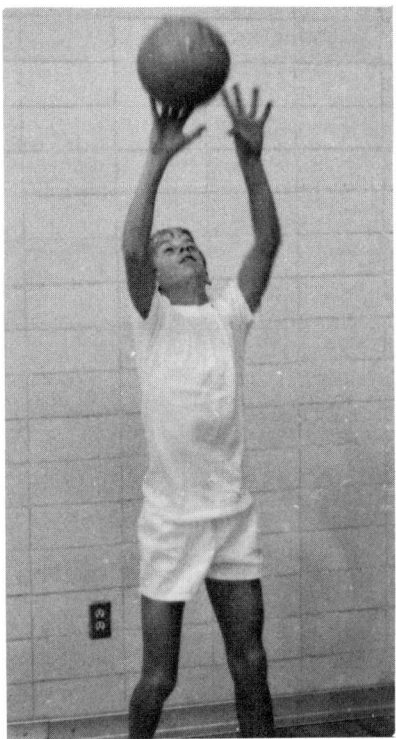

Figure 11-23

Hitting Skill Progression
Underhand hitting skills:
- Bounce the ball, then hit it upward.
- Hit a ball tossed from a partner.
- Hit a bounced ball to a partner who will hit it after it bounces.
- With a partner, hit the ball back and forth allowing only one bounce between hits.

- Throw the ball against the wall and hit the return with an underhand hit.
- Count consecutive underhand hits with a partner—no bounces allowed.
- While volleying with a partner, hit the ball so it lands in a large circle.
- Play "Two Square" as described in Hitting Skill Games (which follows).
- Play "Four Square" described in Hitting Skill Games.

Sidearm hitting skills:
- Hit for distance.
- Hit over a net at variable heights.
- Play tether ball.

Overhand hitting skills:
- Toss the ball in the air and catch it in the proper overhand hitting position.
- Toss the ball in the air and hit the ball upward.
- Toss the ball high in the air several feet away, move under the ball, and catch it in the right position.
- Toss the ball high in the air several feet away, get under the ball, and hit upward.
- Hit a ball tossed by a partner.
- Throw the ball against the wall and hit the rebound with an overhand hit.
- Volley with a group in a circle, hitting the ball high.
- Volley the ball with a partner.

Hitting Skill Games
Two Square
Formation. One child in each square.
Equipment. One utility ball for each two children.
Number of Players. Two for each game maze.
Game. Each child stands just inside the end line of a square. One player serves the ball by bouncing the ball and hitting it underhand into the opposite square. If the opposing player fails to return the ball with an underhand hit, the serving player gets a point. After the service, the ball continues in play until one player fails to return the ball to the opposite square. If the serving player fails to return the ball, the opponent is awarded one point and the service. Play continues until one player gains fifteen points. Note: The ball must be hit upward.
Teaching Suggestions. To simplify the game, the receiver catches the service and returns the ball with a serve. The player gains

a point when his opponent fails to catch the ball after one bounce or fails to hit it so it lands in the opposite square.

For more advanced players, designate the squares A and B. The objective is to stay in square A. If the player in square A makes an error, the player in square B rotates to square A.

More players can play by having a new player rotate in each time a player in one of the squares commits an error. This is sometimes difficult to play with children who have a short attention span.

Four Square

Formation. One child in each square.

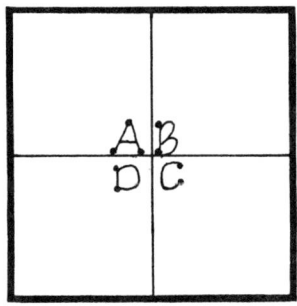

Equipment. One utility ball for each four players.

Number of Players. Four for each game maze.

Game. Player D serves the ball by bouncing the ball and hitting it from behind the serving line into any one of the other three squares. The player in the square into which the ball was served must return the ball to any other player after it has bounced once.

Play continues until a foul is committed. The player committing the foul moves to square D and everyone below him moves one square toward A.

The ball must be hit upward so it lands within an opponent's square. Other fouls consist of causing the ball to touch a line, contacting the ball with any part of the body other than the hands and forearms, holding or throwing the ball, not returning the ball after one bounce, hitting the ball with the closed fist, and causing the ball to go out of bounds.

Teaching Suggestion. The teaching suggestions for "Two Square" may also apply to "Four Square."

Volley Handball

Formation. Two players facing the wall.

Equipment. One utility ball for each two players.

Number of Players. Two in each game.

Game. One player serves by bouncing the ball and hitting it against the wall above the three-foot line. The second player must hit the ball after one bounce. Play continues until one player fails to return the ball above the three-foot line. Players alternate hits.

A player scores a point each time his opponent makes an error. The service alternates. The first player to score fifteen points wins the game.

Teaching Suggestions. A hit which purposely causes the ball to hit near the base of the wall is illegal. Also, more players can play by having a new player rotate in each time a player commits an error.

Tetherball

Formation. Tetherball court.

Equipment. Tetherball rope seven and a half feet long and a pole ten feet long with a mark five feet from the ground.

Number of Players. Two.

Game. One player stands in each half of the circle around the base of the pole. One player starts the game by throwing the ball into the air and hitting it with the hand or fist in the direction he chooses. The opposing player must let the ball pass him once. He then hits the ball in the opposite direction on the second swing around the pole. The player who winds the ball around the pole above the five-foot line is the winner.

Teaching Suggestion. A third child may hold the ball so the rope is taut for the service.

Gradually add more rules to include other fouls in the game. Additional fouls are throwing the ball, touching the ball with any part of the body other than hands, touching the pole, hitting the rope, and playing the ball while outside the playing area.

Beginning Handball

Formation. Players stand behind the service line.

Equipment. Sponge-rubber ball, volleyball, or utility ball; handball court.

Number of Players. Two to four.

Game. Player No. 1 serves the ball by batting it against the ground, causing the ball to rebound against the wall and back into the playing area. Player No. 2 returns the ball by batting it after one bounce so that it again rebounds from the wall.

Play continues until a player misses the ball or causes it to go out of bounds. The player who does not commit the error is given one point. The service alternates. The first player to gain fifteen points wins the game.

Teaching Suggestion. More bounces may be allowed for the beginner. Also, additional players may be included in the game by rotating them in for the player committing the error.

Handball

Formation. Players stand behind the service line, which is fifteen feet from the wall.

Equipment. Sponge-rubber ball, volleyball, utility ball, or tennis ball; handball court.

Number of Players. Two to four players.

Game. Player No. 1 serves the ball by letting it bounce on the floor and then hitting it against the wall so it rebounds back into the playing area. Player No. 2 returns the ball by hitting it after one bounce or before the bounce so the ball will rebound from the wall into the playing area.

Play continues until a player misses the ball or fails to make it hit the wall. The player who does not commit the error is given one point. The serve alternates. The first player to gain fifteen points wins the game.

Teaching Suggestions. More bounces may be allowed for the beginner. Also, additional players may be included in the game by rotating them in for the player committing the error.

Variations. Two-wall handball or three-wall handball can be played to add skill to the game. The ball may be hit at an angle such that the ball will rebound off the side wall, hit the front wall, and rebound into the playing area. The ball must hit the front wall last to be a legal hit. The other rules are the same as handball.

Paddle Tennis

Formation. Paddle tennis is played like tennis except that on the serve the ball is hit after it has been dropped and bounced once. Short paddles or "shorty" tennis rackets are used to simplify the skill.

Bounce Keep-It-Up

Formation. Single circle with the players facing the center of the circle.

Equipment. Utility ball or volleyball.

Number of Players. Six to eight in each group.

Game. One player in each group tosses the ball up to himself and volleys the ball upward and toward another circle player. Players continue to volley the ball into the air and the entire group calls the number of each consecutive hit. The ball must bounce once between each hit. Also, the ball must be contacted with the hands or forearms only and be clearly batted. Each group attempts to improve the number of consecutive hits without a miss.

Teaching Suggestions. A more advanced variation would be to try to volley the ball without a bounce. If the ball is missed, play it after one bounce. If the ball is hit successfully after one bounce, the counting continues.

Bounce Net Ball

Formation. Children in two lines facing the net.

Equipment. One volleyball or utility ball for each group, nets five to six feet high.

Number of Players. Two to six in each group.

Game. One player begins by bouncing the ball and hitting it over the net. Player on the opposite side returns the ball after it bounces. The ball may be played as long as it remains in bounds and keeps bouncing.

The ball must be batted and not caught or thrown. When an error is committed, the opposing team is given the serve and one point. The first team to get fifteen points wins.

Teaching Suggestions. As the skill of the group improves, (a) limit the number of bounces to one, (b) increase the height of the net, and (c) start the service near the middle of the court and gradually move it back. Also, a regular underhand serve without a bounce can be substituted as the skill of the players develops.

The teacher or another skilled player on each side will help the game to progress and control the practice of the group.

Catch Volleyball

Formation. One team on each side of the net in scattered formation.

Equipment. Volleyball, net about six feet high, and a volleyball court.

Number of Players. Ten to twelve.

Game. One player hits the ball over the net. Any player on the opposite team attempts to catch the ball. A player who catches the ball must hit it back over the net. One point is awarded the serving team if the receiving team does not catch the ball. One point is awarded the receiving team if they catch the ball before it bounces. The first team to get fifteen points wins the game.

Teaching Suggestions. Use an underhand serve to hit the ball at first. As skill improves, let each child toss the ball to himself and volley it over the net.

Lead-up Games for Volleyball

One-Bounce Volleyball

Formation. One team on each side of the net in a regular volleyball position.

Equipment. Volleyball, net about three feet high, and a volleyball court.

Number of Players. Six to eight on each court.

Game. The right-back player on the serving team, using an underhand serve, hits the ball over the net to the opposing team. The ball must bounce once and only once before it is returned across the net. Each team may have three hits to return the ball over the net. The ball may be hit only once in succession by any one player.

The game is scored in the same manner as regulation volleyball.

Teaching Suggestions. The team will have better success in returning the ball over the net if the serve is hit before it bounces on the receiving team's side of the court.

The players should be taught to hit the ball cleanly. Also, this game serves as a good opportunity to learn to hit the ball without having to make a powerful hit.

Newcomb

Formation. One team on each side of the net in regular volleyball positions.

Equipment. Volleyball, a volleyball court, and a net at the appropriate height for the children's ability.

Number of Players. Six to eight on each team.

Game. The right-back player serves the ball by throwing it over the net. Players on the opposite team catch the ball and may either pass it to a teammate or throw it over the net. The player who has possession of the ball may take only one step before releasing the ball. The object of the game is to place the ball between players of the opposing team so they cannot catch and return it.

The game is scored in the same manner as regular volleyball. Only the serving team may score points. When either team fails to catch the ball or hits it out of bounds, either a point or side-out is called.

Teaching Suggestion. This game provides a good opportunity to teach scoring procedures and strategy of regular volleyball.

The players should keep the ball moving quickly to catch the opponent off guard.

Keep-It-Up

Formation. Circle on each side of the volleyball court.

Equipment. A volleyball or playground ball.

Number of Players. Six to eight in each circle.

Game. On the signal to begin, one player in each circle tosses the ball to himself and hits to another member of the circle. The players continue to hit the ball *up* and toward other players in the circle. The group calls the number of each consecutive hit until an illegal hit is made or the ball lands on the floor. The objective is to make as many consecutive hits as possible without letting the ball touch the floor. The group with the most consecutive hits in the allotted time period wins the game.

No one may play the ball twice in succession. The ball may not rest momentarily on the hands of a player. The ball may not touch the body below the waist.

Teaching Suggestions. Encourage the players to bat the ball cleanly and to call their own illegal hits. For less skilled players, one bounce may be allowed in order to keep the ball in play longer.

Remind the players to hit the ball high to allow time for a teammate to move under it. Moving into the proper hitting position is very important in order to play the ball correctly.

Variations. Two players may play the game, or the game may be played by an individual player against the wall. A line drawn on the wall will help the players to hit the ball with more control and consistency.

Balloon Volleyball

Formation. Using the same procedure as for regular volleyball, substitute a large balloon for the volleyball. There is no limit on the number of hits.

Cage Ball

Formation. Scatter formation on a regular volleyball court.

Equipment. A cage ball and a sturdy net at volleyball height.

Number of Players. Six to twenty on a team.

Game. The player in the right-back position throws the ball into the air. The other players on his team may assist in hitting the ball over the net with no limit on the number of hits.

The game is played like volleyball with no limit on the number of hits. If the ball is allowed to hit the floor, a point or side-out is called.

Teaching Suggestions. Players should be encouraged to play areas of the court rather than follow the ball, thus providing for more play.

This game will help the players get over any fear of hitting smaller balls. Less skill is needed to play this game; therefore, more players may play the game with success.

Modified Volleyball

Formation. Regulation volleyball positions on the court.

Equipment. A volleyball and a net at a height appropriate for the skill of the players.

Number of Players. Six to nine on each court.

Game. The game is played in the same manner as regulation volleyball with possible modifications which may be used according to the ability of the players.

Modified rules allow for one player to hit the ball twice in succession and three people to hit the ball before it crosses over the net. Allow two serves or an assist on the serve to get the ball in play. Move the serving distance up to accommodate the ability of the players. Allow as many hits on a side as necessary to keep interest in the game.

Teaching Suggestions. Use more players on the court to cover the space, but not so many that there is no opportunity to hit the ball frequently. Provide for automatic rotation so no player stays out of the game longer than for one point. Allow for one bounce to keep the ball in play.

Encourage the players to use a bounce pass for balls at chest level and below. The ball should be hit high to a teammate and low to the opposing team. Stress team play by encouraging passes to teammates.

The players should maintain a good ready position and slide to move under the ball to play correctly.

BATTING SKILLS

Stand with the left side toward the pitcher. Spread the legs comfortably. Grip the bat with the left hand near the end of the bat and the right hand above and touching the left hand. Elbows are bent and away from the body, and the weight is evenly distributed (Fig. 11-24). Swing the bat parallel to the ground. Keep the eyes on the ball. As the bat swings forward, push on rear leg for more power. Follow through with the bat, swinging around the left side as the weight transfers to the left foot.

Figure 11-24

Batting Skill Progression
- Hit a stationary ball off a batting tee (Fig. 11-25).
- Hit a ball pitched underhand (Fig. 11-26).
- Hit a ball pitched overhand.
- Fungo hitting (hitting a ball the batter himself throws up).

Softball Skill Games
Five Pitches
Formation. Participants stand with both feet touching a line which is pitching-distance away from the target.

Figure 11-25

Figure 11-26

Equipment. One softball for every two children, and a wall eighteen inches wide and thirty-two inches high, with the lower edge sixteen inches from the floor.

Number of Players. Two for each target.

Game. One player stands on the line. He throws the ball with an underhand pitch at the target on the wall. Each player is given five pitches at the target. One point is given for each ball which lands in the strike zone or target.

The second player stands near the target and returns the ball to the pitcher. After five pitches the participants change positions.

Teaching Suggestions. Encourage the participants to use proper pitching form and rules.

Hoop Ball

Formation. Player No. 1 stands thirty feet away from the wall while Player No. 2 stands near the wall to retrieve the ball.

Equipment. One softball for each target. The target is a hula hoop taped to the wall, with the lower edge two feet above the floor.

Number of Players. Two for each target.

Game. Player No. 1 throws the ball with an overhand throw at the hoop. He must stay behind the throwing line, which is thirty feet away from the target. Each player is given five throws at the hoop. One point is given for each ball which lands in the hoop.

Player No. 2 retrieves the ball and throws it back to Player No. 1. After five pitches the players change positions. The player with the highest total after a designated number of throws is the winner.

Teaching Suggestions. Vary the throwing distance according to the skill of the participants. Designate the number of throws according to the ability of the children to tally scores.

Goal-Line Softball

Formation. Two teams lined up in front of their goal lines.
Equipment. One softball.
Number of Players. Ten to twelve.
Game. A player on one team must throw the ball from behind the throwing line. He attempts to throw the ball over the opponents' goal line. The ball must bounce at least once before crossing the goal. The receiving team catches the ball before it crosses the goal line; the player who catches the ball throws it from where it is caught.

One point is earned each time the ball is thrown over the goal of an opponent. The team with the highest total points wins.

Teaching Suggestions. Larger balls may be used for less-skilled players. Provide an opportunity for all children to throw the ball.

One Base

Formation. Two batters, a catcher, one baseman, and several fielders.

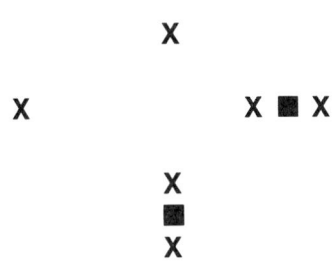

Equipment. One base, one home plate, and one softball.
Number of Players. Nine to twelve.
Game. Player No. 1 throws the ball into the field and tries to run to the base and back home. The fielders field the ball and try to get the ball to the catcher before the runner reaches home. If the runner reaches home before the ball, he scores a run. If the ball reaches home before the runner, the runner is out. The runner then takes a fielder's position and the catcher becomes a batter. The fielders are

numbered or named and work up to become the catcher. The player with the most runs is the winner.

Teaching Suggestion. For more advanced players, the runner may stop at the base and return home on the next turn.

Softball Beat Ball

Formation. One team in the field, the other at bat.
Equipment. Three bases, one home plate, and one softball.
Number of Players. Six to eighteen.
Game. The catchers throw the ball to first as the runner leaves home base. The basemen try to relay the ball around the bases before the runner completes his circuit around the bases. Each baseman must touch the base while in possession of the ball. The baserunner must touch each base while making the circuit.

If the baserunner reaches home plate before the ball, a run is scored. If the ball reaches home plate before the runner, the runner is out. Three outs and the teams change places.

Teaching Suggestions. With a small number of players, the game can be played with "work-up" rules (see Lead-Up Games).

Adjust the distance of the bases to the ability of the players. Also, change the number of times around the bases for the runners and the throwers according to the skill of the group.

Under the Leg

Play regular softball rules with the exception that the ball is thrown under one leg by the batter rather than using a bat. The batter must catch the ball thrown by the pitcher before throwing the ball into the field. If the batter fails to catch a ball which is in the strike zone, he is out.

Five Hits

Formation. One player at bat, one catcher, and fielders.
Equipment. One softball diamond, a batting tee, and one softball.
Number of Players. Four to twelve.
Game. The batter hits the ball off the batting tee. A ball landing in the infield scores one point. A ball landing in the outfield scores two points.

Each batter hits five balls. His score is the total points gained after five hits. After hitting the ball five times the batter changes positions with a fielder.

Teaching Suggestions. Use a batting tee until the children can use fungo hitting. Also, point value can be changed when the participants understand larger numbers.

Lead-Up Games
Hit the Bat
Formation. Group of children facing a batter.

```
                        XXXX
            X           XXXXX
                        XXXX
```

Equipment. One bat and two softballs.
Number of Players. Six to ten in a group.
Game. The batter, using fungo hits, sends the ball into the field toward the remainder of the players. The fielder closest to the ball fields the ball. If the ball is caught on the fly, the fielder becomes the batter. If the ball bounces two times, the fielder becomes the batter. If the fielder can roll the ball from the spot where he gained control of the ball and hit the bat placed on the ground in front of the batter, the fielder becomes the batter.
Teaching Suggestions. Children should not run in front of other children to field the ball. Also, a batting tee may be used for children who cannot hit a tossed ball.

Five Hundred
Formation. Groups of children facing the batter with open space in which to scatter.

```
                        XXXX
            X           XXXXX
                        XXXX
```

Equipment. One bat and two softballs.
Number of Players. Six to ten in each group.
Game. The batter, using fungo hits, sends the ball into the field toward the remainder of the players. The fielder closest to the ball fields the ball. If the ball is caught on the fly, the fielder gets one hundred points. If the ball is caught after one bounce, the fielder receives seventy-five points. If the ball is caught after two bounces, the fielder receives fifty points. If the ball is caught after three bounces, or before it stops rolling, the fielder receives twenty-five points. The first player to receive five hundred points becomes the next batter and all players start again at zero.
Teaching Suggestions. A batting tee may be used for children who cannot hit a tossed ball. Also, for children who field the ball well, points may be subtracted from their score for making an error.

Pepper

Formation. Children standing in a line about forty-five to fifty feet from the batter.

Equipment. One bat and two softballs.
Number of Players. Six to ten in each group.
Game. Using an easy overhand throw, one player in the line throws the ball to the batter. The batter, using a modified swing with no wrist snap, hits the ball at a moderate speed toward the line of fielders. The fielder in front of the ball fields the ball and throws it to the batter. This process should be repeated as quickly as possible to keep the batter busy.

If the fielder makes an error, he moves to the end of the line. If the batter hits the ball over the fielder's head or swings and misses once, he takes his place at the end of the line and the fielder at the top of the line becomes the new batter.

Teaching Suggestions. When the children are batting, caution them to use a correct swing but no wrist snap. Also, the players in the fielding line should use a good ready position to field the ball.

Work-Up

Formation. Regular softball positions in the field with three or four batters.
Equipment. One softball, a bat, three bases, and a home plate.
Number of Players. Twelve to fourteen players.
Game. The game is started and played with regular softball rules. If a fielder should catch a fly ball, he becomes the batter. When the batter makes an out which is not a caught fly ball, he becomes the right fielder and all the fielders move up one position. The rotation is from right to center field, center field to left, left field to shortstop, shortstop to third base, from third to second and to first base, first base to pitcher, and pitcher to catcher. The catcher becomes the last batter. The players may also rotate to the umpire positions.

Teaching Suggestions. When the hitting and pitching skills are not consistent, a batting tee may be used to speed up the game.

The batters waiting their turn to bat should remain in the dugout in a safe area. To prevent throwing the bat, the batter may be required either to carry the bat toward first base with him, or to place one end of the bat on the ground before releasing the bat.

SHOOTING SKILLS

Two-Hand Underhand Shot. Stand with the feet slightly spread. Hold the ball with the fingers, both hands slightly under the ball. Bend the knees slightly as the ball swings down between the knees (Fig. 11-27). Swing the ball forward and upward and at the same time shift the body weight up on balls of feet. Release the ball at about eye level. Follow through toward the basket.

Two-Hand Chest Shot. Stand with one foot slightly in front of the other. Hold the ball with the fingers spread, in front of the chest, and elbows close to side. Bend the knees slightly. Push the ball forward and upward and then extend the knees (Fig. 11-28). Release the ball above eye level with a wrist snap. Follow through toward the basket.

One-Hand Push Shot. Put the right foot ahead of the left. Hold the ball in the left hand against the right hand with the fingers. Shift

Figure 11-27   **Figure 11-28**

the weight forward as the ball is pushed upward. Release the ball above eye level with a snap of the wrist and fingers. Follow through toward the basket (Fig. 11-29).

Shooting Skill Progression
- Shoot the ball through a hoop hung from a basket.
- Shoot the ball into a barrel standing on the floor.
- Shoot the ball into a barrel on a table.
- Shoot the ball at the rim of the standard basket.
- Shoot the ball into the basket while standing within five feet of the basket.
- Shoot the ball into the basket while standing in the free-throw circle (Fig. 11-30).

Figure 11-29   **Figure 11-30**

SPORT SKILLS

- Shoot the ball into the basket while standing behind the free-throw line.
- Shoot the ball while running (lay-up).
- Shoot the ball while jumping (Fig. 11-31).
- Shoot the ball with back to the basket (hook shot).

Teaching Suggestion. For small children use a lighter ball. A partially deflated ball may help some children to find success.

Figure 11-31

Basketball Skill Games

Basketball Keep-Away

Formation. Children in a single circle facing the center.
Equipment. One basketball for each circle.
Number of Players. Six to eight in each group.
Game. One player goes to the center of the circle. The circle players pass the ball across the circle. The center player attempts

to touch the ball. If he is successful he takes the position of the player who threw the ball.

Teaching Suggestion. For practice or variation change the type of pass used by the group.

Rotten Egg Basketball

Formation. Children in a line with a basket at the end of the line.
Equipment. One basketball and a box or wastebasket.
Number of Players. Three to six.
Game. The children are in a line. A box or basket is placed at the end of the line. The ball is placed on the floor at the other end of the line approximately six feet from the last player. The last player runs to get the ball. He passes the ball to the next person in the line. Each player in turn passes the ball to the next player. The last player throws the ball (rotten egg) into the basket. Players rotate positions and the ball is placed on the floor to begin the relay again.

Teaching Suggestions. The distance between players may be increased as the passing skill improves. Also, the height of the box may be changed upward as the skill of the players improves. The final step would be to use a standard basket.

School

Formation. Children stand in a column behind "first grade."
Equipment. One basketball for each group. Numbered circles on floor around the basket.
Number of Players. Three to six in each group.
Game. Players number off and shoot in that order through the game. Player No. 1 shoots from the first-grade circle. If he is successful in making a field goal, he continues and shoots from the second-grade circle. When he misses, he stays at that grade level and waits for his next turn. The shooter retrieves his own ball after each shot. Players continue to shoot at the basket in the order in which they are numbered, regardless of the grade they are in. When his second turn comes, he shoots from the grade level where he missed his last shot.

The winner is the first player to be successful in making a basket from each grade level. He then retrieves the ball while the other players complete the game.

Teaching Suggestions. Specify the kind of shot to be used if the children are on an equal level of ability. A barrel may be used for beginners.

Follow the Leader

Formation. Children in a column formation behind the free-throw line.
Equipment. One basketball for each group.
Number of Players. Three to six.

Game. Player No. 1 shoots from any line on the floor he chooses. If player No. 1 does not make a basket, player No. 2 may choose any line on the floor from which to make his shot. If player No. 1 makes the basket, player No. 2 must shoot from the same spot on the floor. After completing his turn, each player returns to the end of the column behind the free-throw line.

Teaching Suggestions. A barrel may be used for beginners. As the skill improves, different types of shooting may be required.

Ten Baskets

Formation. Children in a column formation behind the free-throw line.

Equipment. One basketball for each group and a set of numbers for each group.

Number of Players. Two to six.

Game. Player No. 1 shoots from anywhere on the foul line. If he makes the basket he goes to the scoreboard and turns up the number one card. Each player in turn shoots once at the basket. If a basket is made, he turns up the next number. After completing a turn, each player returns to the end of the column. Each player retrieves his own ball and passes it to the next player in the column. The first team to reach ten is the winning team.

Teaching Suggestion. For variation each team could try to improve the number of baskets made within a time limit.

Lead-up Games for Basketball

Captain Ball

Formation. Basketball court with five circles on each half of the court.

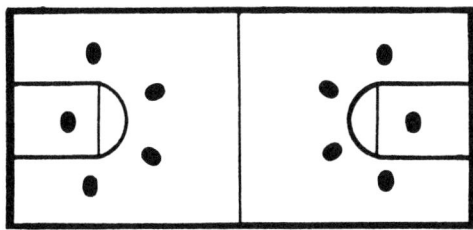

Equipment. One basketball.
Number of Players. Ten on each team.
Game. Five forwards on each team occupy the circles on their half of the court. The guards stand outside the circles on their opponents' half of the court. The game is started in the center of the floor with a jump ball by two opposing guards. The guards dribble and

pass the ball to the center line, where they pass the ball to one of their forwards in a circle. The forwards try to pass the ball to the captain, who is in the circle closest to the basket. One point is given each time the ball is passed successfully to the captain. Each time a point is made, the players on both sides of the floor rotate one position.

Players may not step on the lines forming the circles or on the sidelines or center line. For a violation, the ball is awarded to the closest opponent. Personal contact is a foul for which the player fouled is given a free throw.

Teaching Suggestions. For players with good shooting ability, the game may be varied so the captain shoots upon receiving the ball. The points are scored the same as for regular basketball.

If considerable time elapses before a score is made, time may be called and the players rotate.

Sideline Basketball

Formation. Players from each team line up along their respective sidelines.

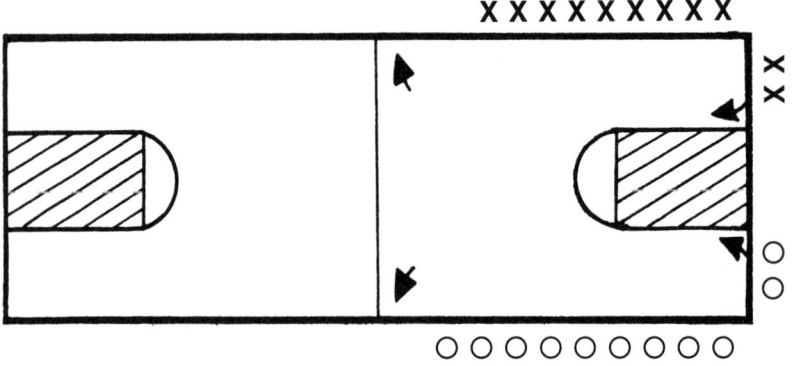

Equipment. One ball, one half a basketball court, pinnies to designate team identity.

Number of Players. Sixteen to thirty-two players.

Game. Two players from each team move onto the court from the basket end of their sideline. Begin the game with a jump ball in the restraining circle. The team gaining possession of the ball becomes the offensive or shooting team. When the ball is intercepted by the opposing team, it must be passed to the sideline players before shooting for a basket. The team in possession of the ball may shoot successive shots until the other team gains possession of the ball.

After a goal is made, or after a time limit, the active players rotate to the sideline near the center line and the four sideline players nearest the basket become the active players.

Regulation basketball rules may be applied.

Teaching Suggestions. This game provides an opportunity for inexperienced children to learn the rules. To provide for height differences, the players line up on the sideline with the tallest players at the same end of the line.

Twenty-One

Formation. Players assume positions for a free throw, with one team in the offensive position.

Equipment. One basketball, one basket, and pinnies to designate team identity.

Number of Players. Two to five on each team.

Game. One player from the offensive team shoots from the free-throw line. He continues to shoot from the free-throw line until he misses or makes three consecutive baskets. Each free throw counts one point. If the shooter makes three baskets, the ball is awarded to the opposing team out of bounds at the center line.

When the shooter misses and if his team gets possession of the ball, they may continue to shoot at the basket. If the defensive team gets possession of the ball, they must dribble or pass the ball to a point at least twenty feet away from the basket to give the defense a chance to set up.

The play continues until someone on either team makes a field goal, which counts two points. The player making the field goal moves to the free-throw line and repeats the process used to start the game. The game continues until one team gets twenty-one points. If a team should end up with twenty-two points, their score becomes eleven and they must work their way up to twenty-one again.

Teaching Suggestions. Encourage the players to call three-second lane violations and other infractions of the rules. Stress passing and teamwork.

12
STUNTS AND TUMBLING

Two recognized objectives of physical education are the development of physical fitness and the development of performance skill. The activities included in this chapter all require strength, flexibility, endurance, and coordination, and by a child's learning the skills and stunts, he will develop strength, flexibility, endurance, and coordination, thus improving his physical fitness as well as increasing his skills. Each stunt has form and function peculiar to it, and development of the skill and the increase in performing ability is satisfying and fun for the child.

The retarded child may have missed the normal experiences of rough and tumble play on the living-room carpet and rolls and cartwheels on the front lawn on summer evenings. Protected as he often is, the retarded child may not be physically strong enough to join safely in these activities in the usual situation. But parents should make certain that the retarded child is not left out of this type of play. The retarded child gains strength, flexibility, endurance, and coordination in the same manner as does a normal child. A retarded child will benefit from the family group activities and from being included whenever possible in the activities of the neighborhood children.

Stunts and tumbling activities make a unique contribution to and greatly benefit the child who takes part. Courage can be developed through performing the stunts, and is especially required for participation in many of the tumbling sequences.

Emphasis in the stunts and tumbling activities should be on exploring new skills, making animal-like movements, solving movement problems, experimenting to determine limits, and learning and trying new skills. The child should be assisted through the stunt when he needs to be helped; he should be encouraged to perform his best each time. The courage required by the stunt will be increased each time he performs it, and can carry over into his other activities. The parent and teacher should make certain the child understands what is being asked of him, and they should provide good spotting techniques—placing a hand on the back of the child's neck or lifting the child through the stunt—as the child attempts each skill. The child's feeling of *self* can be improved as he involves himself in activities that challenge his total body.

Teaching Suggestions

- The group for each teacher should be small—one or two children for each teacher is enough. As the children become more skilled, the size of the group can be increased.
- Mats should always be used.
- As each child performs he should be praised and receive positive reinforcement.
- The pace of the activities should be kept moving. Children waiting too long for a turn will become restless and require discipline, which can change the entire feeling about the activity.
- The teacher should know the activity. The inexperienced teacher does not know or understand the fears a child has about a stunt or the hazards involved in the activities.
- The teacher should progress slowly and increase the skill difficulty gradually. When a child can perform a stunt efficiently, move on to another, more difficult and demanding stunt.
- The teacher should be the spotter for each child until he can perform efficiently, and then the child should be encouraged to perform without a spotter but should always perform.
- Each lesson should be started with a brief active review of the previous lesson. This review will set the mood for the lesson and will help the student recall what was done.
- Each child should be called by name and signals or commands should be used. Example: "Tommy, be ready, tuck your chin and roll."
- When there is more than one teacher for the group, each should plan to use the same lesson outline for each daily lesson, but should adapt the lesson for her own group on any particular day.
- Each teacher should have the same group of children each day. A child develops a relationship for performance with a teacher. The teacher should recognize the amount of effort needed for a single-stunt performance for the first time.
- Tumbling stunts should not be used for relay races. Accidents can happen any time in a tumbling program, and racing is especially hazardous because it often causes the performer to forget cautions.

Individual Stunts

The list and description of activities is placed as nearly as possible in order or progression of difficulty. Each stunt requires balance, strength, flexibility, timing, agility, and coordination. The child can learn how to follow instructions and obey directions.

Tightrope Walking
Starting Position. Stand with both feet on a line.
Action. Walk down the line without stepping off the line.

Heel Click
Starting Position. Stand with the feet twelve inches apart.
Action. Jump into the air and click the heels together and land with the feet apart.

Balance
Starting Position. Stand with the hands on the hips.
Action. Close the eyes, raise one foot, and balance as long as possible (Fig. 12-1).

Lame Dog
Starting Position. Weight on the hands and one leg. Keep the other leg bent and off the mat (Fig. 12-2).
Action. Walk forward.

Figure 12-1

Figure 12-2

Wicket Walk

Starting Position. Stand, bend over, and take hold of an ankle with each hand.

Action. Walk, keeping the knees as straight as possible (Fig. 12-3).

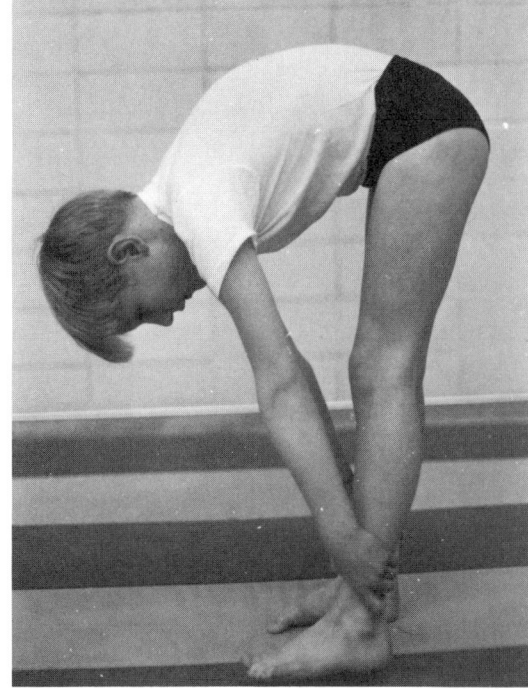

Figure 12-3

Side Roll

Starting Position. Lie on the back, bend the knees to the chest, bend elbows, and put hands on the opposite shoulders (Fig. 12-4).

Action. Roll to either side and come to a position on hands and knees.

Submarine

Starting Position. Lie on the back, placing the hands on bent knees.

Action. Raise the head and push the body along the floor by pushing with the feet and sliding the body backward (Fig. 12-5).

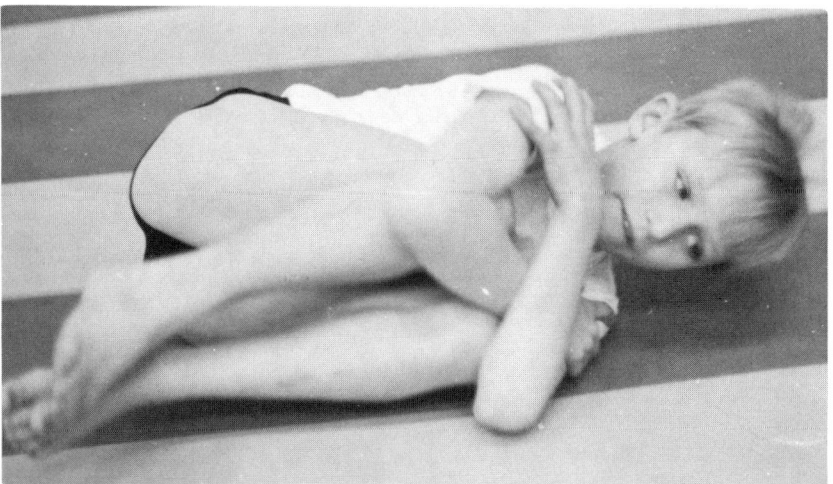

Figure 12-4

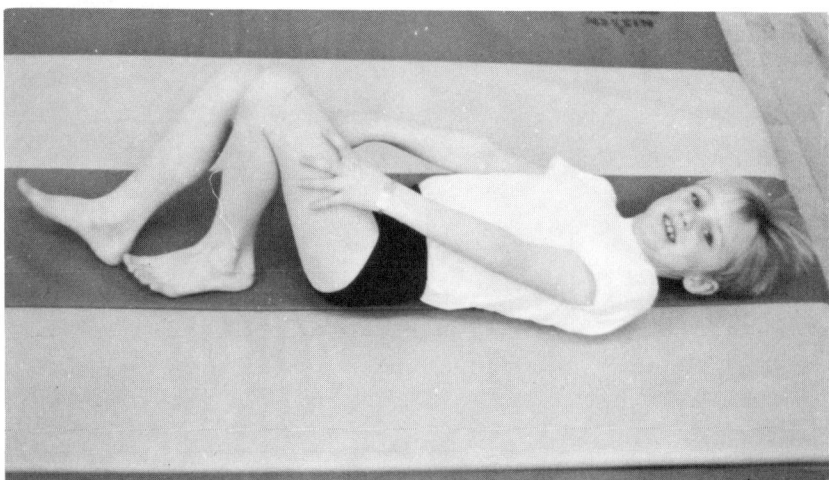

Figure 12-5

Cricket Walk

Starting Position. Assume the squat position, put the hands between the knees and around behind the ankles, and take hold of the top of the feet (Fig. 12-6).
Action. Walk forward.

Tuck Jump

Starting Position. Assume the squat position and hold both knees together with both arms (Fig. 12-7).
Action. Jump forward; do not let go of the knees.

Bear Walk

Starting Position. Assume front-lean position with arms and legs straight.
Action. Lift the right leg and the right arm and move forward, keeping arms and legs straight. Repeat with left side (Fig. 12-8).

Seal Walk

Starting Position. Support body with weight on the hands, and legs extended behind (Fig. 12-9).
Action. Walk on the hands and drag the feet.

Figure 12-6

Figure 12-7

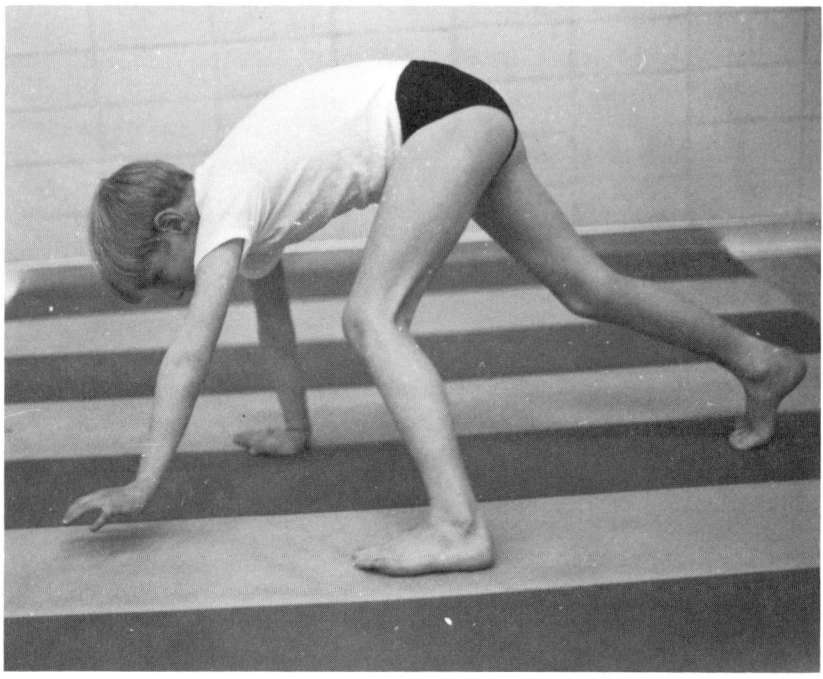

Figure 12-8

Figure 12-9

Crab Walk

Starting Position. Sit on the floor, with hands behind the hips, and raise the body.

Action. Walk on the hands and feet, keeping the body straight (Fig. 12-10).

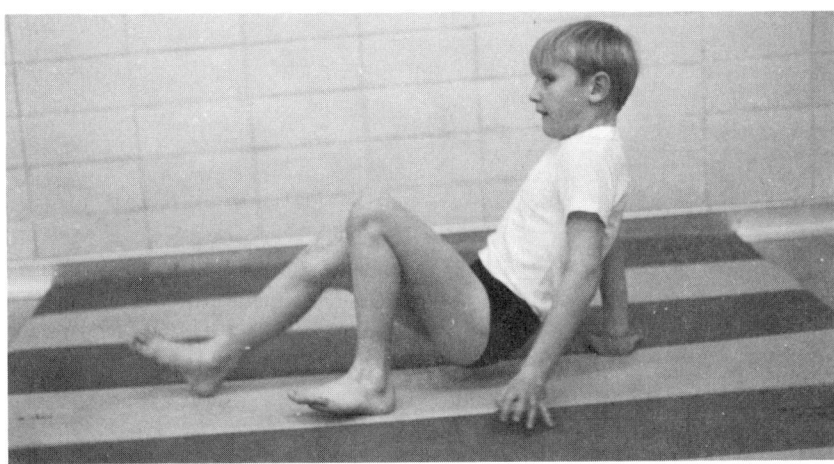

Figure 12-10

Top Spin

Starting Position. Stand with the feet apart.

Action. Jump, turn, and land facing one-quarter turn to the right; jump, turn, and land facing one-half turn to the right; jump, turn, and land facing three-quarter turn to the right; jump, turn, and land making one full turn to the right (Fig. 12-11, 12-12). Repeat the entire sequence to the left.

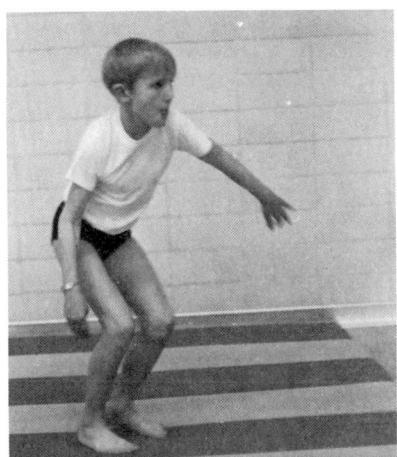 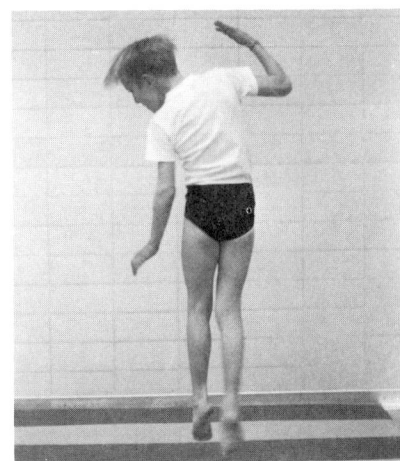

Figure 12-11   **Figure 12-12**

V-Sit

Starting Position. Sit with legs outstretched, hands on the mat behind the body.

Action. Lean the upper body back and raise both feet. Keep legs straight and hold for five seconds (Fig. 12-13).

Timber

Starting Position. Kneel with the body straight and the arms extended at a 45-degree angle.

Action. Fall forward and catch the body with the arms just as the mat is reached.

Rabbit Kick

Starting Position. Assume a squat position with the knees together, the arms extended forward, and the head up.

Action. Dive forward onto the hands, keeping the knees bent and the feet close to the hips. Look at the mat (Fig. 12-14). Return to starting position.

Mule Kick

Starting Position. Stand at the edge of a mat with the hands extended overhead.

Action. Place the hands on the mat and kick the legs above the hips. Look at the mat (Fig. 12-15). Return to starting position.

Figure 12-13

STUNTS AND TUMBLING 201

Figure 12-14

Figure 12-15

Frog Stand

Starting Position. Kneeling, place the hands on a mat even with the knees. Place the head on the mat in front of the hands to form a triangle.

Action. Raise the hips and place the knees one at a time on the elbows (Fig. 12-16). Hold for three seconds. Return to starting position.

Figure 12-16

Partner Stunts and Elementary Combatives
Bouncing Ball

Starting Position. One person (the ball) squats and holds the knees with the arms. The partner (bouncer) stands behind with his hands on the "ball's" upper back.

Action. The bouncer pushes the ball and makes it bounce. The ball responds to the pressure exerted (Fig. 12-17).

Wring the Dishrag

Starting Position. Partners face each other and join hands.

Action. The arms are raised as the partners turn away from each other under the raised arms (Fig. 12-18). They return to face each other as opposite arms are raised.

Figure 12-17

Figure 12-18

Sawing Wood

__Starting Position.__ Partners face each other each with one foot forward and take hold of hands.

__Action.__ Push opposite arms back and forward, pretending to saw wood (Fig. 12-19).

Figure 12-19

Chinese Get-Up

Starting Position. Partners of equal size stand back-to-back with elbows hooked.

Action. By pushing each others' back, lower to a sitting position (Fig. 12-20) and then rise to a standing position.

Seesaw

Starting Position. Partners face each other and join hands. One partner stands and the other squats (Fig. 12-21).

Action. Partners move at the same time and each finishes in the opposite position. Repeat at an increasing rate of speed.

Figure 12-20

Figure 12-21

Twister

Starting Position. Partners stand back to back with legs apart and with the left hand on the left knee. Reach through the legs with the right hand and grasp partner's right hand (Fig. 12-22).

Action. Keeping hands gripped, one child swings his right leg over the partner's back (Fig. 12-23). Then the partner swings his right leg over the clasped hands. They are now facing each other. One child swings his left leg over clasped hands, the other partner swings his left leg over his partner's back. They are now in starting position.

Figure 12-22

Figure 12-23

Siamese Twin Walk

Starting Position. Stand back to back with the elbows hooked together.

Action. Walk together; one walks forward and the other backward (Fig. 12-24).

Rocker

Starting Position. Partners sit facing each other; each one sits on the other's feet. The legs are bent. Each grasps the other's arms at the elbow (Fig. 12-25).

Action. One partner leans back and the other rises from the mat to a standing position. Reverse action and continue rocking.

Push the Donkey

Starting Position. Partners stand one behind the other, both facing the same direction.

Action. The person behind attempts to push the other over a line. The partner in front resists by pushing backward (Fig. 12-26).

Crab Fight

Starting Position. Assume crab-walk position side by side, facing in opposite directions.

Action. On the signal, each tries to push the other off balance (Fig. 12-27).

Back to Back

Starting Position. Partners sit down back to back.

Action. Using the hands and the feet, each tries to push the partner without lifting his own seat from the floor (Fig. 12-28). Keep the head down.

Tumbling Skills

The importance of correct spotting during each of the activities included in this tumbling series cannot be overstressed. It is the responsibility of the teacher to insure safe participation throughout the entire unit of instruction. Spotting correctly is one of the ways to keep tumbling safe and fun.

Spotting Techniques for the Forward Roll

Starting Position. Kneel at the side of the performer.

Action. Place one hand at the base of performer's neck, the other hand at his hips. Give support to the head, keeping it tucked, and help direct the roll with the hand at the hips.

STUNTS AND TUMBLING

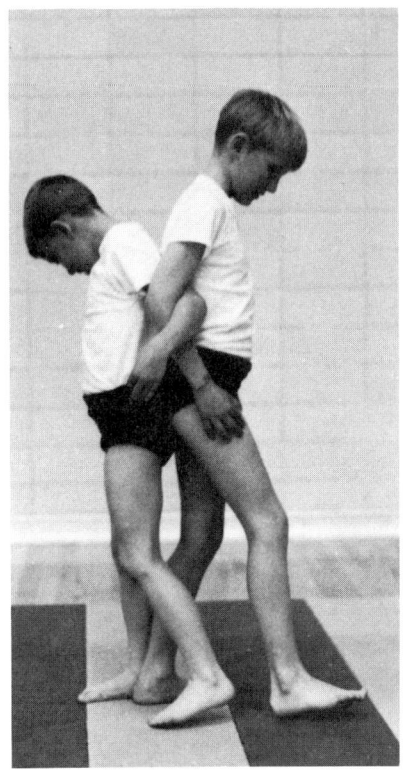

Figure 12-24

Figure 12-26

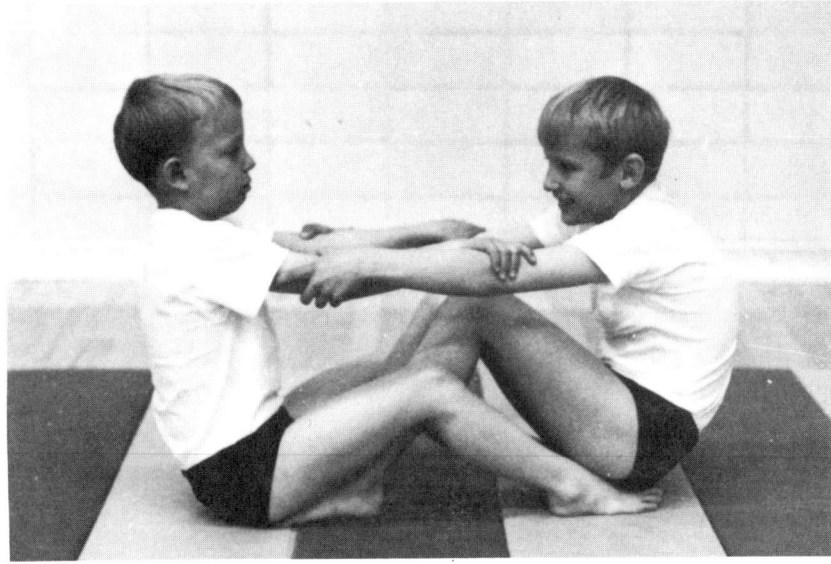

Figure 12-25

Figure 12-27

Figure 12-28

Forward Roll Sequence

Starting Position 1. Kneel on the mat, put hands on the mat in front of the knees, and put head on mat between hands. Keep the chin tucked close to chest (Fig. 12-29).

Action. Lift hips, look between the legs, *roll* to the back of the shoulders, push with feet and hands, and roll over, supporting the weight with the hands. End roll with feet together and knees close to the chest.

Starting Position 2. Squat on the mat and put hands on the mat in front of the knees (Fig. 12-30).

Figure 12-29

Figure 12-30

Action. Keep the chin tucked, brush the head lightly on the mat as the hips are lifted and the feet push. Roll over, supporting the weight with the hands (Fig. 12-31), and land on upper back. End the roll with feet together and knees close to the chest.

Starting Position 3. Squat on the mat with the arms extended.

Action. Rock forward, place the hands, brush the head lightly on the mat, and push with the feet and roll, supporting the weight with the hands. Land gently on upper back. End roll with the feet together and knees close to chest. Repeat action but end roll by continuing forward and finish in a squat position.

Starting Position 4. Stand on the mat. Bend the knees; extend arms downward.

Action. Reach forward and downward, place the hands on the mat (Fig. 12-32) and brush the head lightly on the mat, keeping the chin tucked. Push with the feet and roll over. End roll in a squatting position.

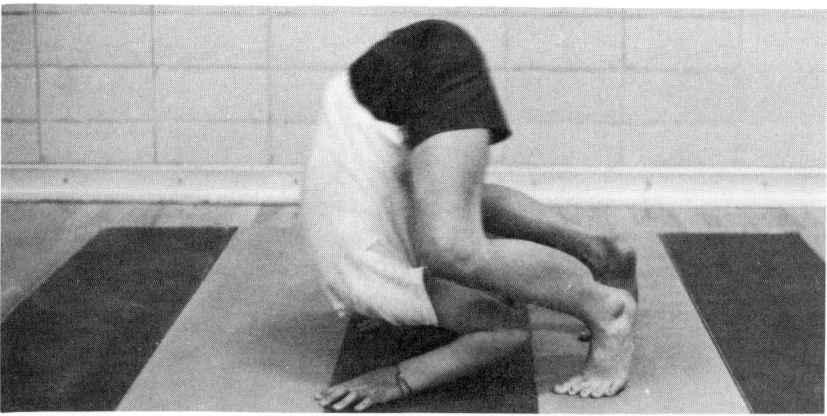

Figure 12-31

Figure 12-32

Starting Position 5. Stand with arms at the sides.

Action. Swing the arms forward and place the hands on the mat. At the same time tuck the head, brush lightly on the mat, lifting the hips, and complete the roll. End roll by standing up.

Do not include dive rolls over other children when working with mentally retarded children. The chance for serious injury is very great.

Spotting Techniques for the Back Roll

Starting Position. Stand at the side of the tumbler and in the line with direction of the roll. Place hands at the hip joint.

Action. As the tumbler starts the roll, lift (do not *push*) the tumbler at the hips (Fig. 12-33).

Figure 12-33

Back Roll Sequence

Starting Position 1. Sit with the knees bent and hands on the knees (Fig. 12-34).

Action. Roll back (Fig. 12-35) until the feet touch the mat behind the head. Return to a sitting position.

Starting Position 2. Sit with the knees bent, hands on the knees, and head down close to knees.

Action. Rock forward and roll back; release the hands and place them on the mat with the thumbs next to the ears and push to complete the roll. Keep the chin tucked. End in a kneeling position. Repeat action but end in a squatting position.

Starting Position 3. Squat with the head close to the knees and the arms around the knees.

Figure 12-34

Figure 12-35

Action. Rock forward; roll back, push with the hands placed on mat by the ears (Fig. 12-36). Roll over and finish in a squatting position.

Starting Position 4. Stand.

Action. Drop to a squat and complete roll as in preceding action (Fig. 12-37).

Starting Position 5. Assume side stride position with knees bent slightly and the arms extended between the knees and reaching back toward the mat.

Action. Sit down, catching the body with the hands. Change the hands onto the mat even with the ears and complete roll. Finish in a stride-standing position.

Figure 12-36

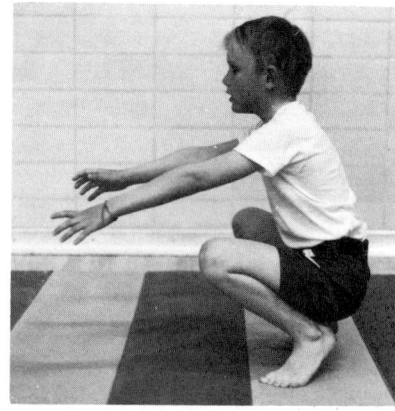

Figure 12-37

Spotting Techniques for the Cartwheel

Starting Position. Spotter stands behind the tumbler and places his hands on the tumbler's waist, using a cross-arm grip (Fig. 12-38).

Action. As the cartwheel is performed, the arms uncross and are parallel at the end of the stunt. Move with cartwheel and give support throughout.

Cartwheel Sequence

Starting Position 1. Each child draws a circle on the mat with chalk or places plastic ring on the mat. Stand sideways to the circle. Bend down to put nearest hand in the circle. Turn body to put other hand in the circle (Fig. 12-39).

Action. Keep both hands in the circle. Swing legs over the circle (Fig. 12-40) and come to a standing position.

Starting Position 2. Same as #1; swing the legs up over the hips (Fig. 12-41).

Starting Position 3. Tumbler stands close to a rope held about knee height by two other children.

Action. Reach over the rope with the arms and kick legs over one at a time.

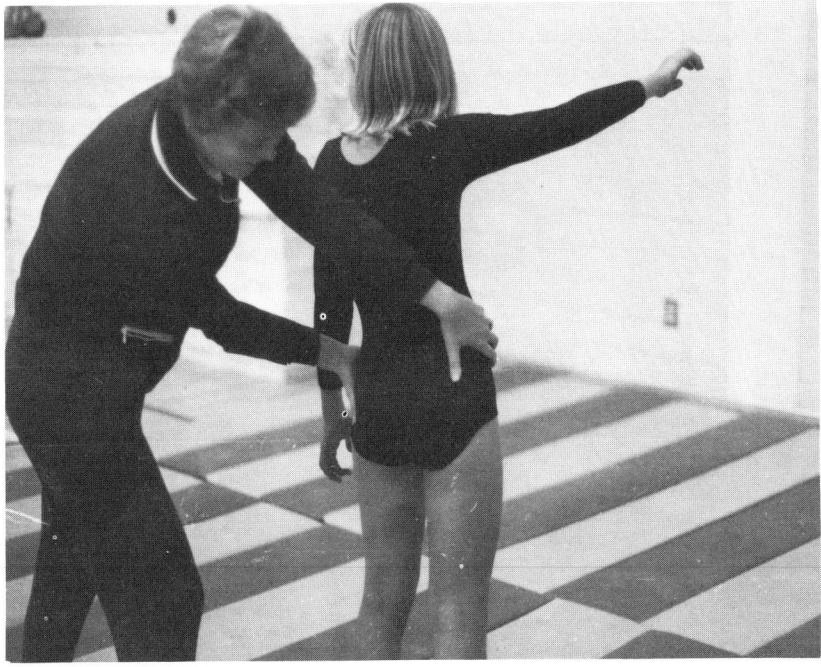

Figure 12-38

Figure 12-39

Figure 12-40

STUNTS AND TUMBLING 215

Figure 12-41

Starting Position 4. Stand with body bent and arms extended toward mat.

Action. Thrust arms to the mat one after the other. Swing leading leg up as other leg pushes off (Fig. 12-42) and land on leading leg.

Starting Position 5. Stand facing the mat, arms back extended overhead.

Action. Kick one leg forward, hop, and step forward. Count 1: place the same hand on the mat to the side of the foot. Count 2: place the other hand on the mat in a line on the mat. Kick both legs up until the hips are over the head. Count 3: place one leg on the mat in the straight line. Count 4: place the other leg on the mat.

Spotting Techniques for Head Stand

Starting Position. Place one hand at the base of the tumbler's neck and give pressure. Place the other hand at the tumbler's hips to give support and direction.

Action. As the tumbler lifts his hips, give support at the base of the neck. Keep his body straight and his weight equally distributed between his hands and his head. *Do not hold the tumbler at the ankles.*

Head Stand Sequence

Starting Position 1. Review frog stand (Fig. 12-43). Take starting position for frog stand; slowly extend the legs overhead and balance. Return to the starting position.

Starting Position 2. Kneel with the hands shoulder-width apart in line with the knees; place the head with front hairline on the mat, *not the top of the head*. Hands and head are in a triangle. Caution: do not balance on top of the head.

Action. Lift the hips above the shoulders, and push the feet upward until the legs are straight and back is slightly arched.

Starting Position 3. Same as #2.

Action. Push off the mat with toes of both feet, flex the knees, and raise the body to a half-way position. Extend both legs.

Figure 12-42

Figure 12-43

13
APPARATUS ACTIVITIES

Apparatus activities provide variety in the physical education program and are challenging for the participants. Retarded children will need to be involved in very structured and organized programs so they will be as safe as possible, gain confidence, and will be able to learn to perform the skills gradually. It will take courage by the students to take part, but they should be urged to perform with the help of skilled teachers. Strength, balance, flexibility, and coordination can be developed through participation in activities using the various pieces of equipment. Activities are included for the trampoline, balance beam, vaulting box, climbing and jumping ropes.

Trampoline

The skills done on the trampoline give the child a freedom of movement not found in any other activity in the physical curriculum. In addition to the skills specific to the trampoline, the child can learn to be a solo performer with other children watching him, he will learn to follow verbal instructions, and he will gain control over his body as he does the various combinations and sequences of the trampoline skills. Most children will benefit from and enjoy the freedom the trampoline provides, and they really will feel good about being able to perform the skills.

A section on skills for the trampoline has been included in this text because trampoline equipment may be available for special education classroom units. The teacher of an instructional unit on trampoline skills must understand the hazards involved with this very popular piece of equipment. Children can be seriously injured during the activity unless special care is taken to provide proper instruction and supervision.

The position statement on the use of trampolines in physical education of the American Alliance of Health, Physical Education, Recreation and Dance is as follows:[12]

(1) No student should be required to engage in trampolining, (2) The program is to be supervised by an instructor with professional preparation in teaching trampoline, (3) Spotters are to be in position whenever the trampoline is being used and all spotters are to be instructed in the techniques of spotting, (4) The somersault is not to be permitted in regular classes, (5) The apparatus is to be locked to prevent unauthorized and unsupervised use, (6) The apparatus will be erected, maintained, and inspected with the manufacturer's recommendations, (7) Policies for emergency care are to be preplanned and actively understood by all affected personnel, and (8) Participation and accident records will be maintained and periodically be analyzed.

Teaching Suggestions for the Trampoline

- Make the turn for each child short. If the waiting time is too long, the value of using the trampoline is lost.
- Give each child a specific number of jumps or stunts to do.
- Remind the child at each turn what he is to perform.
- Keep track of the performing order of the group.
- Remind the child to jump in the center of the mat for safe jumping.
- Get on the mat with a child if that particular child needs your help.
- Ask a child to attempt to repeat verbally what he is to do before he performs the sequence.
- *Never leave the trampoline open and unattended by a trained leader.*

Trampoline Stunts
Easy Bounce
Stand in the center of the mat, bend knees, and jump, pushing down with toes. Swing arms over head (Fig. 13-1). Land with feet apart. Jump five times and get off.

Knee Drop
Stand in the center of the mat; drop to the knees with the feet extended behind, arms extended to the side (Fig. 13-2). Keep the knees on the center of the mat. Push into the mat with the legs and return to standing position. Repeat: feet, knees, feet, knees, feet.

---

[12] AAHPERD Position Statement on Trampolines, "The Use of Trampolines and Minitramps in Physical Education" *Journal of Physical Education and Recreation*, Oct. 1978 P. 914.

Figure 13-1

Seat Drop

Stand in center of the mat. Push into mat and jump slightly. Extend both legs and sit in center of the mat with hands on mat even with the hips. Push into the mat and jump in the center of the mat (Fig. 13-3). Repeat: drop, jump, drop, jump.

Hand and Knee Drop

Stand in the center of the mat; drop to the knees and the hands (Fig. 13-4). Hit mat with the knees and with the hands at the same time. Keep the center of the body at the center of the mat. Push into the mat and place the feet at the center of the mat. Repeat: drop, jump, drop, jump.

Half-Pirouette

Stand in the center of the mat; jump two times. Swing one arm over head and turn toward that arm (Fig. 13-5). Make a half-turn. Jump two times and half-pirouette again.

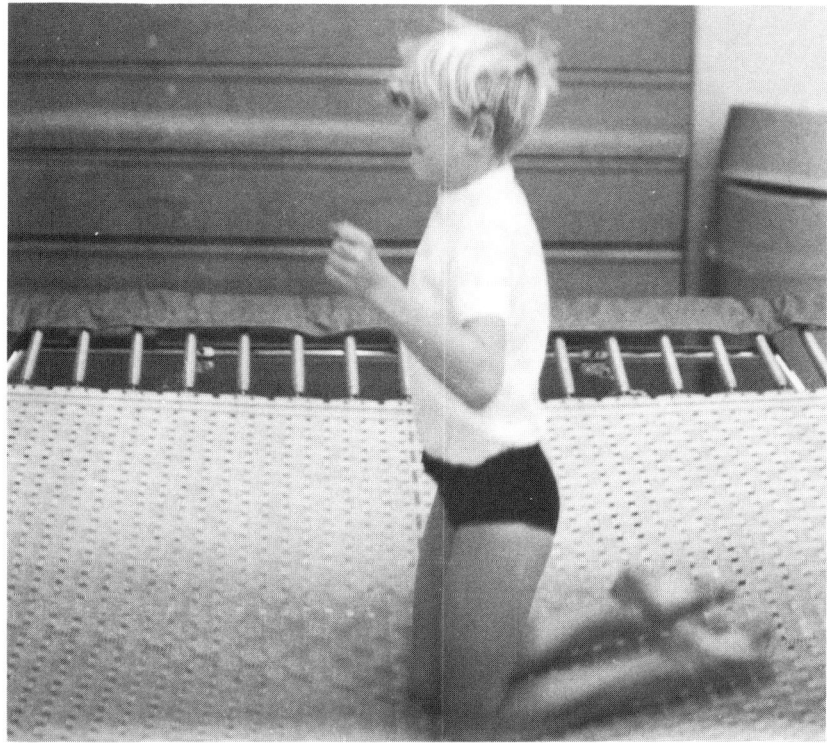

Figure 13-2

Figure 13-3

APPARATUS ACTIVITIES

Figure 13-4

Figure 13-5

Figure 13-6

Seat Drop and Half-Twist to Stand

Stand in the center of the mat facing one end of the mat. Perform a seat drop. Push into mat, and turn and jump facing opposite end of mat (Fig. 13-6). Repeat: seat drop, turn, jump, seat drop, turn, jump.

Swivel Hip

Stand in the center of the mat facing one end of mat. Perform a seat drop, push into mat, and swing both arms over head. Twist body and perform another seat drop facing opposite ends of mat.

A trampoline routine can consist of ten counts with the mat. Simple routines can be made up by the teacher and by the children from the above list of beginning stunts. A simple routine might be: jump three times, spread legs and jump two times, turn around, jump one jump, seat drop and two jumps. A more difficult routine might be seat drop

- to a stand
- half-pirouette
- half-pirouette
- hand and knee drop
- to a stand
- seat drop and turn
- half-pirouette
- deep jump with legs extended
- jump.

BALANCE BEAM

Every child seems naturally attracted to walking on a rail, a fence, or a beam. This skill requires balance, coordination, and timing. A child with motor problems, whether he be retarded or not, will not enjoy this experience because children often feel insecure when on the beam above the ground. They will need to be taught, assisted, and encouraged to perform. Fear enters a great deal into the performance of this skill. Overcoming of this fear can help the child to be more able to solve other problems that he may meet during his daily activities. The teacher should spot or assist the child throughout each stunt until the fear of being on the beam is overcome.

The specific values derived from working on the balance beam are those inherent in perceptual-motor experiences. By walking the beam, a child learns to balance while standing motionless. He can change his balance by weighting one side or the other. He can test his balance by changing his level on the beam. There are some tests available that make use of the balance beam in measuring a child's ability to maintain balance, his laterality, and his perceptual skills in general.

Prebalance Beam Skills

The prebalance beam skill progression is as follows:
- Practice walking first on the floor.
- Practice walking on a line on the floor.
- Practice walking on a board (2x4) that is lying flat on the floor.
- Practice walking on an intermediate beam about two feet from the floor.
- Practice walking finally on a high beam five feet from the floor.

Balance Beam Skills

The skills described are all done on the low beam, but they all can be performed on a higher beam when the child is ready. When performing the skills, it is important to remember that good posture is to be maintained throughout.

Walking Forward. The arms are raised to the side, the head is up, and the body erect. The eyes should be watching for the end of the beam. (Do not watch the feet.) Place one foot in front of the other, feel the beam, and walk down the beam (Fig. 13-7).

Giant Steps. Observe erect posture with the arms raised. Take big steps and progress down the beam (Fig. 13-8).

Figure 13-7

Figure 13-8

Big Step-Little Step. Take one big step and one little step and progress down the beam.

Sideward Steps. Stand on the beam with the side facing the end of the beam, hands out to the sides, and the body erect. Step to the side with the leading foot and bring the other foot up to it. Repeat to the end of the beam (Fig. 13-9).

Side Crossover. Side position as in #4. Cross the nonleading foot over in front of the lead foot, step to the side, and progress to the end of the beam (Fig. 13-10).

Backward Walk. Stand on the beam, take a step backward, place one foot directly behind the other, feel the beam, and progress to the end of the beam (Fig. 13-11).

Pivot. Stand on the beam at the center facing one end of the beam. The feet are one step apart. Rise onto the balls of both feet, turn slowly, face the opposite direction, and carefully put the heels down on the beam. Arms can extend sideways to assist in the lift and turn (Fig. 13-12).

Walk-Pivot-Return. Walk to the center of the beam, pivot, and walk to the starting end of the beam.

Walk-Pivot-Continue. Walk to the center of the beam, pivot, and walk backward to the end of the beam.

Scale Balance. Stand on the beam, balance on one leg, raise the other leg straight backward, and extend both arms forward. The body is in as horizontal a position as possible (Fig. 13-13).

Arabesque. Stand on the beam on one leg. The other leg is bent at the knee and the knee is raised. The arms raise overhead and the body is erect.

Figure 13-9   Figure 13-10

APPARATUS ACTIVITIES

Figure 13-11

Figure 13-12

Figure 13-13

Knee Scale. Kneel on the beam. The weight is supported on one knee and foreleg, and on both hands. The other leg is extended backward and the head is up.

Mounting the High or Intermediate Beam. Sit sidesaddle on the beam. Swing one leg over the beam. Swing both legs forward and backward and place the feet on the beam to the rear. With the hands and feet on the beam, push into a standing position.

Dismounting. Place on hand on the beam for support. Jump off.

Obstacle Course. Place beams of different heights end to end to make a trail or route to follow. The children can just walk all of the beams, or, as they become more skilled, stunts can be performed as the trail is followed.

Simple Routine. Mount, take three steps, pivot, arabesque, pivot, knee scale, stand, dismount.

Balance Beam Jumping Skills

There are many stunts to be performed on the balance beam. The objective of the chapter is to present a sequential progression of skills to provide a parent or the teacher in special education with enough materials to include the balance beam in a program of physical education. The list of jumping skills for the low beam requires balance skill as well as jumping skill.

- Stand on the beam, jump off the beam with one foot on each side of the beam and jump back onto the beam. Progress to the end of the beam.
- Stand on the beam, jump off the beam with both feet on the right side of the beam and jump back onto the beam. Repeat by jumping off the left side of the beam and back on the beam. Progress to the end of the beam.
- Stand on the floor beside the low beam. Jump onto the beam and jump off the beam, landing on the floor at the other side of the beam. Continue to the end of the beam.
- Stand on the floor at the side of the low beam. Jump over the beam to the floor on the other side. Continue jumping over the beam as you progress to the end.

Additional skills and stunts for the balance beam can be obtained by contacting the gymnastic teacher at the local high school or college, or by reading the competitive gymnastic books available in the library.

VAULTING

Every child should experience jumping over boxes, bushes, or barrels. The mentally retarded child can learn to do this vaulting if the teaching is progressive, and if safety is maintained at all times.

The vaulting box is an ideal piece of equipment. It can be lowered or raised as the performer gains skills. It is padded on top for safety and all the parts store together.

Proper spotting techniques are essential for every vaulting activity. The spotter stands facing the vaulter and on the opposite side of the box, in a forward stride position with the arms up and forward. As the vaulter leaves the box, the spotter takes hold of the vaulter's nearest arm above and below the elbow and controls the vaulter as he leaves the box as he lands. In all of the following stunts the spotter will be in position and is to be actively spotting.

Skill Progression

- Stand facing the box. Place the hands on the top of the box. Jump, lifting the hips and keeping the feet close to the box. The head is between the arms and the eyes are looking at the top of the box (Fig. 13-14).
- Stand on the box and jump off.
- Stand on the floor with the hands on the top of the box (box at midthigh level); jump and place the knees on the top of the box. Stand up. Jump off.
- Place the hands on the box and jump, placing the feet between the hands on the top of the box (Fig. 13-15). Stand up. Jump off.
- Place the hands on the box. Jump and move the legs between the arms to the other side of the box and sit on the box. Push on through and land on both feet.

Figure 13-14

- Take four steps; place the hands on the box. Jump and place the feet on the top of the box. Push on through (Fig. 13-16) and land on the feet on the mat.
- Take a short run. Place the hands on the box. Jump and push legs through and land on the feet.
- Take a longer run and repeat #7.

Figure 13-15

Figure 13-16

Flank Vault

The flank vault is the basis for this skill progression:
- Place the hands on the box. Swing both legs to the side and place them on top of the box (Fig. 13-17). Push with the legs and swing them over the box. The spotter stands on the side of the jumper opposite the legs.
- Place the hands on the box. Swing both legs completely over the box (Fig. 13-18) and land on the feet.
- Take a short run. Swing the legs over the box and land on the feet.
- Take a longer run. Swing the legs over the box and land on the feet.

Figure 13-17

Figure 13-18

Wolf Vault

Skill progression based on the wolf vault:
- Place the hands on the box. Jump; swing one leg to the side as in the flank vault, one leg bending between the arms as in the squat vault. Land on the top of the box (Fig. 13-19). Push with feet and vault over the box. Land on the feet. The spotter is on the side of the vaulter opposite the extended leg.
- Place the hands on the box. Repeat #1, but do not land on the top of the box.
- Take a short run. Place the hands on the top of the box. Vault as described in #1.
- Take a longer run. Vault as described in #1.

The vaulting box can also be used as a jumping box. The jumper stands on the top of the box and jumps from the box while doing specific skills such as:
- Jump and do a half-turn.
- Jump and do a full turn.
- Jump and clap hands over the head.
- Jump, turn, and clap the hands over the head.
- Jump and extend both legs forward.
- Jump and bend both knees up to the chest, etc.

In all the activities in this chapter, safety must be stressed constantly. These activities are dangerous and care must be taken to protect the child from injury. Proper equipment must be provided. Mats are essential; without them activities involving stunts, tumbling, and apparatus should not be included. The expense may be great, but money can be made available for programs and mats, and equipment can be provided. It may be possible to borrow equipment. Tumbling mats and other equipment are not in use constantly by high schools, so special-education programs should be able to use them during the "off season."

Figure 13-19

ROPES
Jumping Rope Skills

The physical fitness benefits received from jumping can hardly be matched in any other activity. Jumping rope is a part of childhood experienced by all children and is shared with them by adults. Every child can enjoy this activity and can share with others these joys of childhood.

A retarded child must know how to use the rope for jumping. He should not be allowed to use the rope for catching other children, or be allowed to swing or throw the rope at other children. A rope is a potentially dangerous piece of equipment, and the parents or teachers should make certain that activities using ropes are well organized and well supervised.

Jumping Sequence for Short Rope Skills (Single Child)
- Practice jumping in place. Keep the rhythm even and use no rope.
- Jump over a line on the floor. Keep the rhythm even and use no rope.
- Place the rope on the floor. Jump over and back, keeping the rhythm even.
- Hold one end of the rope in each hand. Place the rope in front of the toes and jump. Swing the rope overhead and back to the starting position.
- Practice #4; keep the rope moving and continue jumping.
- The child can progress to some of the more difficult single-rope skills such as crossed arms, backward jump, and crossed feet.

Long-Rope Learning Sequence (One or More Children)
- Stand side by side along a line. Jump over and back across the line.
- Stand side by side to the rope. Jump over and back across the rope.
- Two children hold a rope, swinging it slowly for others to jump over.
- Practice #3, swinging the rope wider and wider.
- Stand by the rope. As one child jumps, the turners turn the rope over his head and continue turning until the jumper misses.
- The jumper is standing outside the rope beside one of the turners. The teacher is next to the jumper and holds his hand. As the rope turns the teacher "hands" the jumper into the rope, being careful not to push him or jump in with him.
- Practice #6 without "handing" the jumper in. The teacher should give verbal cues to show the jumper when to move.
- The jumper leaves the rope as soon as he has jumped the designated number of times. Jump, run, and follow the rope is the motor pattern for getting out of the rope.

    Children should use many of the jumping rhymes known and

loved all over the world. Some of them are presented here. The neighborhood children are good sources for others.

Charlie Chaplin
Charles Chaplin went to France
To teach the ladies how to dance.
Heel and toe and away we go.
Heel and toe and away we go.
Bow to the captain,
Kneel to the queen,
And give a salute to the big Marine.

Charlie Chaplin
Charlie Chaplain sat on a pin.
How many inches did it go in?
1,2,3,4,5,...

Cinderella
Cinderella dressed in black
Went upstairs to peak through a crack.
How many people did she see?
1,2,3,4,5,...

Cinderella dressed in blue
Went upstairs to clean the flue.
How many flues did she clean?
1,2,3,4,5,...

Cinderella dressed in brown
Went upstairs to make a gown.
How many stitches did she use?
1,2,3,4,5,...

Down by the Seashore
Susie broke the milk bottle
And blamed it onto me.
I told Ma,
Ma told Pa,
Susie got a licking
So ha ha ha.
How many lickings did she get?
1,2,3,4,5,...

Down in the Valley
Down in the valley where the green grass grows
Sat little Mary sweet as a rose.
Along came a billy goat
And kissed her on the nose.
How many kisses did she get?
1,2,3,4,5,...

Minny and a Minny
Minny and a minny and a ha ha ha.
Kissed her fellow on a Broadway car.
You tell Ma and I'll tell Pa,
Minny and a minny and a ha ha ha.

Raspberry
Raspberry, raspberry, raspberry jam,
Tell me the initials of your old man.
A,B,C,D,E,...

Strawberry Shortcake
Strawberry Shortcake, cream of tartar,
Tell me the name of your sweethearter.

Teddy Bear
Teddy Bear, Teddy Bear, go up stairs;
Teddy Bear, Teddy Bear, say your prayers.
Teddy Bear, Teddy Bear, switch off the light;
Teddy Bear, Teddy Bear, say good night.

Verbalization experiences like these rhymes will help the child in his general conversation. The rhymes should be sung in a singsong rhythm and each of the children should be encouraged to participate in the singing, whether it is his turn or not.

Other Rope Activities

Jumps
Some additional rope activities involving jumping:
- **High Jump.** Jump over a held rope. The rope is slowly raised after each child has had a turn.

- **Long Jump.** As each child has had a turn, gradually widen the distance between two ropes laid on the ground.
- **Over and Under.** Two ropes are held parallel. The one closest to the jumper is held at knee height and the one farthest away is held at waist height. The child jumps the closer rope and rolls under the farther rope. The height of the two ropes is gradually reversed.
- **Zigzag Ropes.** One rope is held low so it touches the floor. The turners shake the rope sideways to make it zigzag. The child jumps over the rope, trying to keep from being touched by it.

Hanging Ropes

Rope swings are among the activities provided by hanging ropes:
- Sit on the knot and swing back and forth.
- Stand on the knot and swing back and forth.
- Increase the swing of the rope.
- Climb onto a box, get on the rope, and swing.
- Repeat #4 and at the height of the swing, jump off.

Hanging ropes also provide opportunities for rope climbing:
- Lie down under the rope and grasp it. Using a hand-over-hand movement, pull from lying position to a sitting position.
- Lie down under the rope. Using a hand-over-hand movement, pull from lying position to a standing position.
- Repeat pulling to a standing position but return to lying position by slowly climbing *down* the rope. Keep the legs straight through the practice.
- Stand on the knot with the rope between the legs; wrap the rope around to the back of the calf of the right leg and under the arch of the right foot. Place the left foot on the top of the rope and next to the right foot (Fig. 13-20). Reach up the rope with the hands. Bring the knees up toward the waist. Reach up the rope again with the hands. Repeat the leg action and continue up the rope. Climb down slowly, arms and then legs. Do *not* slide. A climber should save enough energy to climb down the rope. He should not expend all his energy in the climb up.

A retarded child should be told how high to climb and he should be spotted throughout the activity. The rope can be painted to designate different heights. The child should be talked to and encouraged to go up, but only to the predetermined height.

Figure 13-20

14
AQUATIC ACTIVITIES

Aquatic activities are accepted as being important for the normal child because they include many and varied skills and provide some knowledge of safety rules. They are doubly important for the child with learning problems. The retarded child has been cheated in his ability to make judgments, to understand fears, to make choices, and to remember warnings and cautions. There seems to be a natural attraction between every child and the water. All children are drawn to the water, with its movements and mysterious colors and shapes. Every child is captured by the water and is drawn to this fascinating hazard that can be his total undoing if he doesn't develop swimming skills and the ability to understand the rules of participation.

Swimming

Swimming skills can provide the child with the opportunity to develop the components of physical fitness—cardiovascular endurance, muscular endurance and strength, and flexibility. Swimming can also provide the student with the opportunity to learn balance, improve agility, develop coordination and speed. The water gives freedom of movement for some children because of its bouyancy and the body position required by swimming. There are natural opportunities for strength development because of the resistance of the water. A child can experience success with the help of a good teacher, and his self image will be enhanced with each, often very small, success. In the pool, the child learns many of the same skills that his normal friends and family members are learning, so his disability becomes less noticeable. Swimming is fun and this fun is shared with others.

The general outline for teaching swimming is essentially the same for the retarded child as it is for the normal child. Each learner must make progressive advancement along the skill development list in order to become an accomplished swimmer. The retarded child usually will progress more slowly than will the normal child; therefore, the teacher must be prepared to spend much time on each skill. Because of the seemingly slow progress being made, the teacher's patience will often be tested. Each class period, even those lessons in which the child appears to have learned nothing and has made no progress, will help the child learn to swim, and will eventually make him more skilled at it. It is important at the very least for every child to learn to swim well enough to save himself should the need ever occur.

The child should be taught swimming skills that include adjustment to the water, bouyance skills, propulsive skills and skills of personal safety. He should know his own abilities and be aware of his limitations. Even if he does know how to swim, he should know that he does not get into the water without adult supervision.

The Objectives of the Swimming Program

The objective of any swimming program is to teach the child to swim well enough to be safe in the water. This is especially true of a swimming program for the retarded child. Fun is the method by which safety and skills are taught.

Values of Swimming

Some additional values of learning to swim are:
- Swimming may serve as a tool for the retarded child to become a member of a peer group, perhaps being the only experience in which he is truly a participating member and not just a spectator.
- Swimming offers a child the opportunity to experience success while having fun. Each success may be small, a single skill learned, but these single skills add up to true learning and fun.
- Swimming, because it may be a new experience, may help to increase the attention span of a child, which could carry over into other activities, thus enriching the total learning experience.
- Swimming may be the one activity in which the retarded child can share equally with the members of his family because everyone has had the same experiences when learning to swim.
- Swimming may help the child develop his ability to follow instructions and directions, thus helping him in these same areas at school and at home.

Program Organization

Safety. The organization for a swimming program for the mentally handicapped is like any other well-organized swimming program. It must be thoroughly understood that swimming is a dangerous activity and that a mistake in judgment on the part of the director or by the instructor may result in an accident for one of the students. *Safety* must be the first consideration with any swimming program.

Pool. Any available pool should be included in the planning. There are many nonscheduled hours in most pools. These hours are the least desirable ones for the public. They may occur during the morning when children are in school and mothers are home with housework, or they may be at noon or at normal dinner hours. Pool owners can usually be encouraged to make the pool available for special education use during these hours, very often free of charge.

Schedule. Learning is better with frequent short periods of instruction than it is with infrequent long periods of instruction. It is better to let two groups swim twice a week for thirty minutes each than each group swim once a week for an hour. When the class periods occur once a week, the nonpracticing time is too long; this results in too much time in which to forget and the teacher is always starting over.

Instructors. It is necessary to have one instructor for every trainable student and one instructor for every nonswimming, educable student. An instructor can teach four to five swimming educable students. The person in charge of the program should be well prepared in aquatics. The more practical knowledge and experience each instructor has, the better the instruction in the program will be. Persons who themselves are good swimmers can make excellent teachers if they are given assistance and guidance by the aquatic program director. All communities have experienced and well prepared swimmers willing to volunteer their services if the need for their assistance is made known. Volunteer service is as reliable as paid service, and can give the program community contacts that can help in all areas of special education. Often service clubs such as Lions, Junior League, and various religious groups will assist in an aquatic program. There may also be groups like Big Brothers and church groups with members who will help.

Another source for instructors lies with the parents of each child. Even if these parents are not experienced swimming teachers, they can be taught to be instructor aides to help in giving swimming instruction. The parent helpers will probably be more successful if they are assigned to help a child other than their own.

Suits. Parents usually provide a swim suit for their own child, but a child should not be excluded from the program because of a parent's inability to provide one. Most swimming families have outgrown suits and will be eager to put them to good use.

Cautions. All children in the swimming program should have a permission card signed by the family physician and by the parents. Special attention must be paid to the child who is subject to convulsive seizures. This child should not be excluded just because of the seizures, but someone experienced in handling the seizure should be in the water and near the child or at the pool edge at all times. The swimming instructor should not be expected to handle this problem.

Children should be encouraged to dry themselves thoroughly following the swimming period. Children may be subject to colds, and wet hair will compound this problem. If each child brings an extra towel, he can get dry enough to keep from getting chilled.

METHODS OF INSTRUCTION

The American Red Cross suggests that emphasis should be placed upon breath control, the face-down float and recovery to standing position. These three skills are basic to all swimming, and when a child can perform them successfully, he is ready for more exciting and challenging swimming.

An instructor should work in the water with the child as long as the child is involved in learning the basic skills of swimming. This not only gives the child confidence in the instructor but it provides a safety factor for the child and makes it possible for the instructor to share in the water experiences.

As soon as the child can perform the basic skills, he should be placed in a group for instruction. The sooner the child can function in a group, the sooner he will be able to live in a group. Swimming can be a great help in preparing a child for successful group participation. By placing a child in a group, an instructor will be freed to assist another beginning child, thus increasing the number of participants a limited number of instructors can teach.

Swimming Skill Progression

The list of skills is not only easy for the instructor to follow, but is presented in a step-by-step procedure with one skill built upon the preceding one. The instructor should become acquainted with the list to be able to move smoothly from one skill to the next. At the end of each lesson, he should check on the skill sheet the progress made by each child.

Entering the Water

To help the child enter the water:
- Let him climb backwards down the ladder to the arms of the teacher (Fig. 14-1).
- Let him sit on the side of the pool and be lifted into the water.
- Walk with the child down the steps and into the water.

Figure 14-1

(Do not teach the child to run and jump into the pool as his first entry into the water. This skill should be included in the lessons but should not be used at the entry level.)

Adjustment to the Water

These first nine activities are designed to help the child adjust to the water:
- Hold the child in your arms and gently bounce with him in the water. Do not splash or duck him or allow him to splash other children.
- Go a little farther under the water each time and stay a little longer each time.
- Let the water drop from your hand onto his shoulder, his hair, his chest, his chin, and his nose. Do not toss the water at him; just let it drop onto him (Fig. 14-2). Encourage him to do this to you.
- Hold the child at the underarms and gently swing him from side to side, forward and backward.
- Hold the child at the underarms and circle with him slowly; then circle with him fast. Keep his head up and let him feel the water flow past him.
- Take hold of both the child's hands and pull him slowly forward (Fig. 14-3). His face is out of the water.
- Take hold of both the child's hands and circle with him. Practice numbers 6 and 7 several times. Explore the pool, talk to the child, and show him new places in the pool.

Figure 14-2

Figure 14-3

- Repeat number 7 and let the child kick. Tell him to kick hard and make a big splash while you pull the child fast.
- The child takes hold of the edge of the pool. The instructor takes hold of the child's feet and helps the child kick from the hips and with a slight bend at the knees. There is no need to stress to the child the direction of the kick if the child is helped through the kicking process.

Beginners Swimming Stroke—Crawl

Mastery of the next twenty-one skills will enable the child to swim the beginners stroke:

1. Stand in shallow water with the child. Take a deep breath, shut your lips, close your eyes, and put your face in the water. Come up and wipe the water from your eyes and smile. The child copies you.

2. The instructor can use tricks to keep the child interested. Straws to blow through, table tennis balls and balloons to blow along the water (Fig. 14-4), and pennies, rocks, and diving rings on the bottom of the pool will all help to get him under the water and used to the feel of water in his hair and eyes.

3. Take hold of both the child's hands. Ask him to put his face in the water.

4. Take hold of both the child's hands. The instructor pulls the child and the child puts his face in the water.

5. Ask the child to put his face in the water without the instructor holding his hands.

6. The instructor should move about three feet away from the child and encourage the child to put his face in the water and walk to the instructor while his face is in the water.

7. The instructor should extend both of his arms and let the child grasp the left arm and wrist of the instructor with both hands. The instructor's right arm is under the child's body to give added support. The instructor walks sideways and pulls the child forward (Fig. 14-5).

8. Repeat number 7. Pull the child forward with his face in the water.

9. Repeat number 8 and tell the child to kick as he is pulled forward.

10. Show the child the jellyfish float, let him try it with help from the instructor.

11. Show the child the prone float; support him as he tries it. Assist the child to a standing position.

12. Teach the child to regain a standing position. From a front float position, bring both knees to the chest and pull down with both arms. Raise the head, force the feet to the bottom of the pool, and stand up. This should be practiced until the child can regain his standing position from a front float easily.

13. Stand a few feet from the edge of the pool in about three feet of water. Hold the child at the waist. The child extends his arms and puts his face in the water. The instructor pushes the child to the edge of the pool with enough force to get him to the edge but not enough to crush him into the edge (Fig. 14-6).

14. Repeat number 12 several times, increasing the distance from the edge of the pool.

15. Repeat number 13 and tell the child to kick as the instructor pushes him to the edge of the pool.

Figure 14-4

Figure 14-5

Figure 14-6

16. In shallow water the instructor faces the child and takes hold of both his hands. The instructor moves the child's arms through the crawl pattern (Fig. 14-7).

17. The child moves his arms in the crawl pattern without the instructor's help.

18. The child puts his face in the water and moves his arms through the crawl pattern.

19. The instructor holds the child at his waist in about three feet of water and about five feet from the edge of the pool. The child puts his face in the water. The instructor pushes the child toward the edge of the pool and the child kicks and moves his arms through the crawl pattern.

20. Repeat number 19 several times, increasing the distance from the edge of the pool each time.

21. The child stands on the bottom of the pool, pushes off, and swims. Practice many times, increasing the distance to be covered each time.

Back Swimming Position—Finning Backstroke

These ten skills will enable the child to do the finning backstroke.

1. The instructor stands behind the child while the child lies on his back. The instructor should support the child at his shoulder blades or at his armpits (Fig. 14-8). A gentle nudge on the child's seat with the instructor's knee will get his hips in a floating position.

AQUATIC ACTIVITIES 245

Figure 14-7

Figure 14-8

2. The instructor should pull the child across the pool. The child's head is back and his arms at his sides.

3. The child takes a breath of air and holds it. The instructor then "fins" one of his hands and returns it to its side. Repeat "fin" movement with the other hand and finally both hands together.

4. Repeat number 3 several times, increasing the time the instructor's hands are removed from under the child's shoulders.

5. Repeat number 4 and let the child kick. Pull the child across the pool and instruct him to kick and float by himself some of the distance.

6. The child holds onto the edge of the pool with his knees between his hands. Ask him to lie back on the water, keep his chin up, and kick his feet. The instructor should be ready to catch the child when the forward movement stops.

7. Repeat number 6 several times, increasing the distance to be covered. The instructor catches the child when the forward movement stops.

8. Teach the child to regain a standing position. Sweep both arms toward the feet, bend at the hips, forcefully extend the legs toward the bottom of the pool, and stand up. Practice many times until the child can regain a standing position easily.

9. While the child does a back float, bring his hands up the sides of his body to the armpits and push them back down along the body. Keep the arms close to the body.

10. Tell the child to do a back float, then kick and do the finning pattern with the arms.

Combined Skills

The last nine skills of the progression are combinations of the skills already learned:

1. The child does the beginners stroke and turns over to the back swimming position. The instructor should help if needed at the time of turning over. Instruct the child to give a strong kick immediately upon turning over.

2. Tell the child to combine the crawl, turning over, and finning. Sometimes start on the back, turn over, and finish with the crawl. The child should be able to turn from either position easily and continue swimming.

3. Tell the child to jump into waist-deep water. If necessary the instructor can catch the child the first few times.

4. The child jumps into the water (Fig. 14-9), pushes off the pool bottom, swims and turns over, and swims to the other side of the pool.

5. Ask the child to jump into deeper water. Progress slowly. Orient the child to be in the water without the teacher. Teach the child to respond to signals and to reach for a pole if he needs assistance. Do not allow the child to grab at the instructor when working in deep water.

Figure 14-9

    6. Practice the crawl and turning over and finning combinations in deep water.

    7. Teach the child to jump into deep water.

    8. The child jumps, levels off, and swims in deep water.

This list is a step-by-step experience designed to help the instructor build skill upon skill to increase the swimming ability of the children in the program. The best way to drown-proof a person is to help him become the best swimmer he can be. He must understand the dangers around the pool and he must have understanding and respect for the pool organization.

The following Swimming Skill Chart can be used by the teacher to record the progress of each child.

SWIMMING SKILL CHART

Entering Get into water							
Adjustment							
Drop water on head							
Teacher pulls student							
Teacher pulls and student kicks							
Hold to side and kick							
Put face in water							
Teacher pulls—student puts face in water							
Teacher pulls—student puts face in water and kicks							
Walk to teacher							
Jellyfish float							
Front float							
Crawl —Teacher pushes student to pool edge							
Teacher pushes and student kicks							
Move arms for the crawl							
Teacher pushes—student moves arms							
Swim beginner stroke							
Back Crawl—Teacher supports for back float							
Back float							
Back float with kick							
Back float and kick and move arms							
Combined skills—Turn from front to back—keep floating							
Turn from back to front—keep floating							
Jump into shallow water							
Jump into deep water							
Jump and swim							

Water Exercising

The purpose of water exercises is the development of physical fitness by taking advantage of water resistance and bouyancy when performing specific exercises for selected muscles of the body.

Everyone will benefit from doing exercises in the water, but some children, because of the nature of the retardation or their physical disability, cannot be included in formal swimming lessons. These children will benefit especially from taking part in the strengthening, flexibility, and relaxation exercises done in the water.

Flexibility Exercises
- **Heel Cord Stretch**

    Starting Position. In chest deep water, stand facing the pool wall with the arms extended and the hands grasping the pool edge. One leg is extended back, and the weight is on the other leg.

    Action. Keep both legs straight. Move the body forward until the stretch pain is felt in the back of the supporting leg.

    Duration. Hold 10 seconds and repeat with the other leg. Do 5 times.
- **Lower Back and Leg Stretch**

    Starting Position. Stand with one side to the pool side. Hook one foot over the pool edge. Keep both legs straight.

    Action. Bend at the waist and reach forward with the opposite hand toward the raised foot (Fig. 14-10).

Figure 14-10

Duration. Hold 10 seconds. Repeat to the other side. Do 5 times.
- **Arm and Shoulder Stretch**
Starting Position. Stand with the back to the pool walk, keeping the heels close to the wall. Reach the arms out behind and grasp the pool edge (Fig. 14-11).
Action. Lean forward away from the pool side. Look up and arch the back by pushing the hips forward.
Duration. Hold 15 seconds. Relax. Do 5 times.

Figure 14-11

Strengthening Exercise
- *Running*
Starting Position. In chest deep water, hold the arms above the water at 90' angles with the fists clenched (Fig. 14-12).
Action. Swing the arms above the water and run as fast as possible.
Duration. Run 20 feet 3 times during the exercise session. (For variety, the student can jump, hop, or skip.)
- *Push Away*
Starting Position. Face the wall and grasp the pool edge with the hands. Keep the arms straight. Place the feet on the bottom of the pool, close to the pool wall (Fig. 14-13).
Action. Pull the body to the pool edge. Push away to the starting position (Fig. 14-14).

Figure 14-12

Figure 14-13

Figure 14-14

Duration. 20 times.
- **Backward Arm Circles**
  Starting Position. In shoulder deep water, extend the arms to the side, fists clenched.
  Action. Make circles with the arms backwards. Keep arms straight.
  Duration. Make 20 circles.

- **Leg Lifts**
  Starting Position. Face the pool wall, hold onto the pool side. Lean hips forward so the front of the body is touching the pool wall.
  Action. Raise one leg backward. Keep the toes pointed and the body straight.
  Duration. 10 times with each leg.
- **Leg Circles**
  Starting Position. Face the pool wall. Hold onto the pool edge. One leg is extended backwards.
  Action. Circle the extended leg in large circles.
  Duration. Do 10 circles in each direction with each leg. Repeat 5 times.
- **Leg Bends**
  Starting Position. Stand with the back to the pool wall. Hold onto the pool edge with arms extended. Bring the knees to the chest (Fig. 14-15).
  Action. Roll the legs to the right, to the center, and to the left (Fig. 14-16).
  Duration. 10 complete cycles.

Figure 14-15   **Figure 14-16**

Relaxation Exercises
- **Arm Swimgs**
  Starting Position. Stand with the side to the pool wall. Hold onto the pool edge with the nearest hand. The outside arm is in the water by the side of the body.
  Action. Swing the outside arm over the head and return to the starting position. The upper body can lean toward the action of the arm (Fig. 14-17).
  Duration. 10 times on each side.

- **Body Float**
  Starting Position. Face the pool side. Arms are extended. Hold onto the pool edge with both hands.
  Action. Dip the body down into the water. Keep the face above the water. Release the feet from the pool bottom and allow the legs to float to the surface. Bend the knees and place the feet on the pool bottom.
  Duration. 10 times.
- **Leg Raises**
  Starting Position. Stand with one side to the pool wall. Hold onto the pool edge with the nearest hand.
  Action. Raise the outside leg slowly to the rear, to the side, and to the front of the body. Keep the body straight (Figs. 14-18, 14-19, 14-20).
  Duration. 10 times on each side. Repeat 5 times.

Games and Water Learning

Games and other water activities can be used to reinforce classroom concepts as well as the skills of swimming. Learning to play in the water prepares a child for formal swimming instruction and can also, for example, teach the mathematical concepts of dividing, doing fractions, recognizing shapes and sizes, and multiplying numbers. Body image, self concepts development, balance, perception, coordination, and endurance can also be learned by water play but all must be established as specific objectives of the activity for such learning.

The games and activities included all require some swimming skill. They also require the child to follow some specific instructions. They are fun, but are designed with specific well-defined objectives.

Obstacle Course

Equipment. Anchor large hoops to the pool bottom with short ropes and sand-filled bleach bottles.
Activity.
- Swim through the hoops and come up for air whenever necessary.
- Swim through one hoop and dive over the next hoop; repeat through the entire course.
- Go through the entire course with only one breath.

Skills developed. Underwater swimming, surface dive, and breath holding.

Musical Hoops

Equipment. One hoop for each child except the child who has been designated as the "It."

Figure 14-17

Figure 14-18

AQUATIC ACTIVITIES

Figure 14-19

Figure 14-20

Activity. Each player except the "It" is inside a hoop. Music is played and the children inside the hoops walk around in the water, moving with the hoops. When the music stops, all the children leave their hoops and try to get into another one. Whoever is left without a hoop is the new "It."

Skills developed. Ability to go under water with the eyes open.

Sponge and Bucket Relay

Equipment. One sponge and one small bucket for each relay team.

Activity. The child dips the sponge into the shallow water and wrings the water into the bucket. When the bucket is full, he pours the water over his head and the sponge and bucket is passed to the next child.

Skills developed. Hand strength. Teamwork with other children.

Poker Chip Pick Up

Equipment. 50 or more colored poker chips.

Activity. The chips are thrown into the water. On signal "Go," the children dip into the water for the chips and gather up as many as possible on one try.

Variation. Assign each child a color; he is to pick up as many of that color as he can on one try.

Skills developed. Ability to go under water with eyes open. Breath holding.

Relay Races

- Run through the water to selected goal and back.
- Run backwards.
- Carry objects above the head—balls, bottles, kickboards.

Skills developed. Ability to take turns. Obeying the rules of each selected relay. Waiting for another racer.

15
TRACK AND FIELD

Track and field events are good self-testing activities, enabling each child to challenge himself at his own level of ability. The conditioning inherent in the performance of these activities makes them valuable components of any program. Running, jumping, and throwing are basic skills used in most sports and games, and therefore the ability to perform them well will enhance the enjoyment of other activities.

Several opportunities are available for handicapped children to participate in organized competition sponsored by service organizations. Many prominent citizens in the community are willing to contribute their means and time to foster opportunities for these children. (See Chapter 17 on competition for specific information.)

Track and field activities are easily adaptable to differences in ability. Even children confined to wheelchairs can participate in many of the events. The nature of the activities provides natural incentive to participate. Everyone enjoys the thrill of running against the clock, the challenge of determining how far he can jump, or seeing how many feet he can throw a ball.

Teaching Suggestions
- Practice the events in a setting which is similar to the competitive situation.
- Use immediate goals to challenge the children. Mentally retarded children need a mark or a flag as a target to help them realize their jumping ability.
- When competition will be started with a gun, practice with the gun to acquaint the children with its meaning and sound.
- The use of immediate rewards, such as a ribbon or badge with their achievement on it, will help mentally retarded children to understand their accomplishments.

- The children should warm up prior to participation in the event. Stretching exercises and light jogging are good.
- Teach one event at a time and practice it until it becomes familiar to the children. It should be reviewed as other events are taught.
- When more than one event is taking place, a leader for each is needed.
- When the children practice for competition, use the same type of equipment which will be used in the meet.

50-Yard Dash

See Chapter 5 for an additional analysis of the running skill.

Crouch Start. The following instructions are to be given:
- "Take your marks." Place the foot of the front leg two handspans behind the starting line. Place the knee of the back leg even with the toes of the front foot, the thumb and forefinger parallel to the line with the fingers together, and focus the eyes down the track (Fig. 15-1).
- "Get set." Shift the weight up and forward to a position in which the weight is balanced on the hands and front foot, with some weight on the back foot, and the hips level with the shoulders (Fig. 15-2).
- "Go!" Push off with the rear foot and vigorously extend the front leg. Step just in front of the line with the rear foot and reach forward with the opposite arm.

Figure 15-1

Running the Dash. For the first three or four steps, use the arms vigorously by reaching forward and backward in opposition. Use short, driving steps with high knee action and lean forward. Gradually rise to a slight leaning position and increase the size of each step until the desired running pace is reached.

While running the dash, lean slightly forward and relax as much as possible. Reach forward and backward with the arms (Fig. 15-3). The arms should be slightly bent and the hands should reach forward until they are about shoulder high and backward to the hip. Run on the balls of the feet with the toes pointed forward.

When finishing the race, run past the finish line at top speed and gradually slow to a jog and then a walk.

Measurement. The race may be against a stopwatch or against other children. It is easier to obtain the best performance when the children run against each other. Use a finish tape which will help the children to see the end of the race.

Rules. Everyone must be stationary before the starting signal. Everyone must run in his own lane.

Variations. The distance may be changed to meet the ability of the children. A 30-yard dash is good for younger children. A standing start may be used when it is difficult for the children to maintain their balance from a crouch start.

Figure 15-2

Figure 15-3

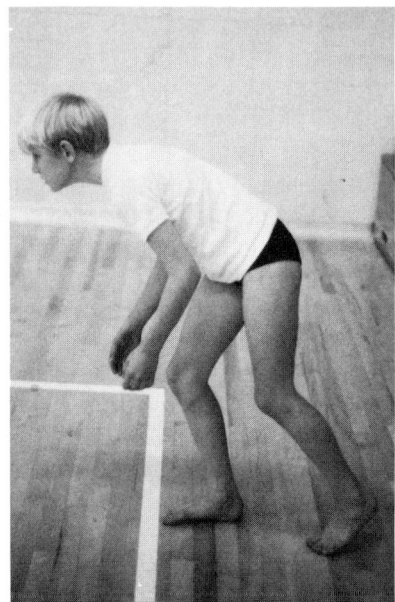

Figure 15-4

300-Yard Walk-Run

Standing Start. A forward-stride position should be assumed just behind the starting line. The knees, ankles, and hips should be slightly bent and the body should lean slightly forward in anticipation of the starting signal. With the signal to "get set," assume a position ready to push forward (Fig. 15-4). On the signal "go," push forward and move the arms in opposition, getting into the normal running stride as soon as possible.

Running the Race. Run at a pace which can be maintained over the required distance and still accomplish the distance in the shortest time possible. If the pace cannot be maintained, slow to a jogging or walking pace until recovery is great enough to run again.

220-Yard Pursuit Relay

Preparation. Space four runners from each team fifty-five yards apart. The first runner assumes either a crouch-start position or a standing-start position, with the baton held by the lower half in the left hand. The other three runners assume a standing-start position facing the finish line.

Running the Relay. On the starting signal, Runner No. 1 races toward Runner No. 2. Runner No. 2 watches Runner No. 1 by looking over his shoulder. As Runner No. 1 approaches, Runner No. 2

extends the right arm back with the palm turned up, the fingers together, and the thumb out. When No. 1 gets about three yards away, No. 2 begins to run forward. No. 1 should place the baton into the hand of No. 2 firmly and both performers should watch the baton and hand during the exchange. (Note: More advanced runners may make the exchange using a blind pass with the second runner looking forward, as in Fig. 15-5.) After receiving his baton, Runner No. 2 should transfer the baton to his left hand to carry it toward Runner No. 3. The same type of exchange is used by No. 2 and No. 3. No. 4 runs with the baton across the finish line.

Rules. Each runner must stay in his lane running and following the baton exchange until all runners have completed the exchange. The exchange of the baton must be carried out within twenty-two yards. If the baton is dropped, the runner who last had possession must pick it up.

Figure 15-5

200-Yard Shuttle Relay

Preparation. Two runners for each team are placed at opposite ends of the 50-yard area. The first runner assumes either a crouch-start position or a standing-start position with the baton held vertically at the lower end in the left hand. The other three runners assume a standing-start position facing the approaching runner.

Running the Relay. At the start signal, the first runner races toward the second runner. Runner No. 2 waits with the palm of the right hand facing Runner No. 1, with the fingers together and the thumb out. The first runner places the baton firmly in the hand of Runner No. 2 (Fig. 15-6). The second runner may begin running after receiving the baton from the first runner, but not before. The same procedure is used by the second and third runners, passing right hand to left hand. Runner No. 4 races across the finish line, which is the original starting line.

Rules. Each runner must stay in his lane. The receiver must stay behind the restraining line until the baton is received. If the baton is dropped, the runner who last had possession must pick it up.

Figure 15-6

50-Yard Hurdle Race

Preparation. Four hurdles, 2½ feet high, are needed for each lane. Place the hurdles 26' 3½" apart, with the first hurdle 39' 4½" from the starting line. The hurdles should be placed so they will tip forward if hit by the performer.

Running the Race. The race is run like a 50-yard dash with the addition of the hurdles. The technique used to clear the hurdle is similar to the normal running stride, not a jump. The lead leg is lifted toward the chest to extend the step over the hurdle (Fig. 15-7). The foot should land on the ground close to the hurdle to continue the running technique as quickly as possible. The trailing leg passes over the hurdle with the knee out to the side of the trunk and the toe turned out to avoid hitting the hurdle (Fig. 15-8). The body should lean into the reaching stride and the arms should reach in opposition. The trailing

TRACK AND FIELD

Figure 15-7

Figure 15-8

leg should snap down to regain the running position as soon as possible (Fig. 15-9). (Note: In teaching the hurdle technique, a loose rope can be held as low as necessary for the children to step over. Gradually raise the rope and continue to work on the correct position of the front and trailing leg.)

Rules. Each runner must go over the hurdle with both legs. Knocking down a hurdle is not a violation as long as the runner goes over it.

Each runner must stay in his own lane, and the other rules for running dashes should also be applied.

Figure 15-9

Standing Long Jump

Preparation. A nonslip takeoff surface is needed. The landing surface should be turf or a mat with some give to absorb the force of the landing.

Jumping Technique. Stand with the toes behind the starting line. Assume a position with the weight on the balls of the feet, the arms bent and forward, and the knees and trunk bent in a semi-sitting position (Fig. 15-10). Rock the weight back onto the heels and swing the arms backward (Fig. 15-11), then rock forward again as the arms swing forward into the jumping position. Extend the legs and trunk as the feet push upward and forward (Fig. 15-12). The arms should swing upward at a 45-degree angle with the head and chest lifted upward also. Lift the knees, reach forward with the legs and land on both feet (Fig. 15-13). Lean forward to prevent falling backward.

Measurement. The measurement is taken from the front edge of the takeoff board to the closest point of contact made by the performer.

Rules. The feet must be behind the takeoff board, both feet must be used, and no preparatory jump may be used.

Figure 15-10

Figure 15-11

TRACK AND FIELD 265

Figure 15-12

Figure 15-13

Running Long Jump

Preparation. A nonslip takeoff board and a landing pit with sand or sawdust in it is needed. The takeoff board should be preceded by an approach area approximately 150 feet long.

Jumping Technique. Start on the takeoff board and run back the desired distance to measure the approach. Mark the point at which the foot to be used for jumping reaches the desirable approach distance. The takeoff should be long enough to reach approximately 80 percent of maximum speed and not tire the performer. The takeoff foot should hit the board with the knee and ankle bent, ready to extend (Fig. 15-14). As the push is made by the takeoff foot, the arms and head lift up at a 45-degree angle. The aim of the performer is to jump upward and let the forward speed carry the body forward as far as possible.

While in the air keep the head and chest up and reach forward with the legs into a sitting position. As the landing is made on both feet, swing the arms backward to thrust the body forward (Fig. 15-15).

Rules. The measurement is the same as that used for the standing long jump. The takeoff must be from one foot, and the foot must not be over the board.

Figure 15-14

Figure 15-15

High Jump

Preparation. A pair of jump standards and a crossbar, and a soft landing pit are needed.

Jumping Technique. The jumper should start at least four or five strides from the crossbar. The approach is made at a 45-degree angle. The takeoff should be an arm's distance from the bar. The method of jumping may vary according to the jumper, the easiest being scissor jump. At the takeoff point, the push-off comes from the foot away from the bar. The leg closest to the bar is kicked up and over the bar while the arms swing upward to help lift the body. The legs should be straight after the push-off. The performer passes over the bar in a sitting position and lands on one foot at a time (Fig. 15-16).

A more advanced method of jumping is the straddle roll. The takeoff is on the foot closest to the bar. The outside leg kicks up and the arms swing upward. After reaching the peak of the jump, roll over the bar and face it by turning the head and reaching with the outside arm (Fig. 15-17). Land on both feet and one arm (or on the shoulder and back if a sponge pit is used) facing the direction of the approach area.

Rules. The measurement is from the upper edge of the crossbar to the ground. Each jumper is given three chances to clear each height. A third miss at any one height disqualifies the performer. A miss consists of knocking the bar off the standards.

Figure 15-16

Figure 15-17

Softball Throw

Preparation. An approach area with a scratch line is marked off at the edge of the throwing area. Markers should be available to mark the throw for each performer.

Throwing Procedure. See Chapter 11 for an analysis of the throwing technique. An overhand throw should be used by the contestant. When throwing for distance the release should be at a 45-degree angle (Fig. 15-18). Three trials are given the performer to achieve his greatest distance.

Rules. The performer may not step on or over the throwing line, and an overhand throw must be used.

Measurement. Measurement is the distance from the throwing line to the place where the ball first touched the ground. Only the best throw need be measured.

Figure 15-18

Soccer Ball Throw

Preparation. Same as for the softball throw.

Performance. A sidearm throw should be used. Start with the side to the throwing area. Hold the ball on the fingers and tucked against the forearm. With the weight on the back foot, swing the throwing arm backward and point the free arm toward the field. Two or three warm-up swings may be used to get momentum for the final release. On the last swing, the weight is transferred forward to rotate the hips and trunk, which in turn helps swing the throwing arm forward and upward at a 45-degree angle (Fig. 15-19). Following the throw comes a reversal, in which the recovery of the body momentum by the back foot prevents falling over the line. The soccer throw is a good lead-up to the discus throw.

Rules. The performer may not step on or over the throwing line. Three trials are given the performer to achieve his greatest distance. Measurement is the distance from the throwing line to the place where the ball first touched the ground. Only the best throw need be measured.

Figure 15-19

16
ACTIVITIES OF OUTDOOR PLAYGROUND EQUIPMENT

The pieces of equipment on a playground can provide unique opportunities for learning. Permanently placed on the playyard, and well away from ball fields and other physical education activity centers, these pieces of equipment may stand unused and unappreciated much of the time simply because they are ignored. The structures can be designed for many age groups to use, or can be designed for use by only the primary or the intermediate grades. Schools can spend money on commercially designed equipment packages, or they can design the playground and have it built (or build it themselves) to suit specific needs of specific children.*

Safety is the first consideration of a well-designed playground. The materials should be of good quality, the workmanship must be guaranteed, and the installation lay-out must consider safety in relation to the entire playground as well as among the individual pieces of equipment.

Playground equipment must be *challenging* to children. A degree of anticipated danger will give the child a sense of accomplishment when using the equipment and when completing a task.

The equipment should be *interesting* and *attractive*. The whole playground should not become an eyesore to the school or to the community.

The equipment should be *easily maintained* and *kept clean*. Children will not use the equipment if they get dirty from the tires, injured from poor welds or joints, or slivers from wooden railroad ties.

Provide *variety* in the activities that can be done on the equipment—such as climbing up and down, going through, sliding down, and swinging opportunities. The equipment can be placed in

---

*Hogan, P. *Nuts and Bolts of Playground Construction*. West Point, New York: Leisure Press.

an obstacle course pattern so the individual pieces fit together, but can also be used singly.

The activities on the equipment should be *fun* to do. The children will return to the equipment if they enjoy what they are allowed to do.

Two different playgrounds are shown (Fig. 16-1) (Fig. 16-2). One is constructed mostly of tires of various size and 8x8 redwood beams, with very few pieces of metal equipment. The other combines metal equipment and redwood beams into an interesting and attractive combination equally divided between metal and wood. Both examples are as safe as possible, and are contained in small areas of the schoolyard.

The apparatus on the playground provides opportunities for free play during recess and recreation time, and can also be a learning laboratory for skill development. The teacher can:
- plan physical education activities using the various pieces of equipment with specific educational objectives in the lesson;
- design obstacle courses that challenge children;
- provide a competitive outlet for appropriate activities; and
- determine specific skill objectives for each child and check off the skill when it is mastered. If the equipment is used for skill development as well as for recreation, the children will improve their recreational performances, injuries will be fewer, and the equipment will be used to its maximum.

Benefits to the Child

Benefits to the retarded child are the same as for other children. They include:
- Freedom to explore his own ability with the equipment.
- Courage as he gains skill.
- Development of creativity in physical education activities.
- Strength development in the muscles used in climbing, swinging, and holding on.
- Improved balance.
- Awareness of activities other children are performing.
- Sharing the pieces of equipment with others and learning to take turns.
- Learning to be cautious when caution is appropriate.
- The opportunity to show-off in a controlled situation. Self image will improve as the number of skills increase.
- Improvement in ability to perform skills by imitating skills other children are performing.

Figures 16-3 through 16-15 show some of the activities that can be performed on the various pieces of equipment. Children can explore and can help the teacher set standards for performance evaluation. Children can also create new and different skills for their peers to learn.

Figure 16-1

Figure 16-2

Figure 16-3

Figure 16-4

Figure 16-5

ACTIVITIES OF OUTDOOR PLAYGROUND EQUIPMENT

Figure 16-6

Figure 16-7

Figure 16-8

Figure 16-9

Figure 16-10

Figure 16-11

Figure 16-12

ACTIVITIES OF OUTDOOR PLAYGROUND EQUIPMENT

Figure 16-13

Figure 16-14

Figure 16-15

COMPETITION

Children of all ages and abilities receive the same benefits from competitive experiences as secondary school and collegiate athletes. Educators believe these programs are a valuable means of developing the total person. These programs provide learning experiences for the developing child in many ways:
- Social interaction with others, both handicapped and normal.
- Opportunities for successes by achieving goals and personal bests in sports and games.
- Improved self-image and self-discipline.
- Incentives for improving physical fitness.
- Self-confidence to encourage achievement in other aspects of life.
- Opportunities for fun and enjoyment.
- Learning about loyalties, cooperation, sacrifice and courtesy with teammates, coaches and officials.
- Respect for others and their efforts, achievements and frustrations.
- Opportunities to travel, meet dignitaries and respected athletes.
- Motivation to overcome problems and handicaps.

Competition can be provided in many forms. Competitions with one's self to improve a score, such as doing more push-ups, running faster, and jumping further, or to improve a personal best in events like the long jump, the 50 yard run, etc., is one form. Contributions to the team to win a relay or game is another. Achieving goals to receive an award or recognition such as ribbons, medals or points is yet another form of competition. These help the individual to practice hard, to believe in himself and to have a desire to participate and to achieve.

Family competitive activities can provide fun and development in all aspects of family life. Competitive experiences are a means of teaching values to family members. Observing rules, achieving results honestly, and accepting disappointments appropriately are behaviors that can be practiced during family games and incentive programs. With activities as the laboratory for practicing these behaviors, parents can guide family members in the development of these objectives.

All children can participate in competitive activities regardless of their abilities. There are unlimited examples of handicapped individuals participating within the limitations of their handicaps, such as children running races on crutches, blind children racing by listening to others who guide them around the track, the quadriplegic man swimming, and the children in wheelchairs racing and playing basketball. Almost any activity can be adapted to meet the conditions necessary to include the child with a handicap. Bowling is a good example of an activity that can be adapted to individual abilities. If the individual can push the ball down the lane, he can participate. Handicaps can be used to equalize the scores. The game can be adapted to a gymnasium, the lawn or living room.

The activities appropriate for organized competition are numerous and can be as simple as a bean bag game or as complex as football. Family and school competition can be organized for fitness activities, track and field activities or sport games. Family, community and individual interests and background should be considered when organizing local competitions. There are many service organizations willing to assist in the planning and implementation of competitive opportunities. Events such as a cross-country run on the local golf course, a bowling tournament, or track meet are often sponsored by local clubs, businesses or churches.

Many sport organizations sponsor youth programs in the community. Bantam basketball, Little League football, and Pony League baseball are examples of team sport activities. Many national organizations also provide competitive age-group competition. Swimming and gymnastics are two good examples. The Amateur Athletic Union (AAU) provides youth competitions which are held locally with opportunities to participate nationally. The opportunities for competitive experiences are extensive. Parents should be selective and supervise the opportunities to ensure that the experiences are appropriate and developmental, and to provide family support and value instruction.

Many excellent programs are available for handicapped individuals. These programs have local foundations with opportunity for state, national and international competition for selected winners. The most widely known program is the Special Olympics sponsored by the Joseph P. Kennedy, Jr. Foundation. Their program is for all ages, for all skill levels and all seasons.

The mission of Special Olympics is to provide year-round sports training and athletic competition in a variety of well-coached Olympic-type sports for mentally retarded individuals by providing them with continuing opportunities to develop physical fitness, prepare for entry into school and community sports programs, express courage, experience joy and participate in the sharing of gifts, skills and friendship with their families, other Special Olympians and the community.

Special Olympics began in 1968 with a national meet of 1,000 athletes. Today nearly 1 million mentally retarded persons participate in some phase of Special Olympics sports training and competition. Special Olympics offers sports training to mentally retarded people in the United States and 40 foreign countries.

The official sports that can be included in Local, Area, Chapter, and National Games include:
- **Basketball** with senior and junior age groups in team play and run, dribble, and shoot;
- **Bowling** with competition organized into age and performance divisions;
- **Diving** from the one-meter board;
- **Floor Hockey** competition in senior and junior age groups;
- **Frisbee-Disc** for accuracy and distance;
- **Gymnastics** competition in free exercise, tumbling and balance beam;
- **Polo Hockey** team play;
- **Soccer** team play and skill competition of dribbling, passing, shooting, and juggling;
- **Softball** games of seven innings;
- **Swimming** of 25 meter freestyle, 50 meter freestyle, 25 meter breaststroke, 25 meter butterfly, and 100 meter freestyle relay;
- **Track and Field** events of 50 meter dash, 200 meter dash, 400 meter dash, mile run, standing long jump, pentathlon, and high jump;
- **Volleyball** in senior and junior age groups;
- **Wheelchair Events** of 25 meter race, 30 meter slalom, and 100 meter relay; and
- **Winter Sports** of Alpine skiing, cross country skiing and ice skating in senior and junior age groups.

Special Olympians are people 8 years of age or older, and who have been assigned by school systems or human service agencies to programs to meet the needs of the mentally retarded. The Olympians may live at home or in residential facilities. They may attend public or private school, activity centers or workshops, or they may be employed. They may not participate if they are a member of any interscholastic or other team organized to participate in competitive sports.

When Special Olympics athletes participate, they are expected to: follow instructions from their coach; attend practices and take part in sports training sessions; practice at home with their parents, brothers, sisters, or friends; learn to cooperate with other team members and to take part in the Special Olympics games and activities. Parents, guardians, and friends of the athletes can assist with training at home, by volunteering as a coach, by working on a Special Olympics committee, by helping to raise funds, and by coming to the games and cheering the athletes on to victory.

Handbooks are available which give the eligibility rules, the competition division and the sport rules which are adapted for mentally retarded individuals. An awards program is provided which recognizes all participants and their achievements. Coaching manuals for the Special Olympics are provided for professionals and volunteers who help with the program. A sport manual for each sport, containing skill techniques, training procedures, goals, progressive activities and sport skill assessments with recognition for achievements for the beginner, the rookie and the winner, are available for most activities, including the most popular activities of bowling, cross-country skiing, track and field, volleyball and swimming. Individual Sport Skills Assessment Record cards are available for individual participants in the sport programs (Fig. 17-1, Fig. 17-2, Fig. 17-3).

For more information about Special Olympics, contact the Joseph P. Kennedy, Jr. Foundation (1701 K Street NW, Washington, DC, 20006-1581).

Figure 17-1

Figure 17-2

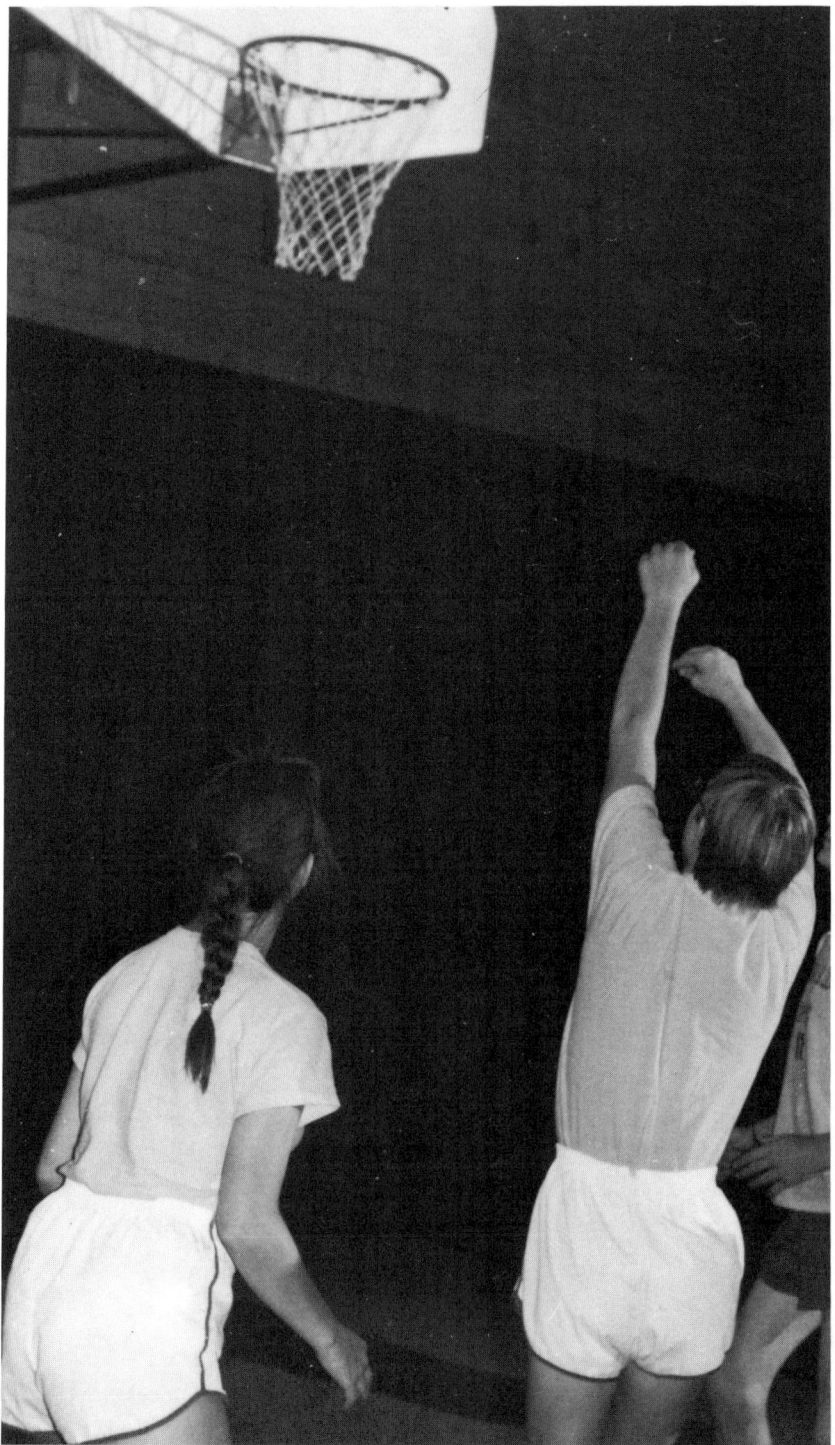

Figure 17-3